# HOLY VIOLENCE

*The Revolutionary Thought of Frantz Fanon*

An Intellectual Biography

## B. Marie Perinbam

**3CP**

THREE CONTINENTS PRESS        WASHINGTON, D.C.

© 1982 by B. Marie Perinham

First Edition
ISBN 0-89410-175-7
ISBN 0-89410-176-5 (paperback)

LC No.: 81-51664

Three Continents Press
1346 Connecticut Ave., N.W.
Washington, D.C. 20036 U.S.A.

*Cover art by Tom Gladden*

| | DATE DUE | |
|---|---|---|
| APR 1 4 1994 | | |
| 2 9 MAY 2002 | | |
| | | |
| | | |
| | | |
| | | |
| | | |
| | | |
| | | |
| | | |

*I am committed to myself and to my neighbor to fight with all my might, with all my strength to prevent the (future) subjugation of people on this earth.*

*. . . you better get used to me . . . I am not going to accomodate myself to anyone . . .*

Fanon, 1952

# Table of Contents

# HOLY VIOLENCE

# VIOLENCE

*The Revolutionary Thought Of Frantz Fanon*

An Intellectual Biography

# Preface

Although the ideas in this book have been painstakingly put together, there is probably nothing new or startling in what has been said. Some of it (like the truth) might even be boring. My only justification for this undertaking is that few monographs, if any, have been written on Frantz Fanon's difficult and complex concept of violence, although the idea has generated considerable controversy.

Certain problems were associated with the writing of this book. First, because Fanon's mind worked with psycho-existential and psycho-political categories, he wrote himself and his feelings into his theory of revolution, to the extent that both his personality and personal experiences were as inseparable from the political ideology, as the man was from his skin. Even in 1952, when his first book *Black Skin White Masks* appeared, Fanon made it clear that his beliefs and actions were no mask. Rather, they were to his being what his skin was to his body: inseparable. Readers expecting a revolutionary ideology developed over a long period of time in a relatively unbiased political laboratory should therefore go no further. Those, however, who are curious about this West Indian man, whose mind was on fire, and "whose pen" was dipped in acid, might wish to explore (among other things) a theory of violence, heard for the first time in the Third World, which reflects the life and experience of a man, who was as committed to the wretched of the earth, as is humanly possible. Thus, although it is analytically preferable to put some distance between the man and his ideas, in reality this proved impossible. Any such attempt would have distorted his ideas, and drained them of their sacred fury.

Second, some problems emerged from the fact that his concept of holy violence developed in a cross-cultural environment: more specifically, in three different parts of the world; in three distinct cultures; and, in relation to three social mileux. In other words, Fanon was born and raised in Martinique (in the French Antilles), and was educated in France. As a partisan in the Algerian war of liberation (1 November 1954 - 19 March 1962), he later lived and worked in North Africa, in Algeria and Tunisia. Thus in less than ten years, from 1952 when *Black Skin White Masks* appeared and 1961 when *The Wretched of the Earth* was published, the idea was formulated in the Antilles, in Europe, and in North Africa. Admittedly metropolitan France was an important common denominator in all three jurisdictions. Yet because of the obvious differences between the three territories, it has proved necessary in some instances to provide certain types of background material when dealing with biographical aspects of Fanon's life. In other cases, however, this has not seemed desirable, especially when explanatory material threatened to disrupt the narrative flow; or worse, when background material intruded on the development of his ideas. There are sections, therefore, where some background knowledge on the part of the reader is assumed. For those, however, who wish to supplement the narrative, an outline of the main events of Fanon's life, and those of the Algerian war of liberation are offered in Appendicies I and II. Hopefully, these latter will mitigate the reader's sense of discontinuity.

The third problem—a methodological one—associated with this work relates to the two preceding ones. Because Fanon's concept of holy violence belonged as much to his life as his revolutionary theory; and because it developed within three distinct political, social and cultural milieux, the method of analysis has varied. Understanding holy violence in Fanon's life and personality, and studying it as a revolutionary theory are methodologically distinct. Therefore, I have focussed more on the birth of the idea in Fanon's experience (which to the best of my knowledge has never been done), than on its place in revolutionary theory. Given the divergences, this seemed the only valid approach. The outcome is therefore more a discussion of the evolution of an idea—by what means, stages and influences—than an attempt to situate it within the framework of revolutionary theory.[1] Save for my conclusions, where I briefly attempt the latter, most of the book deals with the birth of Fanon's idea.

But having said that, there was a fourth problem associated with Fanon's concept of violence: i.e. his empirical data and how he used them. While he drew on all three regions mentioned above for a conceptual framework, his empirical data for the revolutionary ideology came primarily from Martinique and Algeria, with some additional material from those parts of sub-Saharan Africa which he had either visited, or read about. He apparently supplemented these with insights gleaned in conversations with friends, associates, colleagues and co-revolutionaries. Often he used this knowledge impressionistically and intuitively. Thus although Fanon's fieldwork or "hard" empirical data base seems large, a close examination suggests otherwise as most of his empirical data come mainly from Martinique and Algeria at war. Although uncannily insightful, his revolutionary theory is therefore in a sense underdeveloped, all of which may partly explain why some readers experience problems in accepting its universal applicability. It seems more appropriately to belong to wartime Algeria, and to those former colonial territories which won their independence through violent struggle (e.g.

Angola and Mozambique) than to the colonial scenario in general, which Fanon apparently intended.

On turning to the question of "holy violence," it is well to recognize, on the one hand, that Fanon never applied the prefix "holy" to his concept of violence. On the other hand, it is clear that he *had* a concept of violence-beyond-violence, and that he was dealing with a meta-violence; which suggests that his knowledge of wartime violence in Algeria, and its impact, went *beyond* rational comprehension. In effect, as a politicized psychiatrist, he was pursuing the effects of violence into the inner landscapes of the minds, societies and cultures that he was experiencing; and was at the same time studying the impact of revolutionary violence on the collective psyche, on group behavior, and on cultural change. He had therefore reached those internal landscapes of the mind where indirect insights are frequently substituted for direct knowledge, (and where the latter is more often, even more effectively expressed indirectly through figures of speech, such as the paradox and the metaphor), and where they are subsequently projected onto objective reality. Thus while Fanon never prefixed his concept of violence with the term "holy," the concept itself explored social cultural and psychological experiences which went beyond violence, including those which relate to the dynamics of revolutionary violence in a collectivity. Moreover, holy violence combined the secular with the religious, the terrestrial with the celestial, as well as a magical fantasy with reality. As is shown in the conclusion, it also combined the "scientific" with the impact of a "religious" faith. Thus "holy violence" seemed to capture the idea and its implications better than "meta-violence," especially since the former was compatible with the *jihad*, or holy war, which Fanon found in Algeria—in one form or another.

Having indicated what I tried to accomplish in this book, it is best to admit what I did not intend. First, I never attempted a "definitive" study of Fanon's revolutionary theory; and given the problems of collecting data, the task may well be impossible, for the time being anyway.[2] I expect, therefore, that in the future, others will have more, and/or different observations on the subject. Second, I have not attempted a defense of Fanon's concept of holy violence as an independent or universal thought category *per se*, although some may think otherwise. Instead, I thought it best to explore the idea by projecting it on to the specific historical, sociological, cultural, and psychological data that emerged from Fanon's Martinican and Algerian experiences. When seen from these perspectives, the evidence speaks for itself: in Algeria violence worked. By means of revolutionary violence, the Algerian people obtained their objectives which were liberation from France, as well as Algerian national independence. Given these objective circumstances, therefore, the defense of holy violence as a separate and independent thought category is irrelevant. And it is now a-historical to wonder whether, or if Algerian independence could have been achieved by any other means. Third, I make no claims that Fanon's revolutionary theory was a *sui generis*. On the contrary, I show that given his education and experiences, he adopted a technique similar to that employed by most intellectuals: he selectively built on the ideas of predecessors and contemporaries.

On the one hand, interview work for this study was undertaken in Algeria, Tunisia and Martinique. While working on another research project in Senegal and Canada, I also engaged in informal conversations with friends and associates who either knew, or knew about Fanon. On the other hand, library research for the project was undertaken in the United States, in Algeria and in Tunisia. Most of my work was supported by generous grants from the Hoover Institution on War Revolution and Peace at Stanford University, and from the University of Maryland. Without their financial assistance, the research would not have been possible.

I wish to thank the many friends who encouraged me in this project, as well as Dorothy Lukens, Vera Blenkiron, Amelia Bottalico, Darlene King and Margaret Burkett who were responsible for the typing.

# Introduction
## The Meaning of Violence

While most monographs on Frantz Fanon deal sympathetically with his philosophical and political thought—focussing on psycho-political perceptions as well as his theory of decolonization—his concept of violence has drawn sharp criticism.[1] Because the prescriptive use of violence offends humanist traditions and fundamental law, most critics prefer to condemn first and explain later. Consequently few have really examined its full import. Fanon's concept of violence nonetheless deserves serious inquiry. Permeating his later thought, it is varied, and nuanced—despite his stridency—and is more complex than the dictionary meaning of coercion and physical force, and more creative than most detractors suggest. In fact, it includes elements that go beyond violence, which even approach holiness.

This book deals with Fanon's concept of violence, including those aspects which surpassed violence. There is, however, a problem. Fanon's delinquent methodology, contributing to the indiscriminate use of the term, has obfuscated its meaning. By using violence to explain practically everything, in the hands of critics, violence has come to mean practically nothing. It is now commonplace to criticize Fanon for a prodigal methodology, and for a pretentious opaque writing style. Complaining that Fanon was "so entranced with the sound of words that he sometimes obscure[d] all content," Geismar regretted his lack of clarity. Focussing more on a methodology that was at best "implicit," Caute justifiably criticized Fanon for resorting too easily to "triadic" interpretations and abstract overviews—as in the case of the Hegelian dialectic which dominated his thought—at the expense of empirical date. Gendzier joined the chorus of critics by "publicly regret [ting] that he mingled existential notions with political recommendations."[2] And even in his professional psychiatric work, Fanon's prodigal methodology has drawn criticism. Commenting on his use of diagnostic terminology, Paul Adams, himself a psychiatrist, talked about "our disdain for Fanon's tendency to oversimplify," and observed that although his "cases of madness" discussed in *Black Skin White Masks*, and in *The Wretched of the Earth* are "rich in recognizing what society and culture can induce in human beings," they "are lacking in psychiatric sophistication."[3]

His deficient methodology and opaque style, notwithstanding, a careful investigation of Fanon's concept of violence and holy violence (beyond violence) reveals a psycho-political and psycho-philosophical integrity not often found in Third World revolutionary literature.[4] Moreover, violence and holy violence are not free-form revolutionary propaganda. Structured and organized, they are integrated into a socio-historical framework which authenticates their intellectual heritage. Thus despite a prodigal methodology, a close reading of his disorganized and opaque texts reveals a fully developed concept of violence, including holy violence.

Although Fanon never used the term "holy violence," his later works, especially essays in *A Dying Colonialism, The Wretched of the Earth* and, *Toward the African Revolution* reek with violence.[5] Yet it is clear that he distinguished between violence, meaning coercion and physical force; and holy violence, suggesting a destructive force creative beyond belief, and frightening beyond comprehension, compelling and dangerously powerful, irresistible and fearful to approach, easy to comprehend, yet mysterious, terrible and sacred. Clearly then he was referring to two kinds of violence: one which owed its meaning directly to the barrel of a gun; and the other which indirectly derived a complex and paradoxical meaning from its impact on the Algerian people during their war of liberation from the French, 1 November 1954 to 19 March 1962.

The first interpretation attributed to violence is easily understood. It simply means ridding a nation of the colonizer or oppressor. Numerous precedents of this sort have occurred in modern history. The seventeenth century English Puritan revolutionaries thought to rid themselves of a monarchy which had acquired enough power to threaten arbitrarily the security of life, liberty and property. The eighteenth century American Revolution, the first modern anti-colonial war, was an unequivocal statement that a people would not lightly accept the domination of another, even if that other was a leading constellation in the global firmament. The eighteenth and nineteenth century French Revolution exported an ideology throughout Europe and later to French tropical dependencies, that the risk of liberty with dishonor, was preferable to the security of oppression with something that passed for honor. Twentieth century Bolshevik revolutionaries proclaimed to the world that no condition of oppression, no matter how long-standing and inhuman, could snuff out the primeval urge to individual and collective sovereignty. Other twentieth century peoples' and peasant revolutions, in Mexico, China, Indo-China and Cuba have all repeated the message resounding throughout the world since the seventeenth century: that given a fighting chance, most people capable of organized, collective action would neither chose to be "decided-nor-spoken-for," "acted-upon-nor-against"— and neither oppressed nor colonized. History records that when appropriate, they have invariably exchanged existence in the passive voice, for living in the active. It is interesting to note that in none of the above circumstances, was violence the revolutionaries' first choice. On the contrary, in the face of the oppressors' intransigence, it was without exception the last viable option, arrived at only after the agonies of indecision, and executed only with blood, sweat and tears. Therefore, within this tradition of revolutionary violence in modern history, Fanon's violent option is easily understood. After one hundred and thirty years of resistance against the French in Algeria culminating, between the 1920's and 1950's, in the creation of political parties and abortive attempts to reach negotiated settlements, Algerians exchanged the pen for the sword. Revolutionary violence was the last resort.

The second interpretation attributed to violence is more elaborate. By establishing it in a time perspective, Fanon added an historical dimension, which perhaps can be called violence in history. By this latter, he meant the French conquest of Algeria in 1830, followed by decades of "pacification." Systematically, French search-and-destroy policies ferretted Algerians from guerilla mountain sanctuaries, destroying, plundering and vandalizing, until the 1920's when the last desert tribes submitted. Continuing French aggression provoked resistance and counter-violence which ceased only with the Evian cease-fire on 19 March 1962. French violence in history had produced Algerian resistance and counter-violence. Fanon's third interpretation of violence, which as a concept was becoming more complicated, included an invisible and destructive force at work in colonial social structures, which expressed itself in dominant norms. Neither able to see, feel nor hear it, colonized people nonetheless "smelt" the stench of social and psychological decay which French colonial policies had wrought; and where decades of rotting societies and cultures had turned peoples' lives into garbage heaps. Having Algeria and Martinique in mind—the two dependent territories which he best knew—he talked of metropolitan policies silently destroying indigenous social structures, imperceptibly deforming value systems, tacitly rejecting the legitimacy of indigenous cultures, and categorically denying integrity to African histories. When combined with exploitative economic policies, he concluded, colonial policies had "done violence" to the colonies, by alienating people, both on a micro and macro scale, from traditional reference points in society and history.

In addition to these three interpretations, Fanon attributed to violence meanings which are best contextually understood. For example, he sometimes used "violence," and violent terms (e.g. *faire-sauter:* to blow up), when he apparently meant history in the act of being made ( *d'être d'histoire en actes*), or when he intended to create a mental picture of action (*une image d'action*).[6] Elsewhere he referred to peasant "violence"; yet the ambiguous context suggested a common variety of pre-political unrest.[7] At other times, "violence" was a synonym for internal violence, pent up or misdirected aggressions which awaited externalization under appropriate revolutionary leadership.[8] Frequently, he spoke of an "atmosphere of violence," when implications were of unorganized political stirrings among the masses.[9] Sometimes, he spoke of violence "unifying the people," when the context referred to the entire decolonization struggle, including the ideology and commitment to build a new nation.[10] Finally, he frequently misused the term, when another would have been more appropriate. For example, claiming that decolonization was "always violent," he ignored the fact that the end of empire was relatively non-violent in most of Africa, Asia and the Caribbean. Thus in addition to his frequent misuse of the term, it is clear that by "violence," Fanon had at least seven additional or contextual meanings in mind.

Had Fanon only rested with the above meanings, his concept of violence would have hardly differed from that of modern anti-colonial revolutionaries. It is that terrible holy dimension which he added, that aweful *sanctus* which set it apart. Although all modern revolutions, however rational or "scientific," develop mysterious and sacred elements—usually implicit in goals, ideologies, doctrines and slogans—Fanon went beyond the "rational" mysteries, in that he associated violence with powers capable of changing people and societies for the better.[11] He did not specify the nature of this power. He simply stated its impact on the minds and lives of the Algerian people who were committed to the nationalist struggle. Thus when he claimed that violence implemented by people and leaders alike sharpened socio-political and psycho-political insights; or that it "detoxifies" by eliminating feelings of inferiority, thereby freeing the oppressed for political action; or that violence acts like a "royal pardon" and can create "the new man," he was citing the impact without identifying the process or the power behind it.[12] He never did.

What was this quality which set his concept of violence apart, and which suggested a terrible holiness; this esoteric secret experienced—but not necessarily understood—as release and creation? Clearly it existed and did not exist simultaneously; and the way in which he developed it, suggests that Fanon was aware of the simultaneous existence and non-existence of this discreet power, or holy violence. Holy violence did not exist in that it was neither an attribute of the spiritual nor the material world. It had no supernatural life of its own, and no impersonal power manifesting itself in some specific way or place. It had nothing to do with moral goodness, and played no part in *peacetime* normative systems. It could not be seen, weighed, smelt nor measured. In short, it did not exist. Yet holy violence existed in that it was a quality or character attributed to things and people, animals and places, actions and events, *by others*. Perceived as having supernatural powers, as being mysterious and sacred, violence could evoke in others an uncanny awe, an eerie reverence, and an uncritical submission *as if* it were a *bona fide* part of the spiritual or material world. It could, moreover, provoke a mystical experience, suggesting that not only were the powers of violence holy, but that one could acquire holiness by association. Holy violence therefore existed in people's perceptions, and if they believed in its creative powers, this belief became a social fact, capable of changing attitudes, behavior and societies for the better—even if only temporarily.

Accordingly, the perception in holy violence which Fanon sought to portray was that holy violence made men whole. The idea was not far-fetched. The words "holy" and "whole" share the same linguistic root: the Old and Middle English roots *hal* and *hool* respectively. Both originally conveyed the idea of wholeness, and neither was initially associated with moral goodness. Both connoted completeness, an unreduced or unimpaired entirety, and both suggested the idea of a coherent system or organization of parts fitting or working together as one. Holiness later acquired its spiritual and sacred qualities associated with moral goodness and the supernatural. But initially, "holy" and "whole" both conveyed similar ideas.

If it seems that Fanon was working with a paradox, it is because he was. As a man with miscarried literary propensities who wrote two unpublished plays, he relied on metaphors, similies, dramatic imagery, symbolism and irony to cajole, persuade, mock, and even to shock his readers. He used the paradox to create similar effects, much in the same way as he used the Hegelian dialectic to fracture his thought. Of all his paradoxical concepts, holy violence was by far the most stunning. Of course he would have known that the paradox was sometimes difficult to comprehend. Containing two contradictory ideas in the same concept which remained in conflict with each other, both parts of the paradox belonged together, and represented the whole. Contrary to expectation, and seemingly opposed to common sense, the paradox nonetheless expressed realities not capable of any other expression. Although many of Fanon's paradoxes seemed false, invariably they derived self-contradictory conclusions from valid deductions and acceptable premises. Not surprisingly the word originated with the Greek *paradoxon*; and who understood paradox better than the Greeks?

It is generally known that the paradox appears in many major cultures, and is central to some. Both Egyptians and Greeks claimed the phoenix rising with youthful vigor from its suicidal flames. Christian cultures are imbued with the doctrine that man should first become a slave in order to be free; or that the "old man" should die, so that the "new" can live; not to mention the idea of the Trinity where there are three in one, and one in three. The idea of contradictory elements forming a whole also developed in Chinese cosmogony, where no division existed between light and dark, good and evil, the sacred and the profane. Hence there were no separate godheads to represent these contradictory elements. Instead, in this humanistic and spontaneously self-generating world view the polar modes of *yin* and *yang* moderated cosmic forces in the interest of balance and harmony. Paradox tinged with irony also existed in the second of the Buddhist's "noble truths," when at the moment of dissolving into death, man's ignorance (*avidya*) once again chained him to the process of rebirth. Although much more identified with a social order, Hinduism also developed a form of paradox in the union of the gods Siva, the destroyer, and Visnu, the protector, in the composite god Harihara. On another level, the paradox has also been used to express ideas for which there is no other mode of expression. In their Dionysian spring rituals and orgiastic rites, the Greeks "discovered" "divine madness" to express an experience that was simultaneously creative and destructive; and the seventeenth century Sabbateans spoke of the "holiness of sin" because it was the most appropriate way to describe an obscene protest that was at the same time good. Hence, by using contradictory ideas that make nonsense to commonsense, Fanon was not only using a figure of speech proven tried and true, but he was also capturing readers by assaulting their imaginations.

Why Fanon chose to work with the paradox is not clear. It is now generally accepted that protest or resistance groups usually adopt antinomian attitudes. Intent on pulling down an old order, they rid themselves collectively from encumbrances in the existing or restraining moral order and, in turn, create the new. Once beyond morality, they frequently forge new terms, a new vocabulary, sometimes even a new language, to describe themselves, their new values, and of course the "enemy." Seventeenth century puritans, who called themselves "Saints and Brethren," as did members of the early Christian church, identified Spain their enemy, as the "Roman Babylon" with whom "the Lord Himself hath a controversy." Rejecting the "dross and dung" of this world, their revolutionary endeavors were an important "part of God's plan," in whose name they murdered a king, and undertook to destroy ancient monarchical institutions. In some instances the rejection was so complete, that leaving for the New World, they preferred "a good consceence, in a poore remote wilderness, amongst the heathens; than pleasures of England with submission to the impositions of the —prevayling hierarchie." Violations of the new morality were subject to the magistrates' sword—"God having ordained them for that end"—because magistrates "ought not bear the sword in vain."[13]

De Tocqueville reminds posterity that French revolutionaries, now calling themselves "Comrade," gave way to the "desire, inveterate and uncontrollable, utterly to destroy all such institutions as had survived the Middle Ages and, having cleared the ground, to build up a new society in which men were as much alike and their status as equal as possible . . ." Appealing to the "doctrine" of "Liberty, Equality and Fraternity," they too murdered a king, and were more successful than the Puritan Brethren in destroying monarchical institutions. So strong was their antipathy to the *status quo*, De Tocqueville concluded, "that there was no enormity, no form of violence from which these men would not shrink."[14] By the twentieth century the spectre of the Bolshevik Revolution stalked the land. Now the new "Comrades," who spoke through *Izvestia*, their journal of "truth," were the revolutionary saints of the twentieth century. Overthrowing a monarchy and destroying an Empire, they too abolished "all social, religious and national restrictions," in preparation for the new day. In the name of democracy and brotherhood, soldiers and workers, the revolutionaries sanctioned war, destruction and violence. Marching forward "across the mountains of our brothers' corpses, across rivers of innocent blood and tears, [and] over the smoking ruins of cities and villages," they pledged themselves to "our future victories and the complete liberation of humanity."[15]

On a smaller scale, in the Caribbean where Fanon was born, the "I-Man" language of the Jamaican Rastafarian cult also illustrates this antinomian phenomenon, not to mention the movement's use of metaphors, such as "Babylon" to denote the "evil" establishment in the Rastafarian's manichaean world. In each of the revolutionary or protest movements cited above, the paradox played a role, because implicit in resistance ideologies was the assumption that violence and/or resistance in the name of a great cause was not only creative and good: it was uncontrollably necessary. This use of paradox in revolutionary or resistance situations sharpened the meaning of morality beyond morality, which is exactly what Fanon's concept of holy violence suggests.

It is possible, therefore, that Fanon used the concept of holy violence because, like predecessor revolutionaries, he too was creating a new morality complete with the symbolic murder of a king, and the destruction of an older order. The old European morality was a dead eunuch. As has been suggested above, Fanon never used the term "holy violence" *per se*. Had he refined his thought before surprised by death which overtook his prime, he might conceivably have done so because he certainly had the concept. After all, much in the same way as seventeenth century puritans were locked in a struggle with Satan, many Algerians believed that they were wrestling with the infidel in a *jihad*, or holy war. Thus although he never explained, it is likely that Fanon used the paradox—along with other striking imagery and metaphors—to explain a moral category which was beyond good and evil.

But having established that Fanon developed a concept of revolutionary violence and holy violence, a careful reading of his text nevertheless, suggests a distaste for violence. Most biographers have missed this unexpected twist in an obivously tortured mind. Gendzier, for example, suggested that since Fanon "was not given to reflectiveness," he "did not consider non-violence as a tactic in the struggle."[16] Diffuse meanings, and irregular methodology, notwithstanding, Fanon's opaque prose suggests a personal distaste for violence. Clearly he was ambivalent, especially since his violent pronouncements were in conflict with the results obtained from his clinical work as a psychiatrist. The latter had shown that violence in the colonial state could lead to personality disorders, including madness.[17]

Overcoming the "unpardonable debates" with his conscience, in 1956, Fanon admitted to being "frightened" by the dehumanizing effects of violence. Moreover, he confessed, the conflict between his professional goals as a psychiatrist, and those of the colonial state had rendered his position "absurd," the burden of which he could no longer endure.[18] Thus in his later litanies of the "virtues" of violence, Fanon, the war time propagandist, was in conflict with Fanon, the psychiatrist. Specifically, his clinical data had shown that colonial violence had produced neurotic and deviant behavior, such as avoidance behavior, symbolic killings, fratricidal combats, self-destruction and suicide. Violence also had produced deformed psyches, as well as an emotional sensitivity, which reacted "like an open sore" to the "caustic agent" of colonialism. Finally, Fanon suggested, colonial violence had created a favorable breeding ground for other mental disorders, which ultimately brought "colonized people crowding into mental hospitals."[19]

Morevoer, clinical data demonstrated that violence compromised the psychic integrity of its perpetrators. Deleterious effects were not restricted to victims. For example, the violent confrontation of the colonized and the colonizer had bred an impenetrable insensitivity on the part of the latter. Claiming that "they [the natives] only understood the language of violence," the settler was himself capable only of violent behavior in the presence of the native. Even statues erected to the original conquerors were symbols of violence. Hence, living in a violent environment, which was turned against the Algerians' presence, the colonizer lost the capacity to relate to colonized masses, except through violence and pejorative stereotypes.[20]

Finally, pointing to emotional disturbances in personalities of French personnel responsible for administering torture during the Algerian war of liberation Fanon revealed his own horror of violence. Under controlled clinical conditions, he witnessed its destructive forces at work in the personalities of those who sought professional help. He watched state officials become brutalized, cruel, callous, insensitive, immune to human suffering, even while becoming competitive and ambitious in the art of torturing. It can be argued that torturers choose themselves. Yet according to Fanon's evidence, self-selection or otherwise, hardly eliminated deleterious consequences for those perpetrators of violence whom he cited.

The most celebrated cases were those of two policemen, the one a willing torturer, the other somewhat more reluctant. Apparently after a successful career in torturing, the former experienced depression complaining of " 'fits of madness,' " uncontrollable wife beating, and "ruined fists,"—an occupational hazard caused by "softening up" the "bird." Sometimes, in order to preserve his energy, the "Senegalese" were called in to do the "knocking up." But their work was unprofessional. In any event, torturers alternated in shifts, the officer conceded. Despite that, the work was hard, especially since some shifts were as long as ten consecutive hours. Furthermore, torturers competed with each other to obtain coveted information. Accordingly, one did not dare "lay off" for fear of losing the prize for which the next shift would take credit. The torturer wished to continue his work. The alternative, resignation, was unacceptable.[21]

By way of contrast, the second or reluctant torturer in this surrealistic landscape did resign. The replay of torture scenes haunted his restless dreams. That bothered him. He did not like the screaming. Nonetheless, he had become expert at matching the quality of scream with the degree of agony: "two blows of the fist and a wham from the baton" and "the guy" uttered one kind of cry: "two hours strung up by his wrists produced another." But those screams following application of electrodes to the genitals got to him. Of course, there were "the toughies" who did not scream. Then you had to make them—"that's already a victory." One would prefer to avoid all this, the torturer demurred. But the victims as a rule were uncooperative. Some would not even reveal their names.[22]

Knowing as he did that violence dehumanized the tortured and torturer alike, and that terror, counter-terror, violence and counter-violence formed a "tenacious . . . circle of hate,"[23] should Fanon's praise of violence—as physical coercion—be taken at its face value? Hardly. Aware of the deleterious effects of violence within the structure of the human personality, either he could not, or would not think through the ramifications of the violent policy which he was recommending. Admitting to the "absurdity" of his position, Fanon the political propagandist turned a deaf ear to Fanon the psychiatrist. While the latter was "frightened" by the effects of violence, the former brought colonialism to trial for perpetrating violence, and condemned it to death by violence.

But if Fanon displayed a distaste for violence, few have noticed that he gave his *imprimatur* to a non-violent "compromise with colonialism" even approving a "symbolic" armed struggle, so long as principles were not sacrificed, and the masses were instructed. Furthermore, the violent option was a situational one, determined by those in the eye of the anti-colonial storm, and not by a fixed principle.[24] Fanon's fear of the effects of violence, and his limited concession to non-violence place a different perspective on his concept of violence as it is generally understood. Moreover, it invites a cautious comparison with the thought of Mahatma Gandhi (1868-1948) who, a generation earlier, was similarly faced with problems of decoloniza-tion. Sharing Gandhi's abhorance of violence, their metaphors are somewhat alike. Where Gandhi feared that a "chain of violence [could] lengthen and strengthen," into greater violence, Fanon confirmed that it had formed a "tenacious . . . circle of hate." Both acknowledged that "violence is the law of the brute . . . and knows no law but that of physical might."[25] Although as different as chalk from cheese, both Gandhi the Indian barrister and Fanon the Martinican psychiatrist standing a generation apart recognized that colonized people needed rehabilitation from alienation, feelings of inferiority, inaction and despair, before they could successfully undertake the development of an independent nation. Both identifying colonial humanity with a suffering humanity, the barrister and the psychiatrist developed a "therapy" or a ritual and symbolic purification by way of relief. Believing that purification and political awareness occurred simultaneously, both equated the former with self-change, and the latter with the act of decolonization.[26] But here the likeness ended. Although both demonstrated an insightful understanding of the colonial dilemma, the texture of Fanon's personality, the structure of his mind, and his preference for violence rendered their positions irreconcilable. Fanon made an ultimate commitment to violence, and Gandhi did not.

But what of holy violence—the sacred whore who kidnapped Fanon's mind and held it ransom unto death—can that concept be taken at face value? Among other things, the following chapters examine this problem. It is clear however, that as a tool of political indoctrination, Fanon's concept of holy violence was not only fully developed in his writings, but in association with the *jihad*, it stalked the Algerian land. In the minds of many, it claimed the revolution for itself. As the whole world knows, Algerians won their anti-colonial war against France in 1962, by violence. What has not been clear to date is the meaning of this sacred violence which Fanon found in the Algerian war of liberation from France—a violence which was creative beyond belief, and frightening beyond comprehension, compelling and dangerously powerful, irresistible and fearful to approach, easy to comprehend, yet mysterious, terrible and sacred.

## *I*

# Creative Conflict: The Hegelian Paradigm and Beyond

*It is only through staking one's life that freedom is won . . . The individual who has not risked his life may well be recognized as a person, but he has not attained to the truth of this recognition as an independent self-consciousness.*

Hegel

*The stirring up of conflict is a Luciferian virtue in the true sense of the word. Conflict engenders fire, the fire of affects and emotions, and like every other fire it has two aspects, that of combustion and that of creating light.*

Jung

Fanon's concept of violence first appeared in *Black Skin White Masks*, where he introduced the idea of creative conflict. Specifically, he referred to conflict in the Hegelian dialectic: creative conflict which gives rise to a synthesis; and conflict in the master slave relationship where the latter fought for the master's recognition.[1]

Given his interest in the unequal power relationship between the colonized and colonizer, it is not surprising that Fanon was drawn to Hegel's paradigm of the unequal power struggle.[2] Although Hegel treated the concept of mutual recognition within the framework of the lord and bondsman, he was also referring to that universal human phenomenon of the voluntary or involuntary subordination of one person to another. We see examples of this in every day life, in families, in the work place, in governments, and so forth. Hegel used this relationship to analyse the conditions in which the "self" develops and is maintained.

When two people meet, he argued, they are at first distinct and separate. In the process of exchange (Hegel called it "mediation"), their personalities begin to interact (reciprocity), which not only heightens mutual awareness, but also self-awareness. "Mediation" takes place through self-assertion and self-maintainance. But since—as is frequently the case in the ordinary course of events—one person or personality is stronger, has a higher status or is more independent than the other, that person is capable of self-assertion at the expense of the other. A struggle or conflict ensues during which, Hegel argued, they begin to "recognize themselves as mutually recognizing one another." For Hegel this act of recognizing-in-conflict was an enormously creative process, as struggle was the means whereby self-assertion and self-maintainance *vis à vis* the Other (i.e. the other person) was realized. The result was a mutual recognition of "the equality of the selves," which for Hegel was nothing short of the "truth." Hegel never compromised this notion as, according to him, self and mutual awareness of the "selves as equals" could only be achieved by struggle and conflict.

On the next level of dialectical interaction (which is the Hegelian formula for a triadic "process" and "change"), Hegel developed the idea of continuing conflict by suggesting that as long as people keep relating to each other, the potential for continuous opposition exists. "Struggle" and "conflict" begin to take on new meaning. No longer suggesting mere self-assertion and self-maintenance *vis à vis* the Other, the terms now mean "a life-and-death-struggle" within a relationship. The solution, however, is not to terminate conflict. Instead, Hegel added a moral dimension by urging that people "must engage in this struggle, for they must raise their certainty of being *for themselves* . . . both in the case of the other and in their own case."[3]

The parties thus enter into the process of conflict by seeking each other's death or annihilation; because it is "only through staking one's life that freedom is won." "An individual," he continued, "who has not risked his life may well be regarded as a person." But he has not really become fully self-aware, neither is he aware of the other person's consciousness. Why? Because in the last analysis, he is destroyed by the other person's "absolute negation" or absolute opposition.[4] For Hegel this risk-taking in the face of death was the ultimate in creation, not only because it guaranteed survival of the "self" in the face of stubborn opposition, but also because conflict was the *sine qua non* of change and growth. As opposed extremes in the midst of unmitigated struggle, people involved in reciprocal conflict created themselves through mutual recognition—and ultimately through self-actualization.

Where powers were unevenly matched, as in the case of the master-slave relationship, the outcome was different. Here conflict stabilized. Lacking sufficient momentum to maintain the struggle, the weaker party "died" in the face of the "absolute negation" of the stronger. Contending parties separated into "unopposed extremes," and instead of being an "absolute negation"—as in the case of creative conflict—there was an "abstract negation" as lord and bondsman now treated each other with mere indifference, or as stereotypes. Moreover, as the stronger of the two, Hegel continued, the lord was now in a position to exist only for himself, and to exert power over the bondsman. By that same token the latter, now dependent, treated with indifference and perceived in stereotypical terms, became a "thing" that lived only for the "Other" (his master). In this "one-sided and unequal" recognition—because the slave's dependence was a form of recognition—Hegel argued that the lord gained but a pyrrhic victory, as his self-awareness developed in relation to an inferior being whose humanity he had denied. Seeking self-actualization, the master turned to transient pleasures. Ironically, the bondsman fared better. Since he lived by external commands, his self-assertion and intelligence—now deprived legitimate expression—turned into self-will, skill and aptitudes. Moreover, by becoming involved with work, he produced something objective and material with which he could effectively interact. His work became a creative dimension in which he could realize himself. In some respects, he successfully sublimated his need for creative interaction with the lord into work, thereby "realizing himself." At the same time, he forced the lord to recognize him by making his labor indispensable, while simultaneously destroying, in the private resistance of his mind, the power (fear and dread) which the lord had over him. By sharpening his mind through resistance, he realized his self-awareness on his own terms. The slave had "freed" himself.

Although Fanon did not mention it, his concept of creative conflict also resembled Hegel's later treatment of war as necessary and beneficial. In *The Philosophy of Right* (1851)[5]—a work of Hegel's mature years—he argued that international treaties and contracts abrogated state sovereignty, which should in principle be inviolate. Accordingly, Hegel concluded that treaties and contracts were logically invalid, and should be disallowed. The state proved its sovereignty through war, and not through negotiation. Moreover, war not only guaranteed state sovereignty as a logical entity; it also was the means by which people proved their willingness to assert and maintain freedom and independence. War was to the state what struggle was to the bondsman; and the state should accordingly acknowledge war as necessary and beneficial. Although his ideas were incorporated into Bismarckian statecraft, it goes without saying that Hegel was criticized for "glorifying war." The nineteenth and twentieth century liberal mind, nurtured on fundamental and international law, was horrified at the proposition of beneficial conflict.

On the face of it, Hegel's creative conflict and his treatment of war as necessary and beneficial seems a contradiction in terms. In a sense, this is exactly what Hegel, and later Fanon intended, as they were both talking of dialectic change as part of a process, wherein social organisms either created their environment, or found themselves in one which threatened them (among other things) with destruction. If the organism failed to resist the influences in its own environment, it devalued its identity, its inner integrity, and ultimately its sovereignty. By resisting, it preserved all of these, thereby reinforcing the idea of beneficial or creative conflict.

Fanon was clearly fascinated by Hegel's contradictory idea of creative conflict and of a beneficial or creative war wherein one risked even life and limb in order to preserve the spirit which was opposed by the Other. Quoting Hegel, he urged that " 'it is only by risking life that one preserves liberty . . . . Thus human reality . . . is only accomplished in conflict, and by the risk which that implies.' "[6] Finding a similar idea in Aimé Césaire's "Et les chiens se taisaient," his thoughts lingered on the joyful horror of creative conflict as he quoted the Rebel's recollections of his own risk-taking:

> *It was a November evening . . . . We leapt up, we the slaves, nothing but a heap of dung . . . . We ran like people possessed; the balls of fire splintered the air . . . . It was an assault on the master's house . . . . We forced open the door. The master's room was wide open. The master's room was brilliantly lit, and the master was there, very calm . . . and we stopped . . . . I entered. 'Is it you boy,' he said to me quite calmly . . . . It was I. It was indeed I, I said to him, the good slave, the faithful slave, the slavish slave, and all of a sudden his eyes were like frightened cockroaches on a rainy day . . . I struck, the blood flowed: that is the only baptism\* that I remember today . . . . Killed him . . . . I killed him with my own hands . . . . Yes: it was a fruitful death, a copious death.*[7]

As was the case with the Hegelian paradigm, the "normal" reaction is to be horrified at the joy of killing. But this is hardly what Fanon's concept of creative conflict was about. Instead, he was claiming that in a slave-colonial society where whole cultures, societies, histories and races had been "killed" by the colonizer's "absolute negation," survival meant fighting back, even at the risk of self-annihilation and the death of the colonizer. The act of killing was not an end in itself. Rather, one killed in order to avoid being "killed."

Under these circumstances, it is difficult to deny the benefits of conflict in self defense, or even to underestimate its role. When the struggle is viewed as a temporary actuality in a process (or constant change), where resistance recurs in successive levels and phases, the historical perspectives of creative conflict begin to emerge on a grand scale. When he first explored the subject in 1952, Fanon was not ready to deal with emerging creative conflict on such a scale. He was still resolving the conflicts associated with being black in a white world which had rejected him, and questions of a personal identity were still uppermost in his mind. By 1961, however, he was ready to deal with "fighting back" ideas. He had even analysed the various "fighting back" stages, beginning with the insolent "native" who "mocks" the colonizer and "vomits up" his ideas, making sure all the time that his sharpened machete was not far at hand; and ending with the "liberated" man who has learned that the white settler's breath, heart-beat, skin and life are not worth anymore than his own, and are in fact just as fragile in the face of struggle.[8]

However, although Fanon favored the advantages of creative conflict in master-slave relationships (discussed in *Black Skin White Masks*) the

---

\*The word "baptism" suggests the idea of the termination of an old life and the beginning of the new. By killing his "goaler," the Rebel had freed himself, and made a new life possible.

Hegelian paradigm *per se* could not be applied to the Antilles, or to the majority of colonized people, for that matter. Because, Fanon lamented, unlike Hegel's bondsman, the latter especially Antilleans, had failed to fight back. Instead, they had become dependent slaves lacking self-realization. Their position was, moreover, worse, as instead of "opposing" the master (by denying his power over them), they had *adapted* to the opposition—or oppression as the case might be—by accepting European values as the criteria of all value. Hegel's bondsman had rejected the lord's values and stereotype of him. But not the Antillean: he had instead internalized the colonizer's norms, including the latter's perception of blacks and the black world, together with the dubiously complimentary view that all blacks were inferior to the Antillean who was the "cock of the black roost."[9] Accordingly, Antilleans measured status and achievement exclusively against European standards, and competed among themselves for the master's recognition. Interaction could never therefore be creative as long as the Antillean remained a self-serving narcissistic Self, constantly seeking approval from the Other. This relationship nurtured the colonizer's self-declared superior status, and fostered a permanent sense of inferiority on the part of the colonized people. Inferiority was in the culture, and "in the air" as an operative norm. Colonized people not only felt inferior as individuals and as groups, but accepting the master's pejorative stereotypes, were convinced of a cultural inferiority. According to Fanon, therefore, the slave in a colonized situation was opposed by the master to the point where he was denied recognition. Failing to turn the "absolute negation" to his advantage, the colonized person—the slave—was locked into "thingness" and the master held the key. His master had "killed" him.

However, while still locked in "thingness" and denied recognition, he continued, masters decided to free their slaves—which actually occurred in 1848 throughout the French empire. The slave was now free. But since he had obtained freedom without creative conflict, the ex-slave lost the opportunity to re-appropriate his human personality, appropriated in the first place by the master who had locked him into "thingness," and who still held the key. Unlike the Hegelian bondsman, therefore, he was not really free. He had not fought for freedom, nor had he struggled with his master. There had been no experience of creative conflict. Consequently, he was still simply a slave—but this time without a master.

While the Hegelian paradigm focussed on doctrine, logic and rationality, Fanon sought out the social and psychological implications of being a slave without a master. What was it like to live in a world where one never acted, but was merely acted upon; and where freedom was an imposed condition? Not much beyond a change in life styles, Fanon replied. On the debit side, there was no metamorphosis, no "going from one life to another," no "new man" emerging from creative conflict, who had re-appropriated his humanity and confirmed his manhood. Only a thing-slave who had lost a master, and who was terrified at the prospect of freedom. At the same time, he longed for (Fanon used the word "desired") recognition. In the face of Hegelian opposition from the Other, Fanon said, the "normal" reaction is to desire recognition by resisting—an act which he called "the first mile stone to the dignity of the spirit."[10] Desiring and resisting were part of the asking-for-recognition act. But no recognition followed.[11] Hence frustrations and unfulfilled desires of the most fundamental sort continued to gnaw at the core of the thing-slave's personality. He had lost a master, which he regretted, and "gained" a "freedom" of which he was terrified. He was living with unfulfilled yet fundamental desires, and was denied the opportunity to re-appropriate his humanity. On the credit side, he was secure in the knowledge that he could still "keep his place," that he could still speak "pidgin nigger," and that once a year, he would be "permitted to dance in the [master's] ballroom, and to dine at his master's table." For all this, he should say: "Thank you to the nice white man," and be grateful.[12]

Fanon obviously agonized over the realization that his own heritage, and that of other colonized people whose freedom had been imposed on them, did not fit the Hegelian paradigm. *Black Skin White Masks* is in part a cry of shame and sorrow over lost opportunities. But since Fanon seldom missed the irony in a situation, he made much of the free masterless thing-slave as one who blissfully shuffled along, speaking "pidgin-nigger," singing and dancing, imitating the white man while in competition with his black peer group, thanking the "nice white man" for granting freedom, feeling good about dancing in the lord's drawing room and eating at his table. In his more sober moments, however, the free masterless thing-slave knew that he was not recognized, Fanon conceded. He was merely patronized. He was still locked in thingness by non-recognition, and the master was still the master. With powerful imagery, Fanon described the thing-slave as one who "is condemned to bite himself," or "who is capable only of ersatz conflict." How does the poor devil escape from powerless self-destruction to self-actualization and creative conflict? At this stage of his intellectual development (1952) Fanon did not know. He talked about the need for creative conflict, but concluded that it was "too late." The Hegelian paradigm of creative conflict just could not be applied to the Antillean. Some other solution for masterless slaves had to be sought.

Despite its inapplicability, evidence in his doctoral thesis (1951) suggests that the basis for Fanon's concepts of creative conflict and later holy violence was, nonetheless, being laid during his years of medical training. Submitted to the Faculty of Medicine and Pharmacy at Lyon, the thesis: "Troubles mentaux et syndromes psychiatriques dans l'hérédo-dégénérative-spino-cérébelleuse: Un cas de Friedreich avec délire de passion," has been seen by few of his biographers.[13] Like most of Fanon's later work, the thesis is a rambling discussion. Although focussing on neurological research, the analysis includes references to existentialist thought (he had been reading Sartre, Nietzsche, Jaspers, Merleau Ponty and Heideggar, etc. as a student), and cultural anthropology, together with the importance of understanding mental disorders in their social and cultural contexts. The last section is a free-flowing discussion predicated on humanistic values of man's place in society, as well as in the "primitive" state of nature. The neurolgical sections apart, the work is a *pot-pourri* of ideas about Man in Society, which clearly favors the "primitive" over other forms of social organization. However, although there is neither a reference to the Hegelian paradigm, nor to creative conflict in the thesis—the medical profession would surely have frowned on this, and there would have been more than eyebrows raised among his thesis examiners —it is clear that the ideas were germinating in Fanon's mind. A year later they re-appeared as the Hegelian paradigm in *Black Skin White Masks*; and in 1961, they re-emerged in *The Wretched of the Earth* in the concept of holy violence. Thus despite his rambling presentation, on matters relating to creative conflict and holy violence, there is continuity in Fanon's thought.

Since few have seen the thesis, it might be appropriate to indicate that the first section, which was not germane to creative conflict and holy violence, dealt with concepts now found in variants of genetic research; and in another form even in socio-biology: namely, the extent to which genetic codes influence social behavior. He, however, dealt with the pathology of genetic codes, as relying on clinical data, he examined the extent to which  genetic defects in the nervous system produced mental disorders and abberant social behavior.[14]

But having shown the correlation between genetic codes and social behavior, he went beyond this pathological determinism to discuss the importance of interactional social relationships in the development of the human personality—the phenomenon which he later called "recognition." Personality and human behavior are not only the products of genes he argued, behavior is also influenced by the social environment. A healthy social order can produce positive change and growth. A diseased one creates social dis-ease and a diseased personality. Thus, assuming a healthy society, Fanon argued that "a healthy man is a social man," and the "index of a man's psychological health is the extent to which he is totally integrated into his *socius.*"[15]

Thesis notes reveal that in reaching these conclusions, Fanon was influenced by the socio-psychologists Jacques Lacan (1901-1978), Marcel Mauss (1872-1950), and the social anthropologist Lucien Lévy-Brühl (1857-1939). From Lacan, he borrowed the idea of "desire"—which later appeared in the form of desire-for-recognition in unfulfilled repose.[16] The "end of desire," he concluded "is essentially social in origin, in experience and in feeling." He also used Lacan's concept of the "phenomenology of personality" (or the "determinism of psychogenetics") to reinforce the notion that if all fundamental desires found satisfaction in the social order, a feeling of dis-ease, dissatisfaction, and even madness would follow if these desires were denied satisfaction within the social order.[17] Thesis notes, moreover show that Mauss and Lévy-Brühl introduced him to ethno-sociology and the functions of the so-called "primitive mind"—which did not really fit the thesis—but which suggested that Fanon was searching for appropriate formulas to integrate man into his social environment. He was particularly fascinated by Lévy-Brühl's "essential homogeneity" wherein to "the mind of the primitive there exists and permeates, on earth, in the air and in the water, in all the diverse forms assumed by persons and objects, one and the same essential reality, both one and mulitple, both material and spiritual . . . . Thus beneath [a] seemingly strong diversity they present an essential homogeneity."[18] Could a psychological theory of "essential homogeneity" be applied to man in a modern society? Fanon did not know.

It is interesting that Fanon should have raised questions relating to social therapy in 1951 before he went to work at the Saint Alban hospital in central France with the distinguished social psychiatrist Professor François Tosquelles. Gendzier's study revealed the extent to which Tosquelle's "sociotherapy, with its emphasis on the importance of the social role and the social context" had influenced Fanon's view of psychiatry, one to which he remained faithful to the end. And although there was more to Tosquelles' "sociotherapy" than the notion of man's integration into a social environment, Fanon's references to a type of sociotherapy months before taking up his appointment at Saint Alban, suggests that he was already familiar with the concepts. Thus, one can say that his view of psychiatry began with his thesis preparation, and not with Tosquelles, as Gendzier has suggested.[19]

But if the first part of his thesis had nothing to do with the Hegelian paradigm, creative conflict nor holy violence, the second part laid the foundation for ideas which he was later to draw on, both in *Black Skins White Masks* (1952), and *The Wretched of the Earth,* (1961). References are implicit rather than explicit, "visible" only in content analysis which seeks to establish continuity in his thought. For example, clearly fascinated by Lacan's "determinism of psychogenetics," he had used it (as suggested above) to reinforce the notion that if fundamental desires in the human personality were denied social satisfaction, a feeling of dis-ease, dissatisfaction, and even madness would follow. Then turning it around, he suggested that in the face of a "disordered world," which denied recognition, a person had two options: either he suffered at his own hands by permitting a "disordered world" to impose itself on his consciousness; or he *"breaks by violence"* the circle of frustrated desires that bind him. The latter was the price of liberty, he conceded, as breaking the circle became the first step towards emotional recovery; it is not a recommendation for creative conflict, and certainly not an allusion to holy violence, Fanon nonetheless for the first time advanced the vague notion that if the social environment were itself a hindrance to mental health, one could escape the system through violence, or even, perhaps, by destroying it."[20]

But if this were the key reference to creative conflict—which in a supposedly non-political doctoral thesis was already a lot—Fanon stumbled into other materials, not in the least related to his thesis topic, but which later appeared in his concept of holy violence. Specifically, he turned to Lévy-Brühl's idea that the "primitive' never separated himself from nature; and that his theology, symbolism imagery, rituals, above all his myths, reinforced his "essential homogeneity" with nature. Then ignoring the fact that these ideas interrupted the flow of his thesis argument on genetic defects in the nervous system, Fanon launched into a discussion of projection and collective representation in the "primitive's" world, which he also attributed to Mauss and to Lévy-Brühl. Thus in the middle of a conventional discussion on neurological research, Fanon was also telling readers that in the learning process, the "primitive" or uninstructed mind moved from one level of awareness to another level of awareness by identifying with objective or material phenomena, and by imposing subjective necessities, or the impulses of the subconscious mind, on to these objective realities. The uninstructed mind, moreover, communicated with the internal and external worlds through coded "language," such as myths, religious beliefs, symbols, imagery and ritual. In fact the uninstructed mind lived in a coded spiritual universe (usually of its own making) where knowledge of the material world, and of the self was grasped immediately, either directly or indirectly. The "primitive" therefore ended up by "knowing" because he "knows." By separating himself from what he "knows," the primitive later established "knowledge," which when handed down from one generation to the next in coded forms, such as myths, became the means whereby the primitive interpreted causation and explained his world view. His "knowledge" also instructed and socialized group members and posterity; and although "knowledge" was coded in the form of myths and symbols, it was easily understood by those who had been integrated into the culture.

In effect, in his thesis on a completely different subject, Fanon had already gone beyond creative conflict and the Hegelian paradigm. Wandering around in the "primitive's" world of myths, symbols, rituals and his conceptual framework, Fanon not only asserted how "primitives" learn—how their minds move from one level of awareness to another level of awareness—but he had stumbled into key categories for his own concept of holy violence, which incidentally was still ten years away. He had not only grasped the "primitive's" conceptual framework which he was later to use, but he found a way of reaching him through his belief systems and theoretical world view, which Fanon thereafter implemented by means of indoctrination. It is unlikely that the new graduate was aware of this "find" in 1951. At that time, this information was next to useless, sticking out, as it did, like a sore thumb from his thesis on nervous genetic disorders. By 1961, however, Fanon had turned it around. Now it was the "primitive's" learning process and conceptual framework which provided *him* with *his* categories for the concept of holy violence. The empirical "primitive" was the Algerian peasant; and the conceptual framework now filtered through Jung's archetypal forms, had become a formidable "doctrine."

Fanon came upon these ideas slowly. When dealing with Jung's "collective unconscious" in 1952, he applied it to the French, commenting on the hopelessness of trying to escape the myths, imagery and pejorative stereotypes of the black, which had been embedded in French archetypal forms. The white man never "recognized" the black, save through the projections from his own prejudicial mind.[21] Juxtaposed beside the Hegelian paradigm which he discussed in the following chapter, Fanon stressed the need for breaking the circle of unconscious prejudice by violence, and by creative conflict. But when these archetypal forms re-appeared in *The Wretched of the Earth*—after he had gathered empirical data from the Algerian "primitive" or peasantry—they no longer had anything to do with the white man's stereotypes of the black, *but with the black man's (i.e. the Algerian peasants') stereotypes of the white!* Combining them with the peasants' world view and "essential homogeneity," *Fanon used them to go beyond the Hegelian paradigm.* Holy violence, therefore owed as much, if not more, to the Algerian peasant's "essential homogeneity," including his myths, symbols, imagery and ritual, as it did to creative conflict and the Hegelian paradigm. Hence, while Fanon used Lacan to develop important ideas on the social psychology and social psychiatry, which later provided a background for Tosquelle's concepts at Saint Alban Hospital, Mauss and Lévy-Brühl led him into ethno-sociology and the functions of the "primitive mind" which were later incorporated into holy violence.[22] Small wonder, as Geismar reported, his two hour thesis defense was reduced to a battle scene as conservative doctors parried with an unconventional medical mind quoting the "God is dead" German philosopher Friedreich Nietzsche, and the social anthropologist Lucien Lévy-Brühl.[23]

But having stumbled on the idea of breaking the circle by violence, and the functioning of the primitive mind in 1951, Fanon was not sure how to use this information—apart from attaching it to the second part of his thesis. In any event, he was still too involved with creative conflict in the Hegelian paradigm; and at this stage, he seemed less concerned to follow through with the implications of Lévy-Brühl's "essential homogeneity" *per se,* than to establish linkages between the latter and creative conflict in the Hegelian paradigm (which is exactly what he did). Using the notion of projected image, which permeated the primitive's world of magic and religious beliefs, Fanon linked it to Hegel's concept of the dependent bondsman who lived only to internalize the lord's image of him. Neither primitive man nor the dependent bondsman was perceiving himself *qua* self. While the former fused the Self with objective reality—by means of projection—the latter internalized the image which his lord had projected on him. Both primitive man and dependent bondsman identified with the Other. Neither Self, therefore, possessed the self-awareness necessary for personality growth and change.[24] Hegel had demonstrated the effectiveness of creative conflict in developing self-awareness and self-realization in the bondsman, an option which the colonized Antillean had avoided. But what of primitive man? Could creative conflict separate him from nature into which he was embedded? Fanon did not ask the question, believing it unnecessary. In fact, he left the idea dangling, and it was years before Fanon returned to the concept of creative conflict or the Hegelian Paradigm. And Lévy-Brühl's "essential homo-geniety" in the primitive's world, all but disappeared from his professional writings.

Under Tosquelles' influence, for the while, he seemed committed to finding peaceful means by which to integrate man into his environment. Most of his professional work in Algeria (1953-1957), and in association with the hospital centers of Front de Libération Nationale in Tunisia (1957-1961) showed Fanon faithfully replicating—with various degrees of success—ideas learned from Tosquelles.[25] His professional publications after 1952 revealed the same quest for a peaceful formula for social re-integration in the Algerian colonial world. It is clear, however, that the Hegelian paradigm was not far from his thoughts, as even professional writings conveyed the idea of opposition, and non-recognition on the part of the colonizing "lord," and the "dying" personalities of the colonized "bondsmen" annihilated by Hegelian "abstract negations."

Clinical work in North Africa had provided this empirical data. For example, drawing heavily on Algerian data, where Muslims with psycho-logical disorders were tested and diagnosed according to western clinical standards and techniques, (a *profound* lack of recognition to say the least), Fanon perceived a cultural discontinuity which induced personality "death." Clinical data for these conclusions came, for example, from his use of the Thematic Apperception Test applied to Algerian women with emotional disorders at the Blida-Joinville hospital.[26]

There he found women confused and inarticulate when faced with cultural phenomena with which they could not relate. They not only failed to recognize western objects (e.g. not being able to tell the difference between a European boy or girl, or not recognizing a boat from an areoplane), but some were unable to distinguish between objects in a passive or active condition.

As Fanon remarked, they could say "what there is," but not (as is required in the tests) "what is happening." Why? Because "only God knows what is happening," was the reply. Far from suggesting anger and frustration—a meaning which immediately suggests itself to the western mind—the speaker was denying the ability to interpret action in the scene, as this knowledge is known only to God. In the face of this cultural confusion Fanon concluded that "there is no homogeneity between what we are presenting to the sick person, and what she knows: the world that we present to her is unknown, strange and anonymous." He discussed similar discoveries of cultural discontinuity, or non-recognition, in "la Socialthérapie dans un service d'homme musulmans: difficultés méthodologiques," ("Social therapy for Muslims: Some Methodological Difficulties") when he acknowledged the cultural limits of western techniques to diagnose and treat mental disorders.[27]

In "Attitude du musulman maghrébian devant la folie" ("The Maghribian Muslum's concept of Madness"), and "Reflexions sur l'ethnopsychiatrie" ("Some thoughts on Ethnopsychiatry"), together with "Conduites d'aveux en Afrique du Nord" ("Conduits of Consent in North Africa"), he explored the structure of Maghribian culture with the hope of establishing bridgeheads between the patient, diagnosis and treatment on the one hand, and society and culture on the other.[28] Finally in "L'Hôpitalisation de jour en psychiatrie: valeurs et limites"("Psychiatric Day Care: Merits and Limitations"), he discussed the merits and demerits of a psychiatric day-care center which he established at the Hôpital Charles Nicolle in Tunis after 1957. In the article he stressed that patients should never lose touch with their social environments, and demonstrated the need to relate treatment to society.[29] In each article mentioned above, he found cultural data to which he could relate diagnosis and treatment. In the article on the Maghribian concept of madness, for example, he claimed that traditional societies rejected madness, but not the mad person—which is debatable; and that in the diagnosis and therapy, they separated a person's humanity from his or her sickness. Hence, the sick person's humanity was never denied. Similarly, in his article on ethno-psychiatry (shades of Lévy-Brühl?) he elaborated on the importance of relating treatment and diagnosis to the sick person's culture; and in his discussion of cultural conduits or lines of consent, he gave a theoretical treatment of legal guilt in North African presented in culturally compre-hensible terms. Thus, if Fanon's clinical work revealed the "dead" and dying personalities of North African "bondsmen" systematically denied recognition by the French "lord" and his alien culture, it also revealed that when recognition occurred in culturally comprehensible terms, the cure-rate was higher. No longer locked into the Hegelian "abstract negation," the North African "bondsmen" could travel the path towards Hegelian self-actualization.[30]

In his sociological observations of Algerian society both before and
during the war of liberation (1954-1962)—from which he gathered empirical
data later applied to the concept of holy violence—Fanon's conclusions were
similar: when the colonizing "lord" withheld recognition; or worse, when he
recognized the colonized "bondsman" only through "abstract negations" or
stereotypes "piled up [from] a whole mass of judgements, appraisals, reasons,
accumulated anecdotes and edifying examples, thus attempting to confine the
Algerian within a circle of guilt," colonized "bondsmen" were in danger of
being annihilated by opposition and non-recognition.[31] Nowhere was this
better illustrated than in his analysis of the colonizing "lord's" attempts to
unveil Algerian women, and their corresponding reactions.[32] Algerian Arab
women wore the *Haïk*, or veil, Fanon remarked, because it was customary.
Perceiving it as "sadistic and vampirish" attempts on the part of the Algerian
patriarchy to "keep women out of sight," and to deny them "social
reciprocity," "enlightened" French sociologists and ethnographers recommended a program to liberate Algerian Arab women by freeing them from
the restrictive veil. Their plan, accordingly, was "to destroy the structure of
Algerian society" by radically altering the status and function of women.

To a certain extent the colonizer's opposition, or assault on the
fundamental structure of Algerian society was effective. Shamed into
assuming a "French" personality—since her Algerian *persona* was denied
recognition—some Algerian women unveiled and donned European dress.
The courage of these "test-women" was rewarded with French applause, as
"piece by piece, the flesh of Algeria lay bare." The female unveiling, Fanon
commented, was simply not a matter of individual women exposing faces and
extremities on their own volition. Rather, their unveiling was the symbolic
and systematic peeling away at those layers of Algerian culture and society
which the French deemed worthless. Every unveiling, he added, was "a
negative expression of the fact that Algeria was beginning to deny herself and
was accepting the rape of the colonizer. With every abandoned veil," he
continued, "Algerian society seemed to express its willingness to attend the
master's school and to decide to change its habit under the occupier's
direction and patronage."[33] In the face of this opposition and non-recognition,
Fanon concluded, was the "dying" Algerian "bondswoman" who was
succumbing to the struggle and conflict. In the framework of the master-slave
relationship, she had been annihilated by the greater opposition, the tension
of creative conflict was released, and she had become the victim of "abstract
negation."

Throughout his entire North African experiences, Fanon continued to
gather empirical data on "dying" personalities of the Algerian "bondsman."[34]
There were those ambivalent feelings on the part of the Algerian towards
western medicine: it was without question effective, yet it had been introduced
by the colonial "lord" who was also responsible for the oppression and

racism that was reducing him to the status of an unrecognized "bondsman." Then there was the rejection of the "lord's" radio transmissions, which by being an affront to the Algerian sense of propriety, was also a form of non-recognition of the "bondsman." But Fanon also noticed that at the onset of hostilities in 1954, the "bondsmens' " attitudes towards the colonizing "lord" began to change, as the former initiated struggle and resistance against him. Conflict was bringing "dead" and "dying" personalities back to life as diffused anger and resentment were focussed on the "enemy." Separating the science and technology from the "lord" himself, Algerians entered into the creative stage of conflict by not only appropriating their own personalities once possessed by the "lord," but by appropriating his science and technology and turning it to their advantage in the struggle.[35] If these events were occurring in Algeria at war, he mused, might not similar events be possible in the Antilles where free masterless thing-slaves were still shuffling and miming—unrecognized—in the "lord's" drawing room? Fanon hoped that conflict could do for Martinicans what it was doing for Algeria. He was delighted to learn in December 1959 that the French were beating up some rioting Martinicans. "I wish they would gather their dead, disembowel them and parade them through the streets," he jubilated. "They should shout to the people: 'look at what the colonialist[s] have done . . . let us avenge our dead.' " But they did not; and Fanon knew that they would not.[36] The Algerians avenged their dead, however. And it is to them that Fanon turned to substantiate his concept of creative conflict.

But while Fanon was observing Algerians, and developing his concept of creative conflict, he was also working through the Hegelian paradigm in his own life.[37] Like the characters in Emmanuel Mounier's L'Eveil de l'Afrique noire (1948), (The Awakening of Black Africa), he seemed to seek out conflict, opposition and challenges which would enable him to assert his separate—and distinct—self; which may in part explain observations by friends and colleagues in France and Algeria. Although anxious to preserve the Fanon myth, even loyal friends hinted that Fanon was tense and aggressive, irrascible, demanding, and very difficult to work with. Some have attributed this to his sense of guilt, and to his feelings of "persecution" for being black.[38] Others have observed that he only "went along" with people who "completely agreed" with him, which apparently explains why he broke with the French Marxists, Communists, Liberals and even with Sartre.[39] It may also explain why he was in conflict with the other five Chefs de service or division heads at the Blida-Joinville hospital in Algeria, and why he was out of sympathy with M. Kriff, Director of the Blida complex. In his later years, he maintained a permanent posture of opposition, especially to the white man, even refusing to walk on the same pavement with him, seeking instead the other side of the street.[40]

Geismar also reported several incidents of Fanon's irrascible and

demanding behavior, suggesting that especially in his later years, he
deliberately affected an aggressive style when wanting to be taken seriously.
Gendzier similarly commented on his aggressiveness and hostile manner. She
confirms Geismar's assertions that he was disliked in the Tunisian clinic of
Manouba where he worked after his expulsion from Blida in January 1957.
Evidently his innovations and leadership style angered Ben Soltan, the
Director of the hospital, as well as other colleagues, although the Tunisian
Ministry of Health consistently dismissed charges brought against him.[41] In
*The Wretched of the Earth*, he talked about having no more fear of the white
man, and justified discourtesy to the "former colonizer" on grounds that it
was a "quite normal" defense mechanism against those whose mere presence
polluted the social and moral environment. Similarly, he enjoyed both Nikita
Khrushchev's shoe-thumping act and Castro's machine-gun performance at
the United Nations in 1960. They were treating "those miserable capitalists
the way that they deserve."[42]

But there was nothing new about this attitude which Fanon adopted. As
early as 1952, this is exactly the behavior that he said he was going to adopt,
even if it meant sacrificing the polite constraints of bourgeois role-play by
which he had been conditioned. "I am committed to myself and to my
neighbor," he snapped, "to fight with all my might, with all my strength to
prevent the [future] subjugation of people on this earth." "I pledge to face up
to the possibility of annihilation," he hissed while turning over the
Hegelian paradigm in his mind, "in order that a few truths should be made
clear," because "I suddenly find myself in a world where evil occurs; a world
where I am summoned to fight; a world where there is always the question of
annihilation or victory," "If the white man challenges my humanity," he
growled, "I will show him with all my available strength that I am not the
'nice nigga' that he thinks I am." "You better get used to me," he snarled,
because "I am not going to accomodate myself to anyone . . . . One has to be
tough in order to survive."[43]

# Background to Creative Conflict: Martinique

*For the black who works on a sugar plantation in [Martinique]*
*there is but one solution: to fight. He will undertake this struggle and*
*lead it, not because of any Marxist or idealist ideology, but*
*because—he can only perceive life in the form of conflict against*
*exploitation, misery and hunger.*

Fanon

The last chapter discussed Fanon's concept of creative conflict in relation to the Hegelian paradigm. It argued that in the face of intractable opposition from the Other (who was committed to one's destruction), the only way to prevent annihilation was to resist with force. To kill the opposing Other in self-defense was also acceptable. Thus, Fanon was not recommending the joy of killing as an end in itself. Instead, he was defending the use of force in the colonial scenario—where one was constantly opposed by the colonizer—as essential for survival. Under these circumstances, conflict was creative.

But having said that, he was also aware that the Martinican had never seriously resisted his master, and had consequently not really "survived." On the contrary, he went to a great deal of trouble to adjust to the lord's oppression. Unlike the Algerian who re-appropriated his Self from the Other by force, the Martinican was the "happy" victim of conflict in his colonial society, which he did not create, but which was "creating" him. Martinique, therefore, provided the background to Fanon's creative conflict in that it was the first social laboratory in which he saw the consequence of the *absence of conflict* against the "lord" on a large scale. It was, however, also the social laboratory in which he got his first glimpse of the Martinican peasant who refused depersonalization at the hands of the "lord," and who decided to save himself by fighting back.

Fanon knew Martinique well; he was born there on 20 July 1925. His social background was modest: his father was a middle-grade civil servant in the customs department, while his mother kept a shop at home, preparing "fast foods" which she sold to passers-by. Although the family never suffered material need, the Fanons could hardly have been of the upper middle class, as both Geismar and Gendzier suggest.[1] Seven children were born to M. and Mme. Fanon, of which Frantz was the fourth and youngest boy.

In keeping with the stifling values of the colonial black *petits bourgeoisies*, which Fanon mercilessly criticized in *Black Skin White Masks*, the elder Fanons had "bourgeois" ambitions for their children—but which in reality were "white" ambitions—as models from the dominant minority were the only ones available in the colonial world. Even Fanon himself admitted in 1955 that until 1939, blacks in Martinique thought themselves "white" (a common phenomenon in the colonial West Indies) because they were culturally white.[2] After all, didn't everybody know that the Gauls were their ancestors? As he pointed out in this first book, "a good education" was accordingly stressed, as well as achievement, "culture," and refinement (i.e., French manners). A bourgeois woman's reputation was excessively guarded, especially if she was light-skinned and pretty. Moreover, an air of Second Empire decadence and gentility pervaded the social environnent. Black petits bourgeois families "dressed nicely" (i.e., European dress), "behaved nicely" (i.e., "white" manners), and "spoke nicely"—in public (i.e., good French). Friends and associates were carefully chosen, and families went to extremes to avoid being seen—in public—with someone who was not "nice" (i.e., dark-skinned, modest social background and not well educated). The reverse was also true. Families strove to be seen in "nice" places (i.e., frequented by whites), with "decent" people (i.e., of the same or higher social strata) at the "right time" (i.e., the social season). They kept in the closet friends and family skeletons which could tarnish their "nice" image. With this emphasis on style, form and image, the elder Fanons tried to assure that their children would be appropriately situated socially, and that where possible, they should acquire bourgeois finesse. Thus, for example, instead of attending the free primary school, where he would have rubbed shoulders with the children of the great unwashed, Fanon went to the fee-paying all-black Lycée Schoelcher (1934-43), where, incidentally, he came under the influence of Aimé Césaire, later to become a leading man of letters, and Mayor of the capital city, Fort-de-France. Similarly, at one time or another, his sisters were initiated into the genteel art of piano playing.[3] It is unlikely that the Fanon children mixed socially with Martinique's white or béké population, as for the most part, the latter attended private religious schools. It isn't that the society was rigidly or overtly stratified along racial lines. It is, rather, that since appearance, ancestry and association were frequently determinants of social class, plural elements within the society tacitly acknowledged exclusivity, especially where social mixing in public between the sexes was concerned. The effect, however, was the same. On the surface, the society seemed to be rigidly or overtly stratified along racial lines, even though on the inside it was less so. According to petits bourgeois values, FRANCE was the mother country, and it was assumed that bright children would continue a higher education in FRANCE. It goes without saying that the elder Fanons expected their sons, at least, to excell in one of the more "respectable" professions, such as law or medicine.[4]

This stifling environment notwithstanding, Fanon spent a relatively carefree youth. Martinique, prior to the fall of France in 1940, was still a picturesque, tranquil island, almost pre-political in its orientation, with the emphasis instead on racial classes. Like other Caribbean islands—all of them old sugar colonies—Martinique's poverty and pressing social problems were for the most part ignored by those who could mitigate them. There was still the sense that if people were poor, they only had themselves to blame. Social conditions in anglophone territories such as Jamaica, Trinidad and British Guinea were not much better. But at least there were popular political stirrings, especially in Jamaica. During World War II, the metropolitan powers used some of the islands for military bases, and for resettling evacuated European refugees. As was the case with some of the other islands, the arrival in Martinique after 1940 of 10,000 refugees—most of them French sailors from the collaborationist Vichy fleet which the British blockaded for almost three years in the Fort-de-France harbor—was for many Martinicans the beginnings of a painful political awakening. Interestingly, the American occupation of Haiti (1915-34) had produced similar reactions from large segments of the populace, some of whom turned to a deliberate revival of Africanisms, such as music, literature and dance, as well as a new respect for Haitian folk cultures.

Surviving these vicissitudes—which did not seem to have had much impact on the Fanon family—the young Fanon spent much time in the company of friends at the Savanne an old down-town square in Fort-de-France, and by the sea.[5] But for the fact that school work claimed much of his time (he was apparently an indifferent, "mischievous" student)[6] he passed many hours in the kind of world which French fantasies had stereotyped into the "innocent, ingenuous and spontaneous" native world, peopled by "the children of the world" who had "adorably expressive faces."

Yet as a black family of modest means, the Fanons would have figured below many in the social order, and especially below the local whites or békés. They would also have been discriminated against (a form of non-recognition) by the subtle forms of racism which developed in the Caribbean and Latin American world—the sort which distinguishes minute shade gradations, numerous facial features and infinite varieties of hair structure. Not infrequently, one's social status, work, marriage and life opportunities hinged on these subtle differentiations. Yet if Fanon's word is to be taken at its face value, the significance of growing up in a non-recognizing racist society, which did not openly acknowledge its racism, seems to have escaped him. In 1952, he talked about "that little gulf that existed between the near-white, the mulatto and the black," and of the Antillean's mistaken notion of crossing the color line ("magically turning white") by cultural and economic whitewashing, such as speaking a good French, and acquiring wealth, because in Martinique "one is white if one is rich." Yet in 1955, he wrote that "before 1939, there was not on one side the Negro and on the other side the white man, but a scale of colors the intervals of which could readily be passed over." There was the "magically turning white" which he did not seem to recognize as racism because, he continued, "one only needed to have children by someone less black than oneself" in order to correct permanently the chromosone chart. Hence "there was no racial barrier," no discrimination. "There was [only] that ironic space, so characteristic of the Martinican mentality."[7] Unfortunately the development of racial attitudes in Martinique suggests that by the twentieth century, that was not the case, although the social structure was not as rigid as Emmanuel Hansen suggested.[8]

It is hard to believe that even at eleven years of age (1939) Fanon had not faced some form of discrimination in Martinique; harder still to think that he was unaware of it, especially since according to Geismar his two boyhood friends, Mosole and Manville, both had a highly developed sense of racial awareness.[9] His friends notwithstanding, could it be that he did not know that he was black (this has been known to happen in the Antilles); or did he think that he could "magically turn white" by association, by education and through a cultural whitewashing (this too has happened in the Antilles); or did he only become aware of racism in Martinique after he had gone to France, as is suggested in *Black Skin White Masks* (which has also been known to happen)?[10] What is more likely, is that in his youth Fanon probably had nothing but a superficial understanding of Martinican social structure and racial attitudes, and that he thought of his childhood as a happy one. At least the latter is suggested in this somewhat exaggerated claim that "until 1939 the West Indian lived, thought, dreamed . . . composed poems [and] wrote novels." It is also likely that in 1955 when he wrote this statement, his memory had edited out the more unpleasant experiences.[11] Moreover, refusing to be psychoanalyzed—which was not required for psychiatric training in France—Fanon may have "forgotten" the conflicts, hurts and humiliations which he experienced in a society which neither openly recognized him, nor acknowledged its racism. At any rate, this is the impression of some of the male nurses at the hospital at Blida-Joinville in Algeria where Fanon later worked, one of whom observed that "Fanon seemed to suffer from being black."[12]

Adding to problems of restricted recognition in the Fanon family was the fact of lineage. In a colonial and traditionally structured society, where status was ascriptive and determined by family affiliations, the Fanon family had few claims to high status.[13] The latter was reserved for white or near white creole families. "In Martinique," Fanon observed, expressing the correct idea but getting his statistics wrong, "there are two hundred whites who consider themselves superior to 300,000 blacks." Known on the social scale as the *grands békés, békés moyens,* and *petits blancs*, including the poor white *békés en bas feuille, békés goyave,* and *bitacos* (the last three were pejorative terms) to whom Fanon referred, some had been in Martinique since the mid-seventeenth century.[14] Marrying within their white creole circle or with Europeans, the first two groups were "high society," creating and overseeing its rules of conduct, despite the fact that some members were coarse, ill-bred and unlettered. It mattered little, however, as prior to 1939 their lineage and landed wealth guaranteed their status at or near the top of the social order. Even in competition with poor whites for status, the bourgeois Fanon family would hardly have achieved social recognition, as by the twentieth century, social conventions had tacitly upgraded the status of poor whites—which incidentally did not always match their educational or cultural achievements.

But if the young Fanon came of age in a society which failed to recognize him, the family broke one of its sacred conventions. It is now generally known that his lighter-skinned mother—the daughter of an illegitimate union—married into the darker-skinned Fanon family of mixed Indian and black heritage.[15] In the politics of the black bourgeois Martinican family, Elènore Fanon had broken the conventions known to all: that rather than "founder into niggerness," "the race must be whitened"; and that if one married into a darker-skinned family, it was because this was the last resort.[16] Moreover, no doubt following his father's side, Frantz was the "blackest" of his parents' children, a fact which would hardly have gone unnoticed. In the politics of the Fanon family, it is not known how this issue was handled, save perhaps for two clues: Martinicans talk about who is the blackest member of the family, Fanon observed, but they don't really mean that he is the blackest. What they mean is that he is the least white. (He later added that he "wanted to be white [but knew] that that was a joke.") In any event, he concluded, social conventions had really "solved" the problem by creating "a very black, but . . . quite nice" type of people category (i.e., appearance). Thus if people were "black" to the point of being "blue," or if they "disappeared" in the dark when there was a power failure, they could still be "quite nice" if they played the piano, or taught natural science at the girl's academy, or were medical doctors (i.e., appearance, and association).[17]

In the absence of in-depth psycho-data, it is impossible to verify how this non-recognizing environment influenced the personality development of the young Fanon. Few who knew him talk freely about his youth or of his inner self. Geismar and Gendzier have put together a limited personality profile of the man, and Gendzier in particular regrets that more biographical data has not been available.[18] My own work in Martinique and Algeria has turned up little other than what is already known: the numerous anecdotes which point to the fact that Fanon was a restless student who eventually did well academically; and that frequently "getting into trouble," his youthful behavior left something to be desired.[19] Later anecdotes confirm that as a young adult in France, where he pursued his medical training (1947-1952), Fanon was hard working and hard driving. We also know that he was a political activist, and that shunning the cowardly and weak, he sought out the strong.[20] Evidence of his "aggressive" personality had already began to accumulate. While information from professional associates on his experiences in Algeria and Tunisia (1952-1961) confirm his commitment to the anti-colonial cause, they also comment on his growing aggressivity and hositility towards all who opposed him. They speak also of his intellecutal growth and development, enormous energy and capacity for hard work, together with his physical and emotional stamina. Some comment on his "abstract personality," which suggests that becoming obsessed with anti-colonial struggles during the North African period of his life, he reached the point where "The Struggle" seemed to be taking over his entire personality.[21]

Was this zeal to assert, to exert, to excel a form of compensatory behavior? If skin color had denied him the recognition which he justly deserved, were strength, commitment and achievement the substitutes? Was this a larger than life gesture for recognition? His mother had recognized him, and grew to be proud of him. In the dedication which he wrote in her copy of the thesis, he "marvelled . . . at her never failing ardour for life," and assured her of his "profound love." His father would have been proud of him also, had he lived. But dying in 1947—the year in which Fanon left for France to pursue his education—he "never had the joy," as Fanon sadly commented in his thesis dedication, "to see this son succeed at the end of his medical studies." Other members of his family have also recognized him. But to date (1975), Fanon has not been recognized in Martinique; and "Frantz who?" is not an infrequent response to questions about him in Fort-de-France.

But if we are denied specific insights into the influence of the non-recognizing Martinican world on Fanon's personality, *Black Skin White Masks* gives a general sense of its effects on the collective Martinican psyche. In short, parts of the book reveal *the* struggle writ large for social, intellectual and emotional recognition by the Other of one's choice. It was suggested above that Fanon was not recognized in Martinique. One gets the same sense of denial in *Black Skin White Masks,* where the characters seek constantly for recognition. For example, the blackman in France addresses a Frenchman in good French. The latter replies in "pidgin-nigger." There was no act of recognition. "Pidgin-nigger" not only "keeps the black in his place," but it "perpetuates a state of conflict" by relegating blackness to a stereotype. Or, there is Mayotte Capécia's Ce Carbet who " 'would like to marry . . . a white man,' " although she knows that a black woman "will never win the respect of a white man." Finally, there is René Maran's Jean Veneuse "a man of color," who is culturally white. Needing acceptance (recognition) but fearing rejection (non-recognition), he withdraws into himself and experiences neither.[22] In all three instances, the blacks' request for recognition was never acknowledged. They all suffered a sense of absolute loss.

In Martinique, non-recognition and conflict originated in the Caribbean plantation system. One of the "old colonies" of France's first empire, Martinique was acquired in 1635-36, about the same time as Guadeloupe, by an act of possession.[23] With the introduction of the sugar economies shortly thereafter, the master-slave relationships about which Fanon spoke became widespread.[24] By 1685, when the *Code Noir* was introduced, the statutory background to non-recognition was institutionalized throughout the French Antilles. A legal collection which defined plantation relationships, the *Code* was in part a summary of existing norms of race relations. It remained on the books until 1848, although in some colonies it ceased to be administered after the outbreak of the French Revolution. Its appearance at approximately the same time when sugar production was increasing, when slave labor was being substituted for European indentured labor, and when a new managerial group was emerging, was probably no coincidence.[25]

The *Code* was the epitomy of non-recognition. An analysis of its provisions reveals the specific historical background to the type of conflict in master-slave relationships about which Fanon spoke. For example, slaves were not defined in human but in property terms (article 44), and were required to be "labeled"—showing their plantation or place of residence on their clothing—which dramaticaly illustrates Fanon's observations that with no rights to humanity, Antilleans had become "things." By defining appropriate slave behavior, the *Code* also conditioned blacks to a type of role playing which required them to "keep their place" (articles 28, 33, 37 *et passim*). Slaves were forbidden to carry firearms, they were denied rights of assembly and freedom of movement without authorization. Punishments for *Code* violations included whipping, branding and death. Apart from the fact that the *Code* was supposed to guarantee the slave's right to food, shelter and other basic needs, the only undisputed right which the slave had was the right to work. With this kind of historical background, small wonder that Fanon was attracted to the Hegelian paradigm, where the bondsman re-appropriated his Self through work.

Beginning with the royal ordinance of 29 November 1705, eighteenth century legislation reinforced this non-recognition by threatening the French nobility with serious penalties, including the seizure of property, if they entered into mixed unions. Throughout the eighteenth century, Martinican Royal Councils reiterated the ordinance's provisions, in addition to the official statement of 13 October 1766, which forbade mixed unions on grounds of "natural inequality." In the celebrated statement the Ministry of Marine observed that since all blacks have an "indelible stain on their past," they and their descendents "are forbidden to enter the white class." If ever there comes a time, the statement continued, when blacks or those of mixed origins "are declared white" and should lay claim . . . to all rank of dignity, it would be absolutely contrary to the constitution of the colonies."[26] In March 1777, instructions from the Minister Sartine to the Governor and Intendent of Martinique pursued the same "harsh but wise" decisions *apropos* of free blacks: that however far removed their slave origins, they "were permanently marked with the blemish of slavery, and would be ineligible for any public office whatsoever . . . . Neither would they enjoy the perogatives of the nobility." It was absolutely necessary, the Minister continued, "to put . . . distance between the two species—a phrase which Fanon was to use one hundred and seventy-four years later—as "one could not sufficiently impress blacks with the respect which was due to their masters."[27] Thus like Hegel's bondsman, the *Code* and subsequent legislation had denied humanity to the slave and his descendents, and had prevented recognition by the Other. Kept at a distance, he was left with his "Self," and his work.

The abolition of slavery in the French Antilles (27 April 1848) did little to alter the slave's social and psychological orientation. As Fanon observed, the slave had not accelerated conflict by wresting recognition from his master. Instead, freedom had been legally imposed, while custom and the traditional social structure continued to sanction non-recognition. By the twentieth century, tradition and society not only provided the mould which shaped the young Fanon's development, they became the source material for much of his discussions in *Black Skin White Masks*. In Fanon's lifetime (1925-1961), the *békés* or Martinican whites were still the most influential sub-group. Mulattoes, whose appearance revealed "the indelible stain on their past," were discouraged from openly associating with "white society," while the blacks, still "permanently marked by the blemish of slavery," occupied the lower end of the social scale.

Property ownership reflected the emergence of what were essentially racial classes. For example, in Martinique in 1671 when the total population was approximately 10,000, one-third of arable lands, mainly in the fertile north-east and south-central regions, belonged to 681 proprietors of European descent.[28] These white planters, or *habitants*, were not only important in the local community, but they influenced policy decisions in the local Royal Councils by virtue of their economic power base, and control over the local militia. Moreover, possessing "social" power, they were the core of Martinican creole society, and determined "nice" behavior. By the middle of the eighteenth century, "talented mulattoes" were ranked higher than black populations. About one hundred years later (1844), there were approximately 36,626 free persons of color, some of whom owned and managed properties, together with approximately one-sixth of the total slave population. As their numbers and wealth increased, whites became more fearful of them, and repeated oppression and discriminatory acts were justified on grounds that there had been "another plot," or "conspiracy." By the 1820's a system of virtual segregation was introduced, one example of which was the separation of the birth, marriage, and death registers of the whites from those of the free coloreds. Now barred from practicing medicine, pharmacy and other professions, many free blacks and mulattoes turned to small commerce, and the skilled trades such as tailoring, carpentry, cabinet making, leather working, etc. At the lower end of the social scale, the majority of blacks—about 74,000 in 1848—remained relatively poor with limited chances for social change.

By 1914, just eleven years before Fanon was born, there were popular references to "the three families" which controlled the island's biggest business interests. In 1939, when Fanon was fourteen years old, Martinican *békés* held practically a total monopoly of the sugar profits, and 85 per cent of the rum industry. They also held exclusive ownership of the pineapple processing industry, and had diversified their interests, investing in coffee, cocoa, and other plantation crops. They also held considerable stock in the railways, port facilities and mass-media enterprises. By 1959, two years before Fanon died, a handful of "sugar families" were producing more than 2,000 tons of sugar each, of a total of 783,000 tons. Seventy per cent of this was refined in the island.[29] After Fanon's death in 1961, the principle criteria for social classes was still ethnicity, skin color, occupation and wealth. The society still consisted, as Fanon had observed, of "two separate species": privileged creole and metropolitan whites; mulattoes and blacks.

Sub-groups still remained more or less distinct, and as is frequently the case in plural societies, people of different ethnic backgrounds associated with each other mainly during business hours. Mixed socializing in public was usually restricted to males. While whites added commerce, communications, banking and insurance to their earlier agro-industries, bourgeois mulattoes and blacks such as the Fanon family, began entering the liberal arts professions— the only "acceptable" occupations open to them. With the exception of certain free mulatto families, few non-whites—and certainly not the Fanon family— were large land owners. It is hardly surprising, therefore, that Fanon chose "formal education"—as opposed to "society education." Few viable "bourgeois" alternatives remained.

When seen from this perspective, Fanon's feelings of inferiority, and hatred of racism and non-recognition can be explained. He was born into a society which had been officially stratified along racial lines since the seventeenth century. In the twentieth century, evidence of white domination in all major business interests, in society, and in the government was still present. Fanon was aware of this racial stratification and the existence of pre-political racial classes. Yet he seemed ambivalent, sharing his mixed feelings

with the non-recognized characters in *Black Skin White Masks*. He
attributed *their* ambivalence (in part) to alienation from devalued colonial
cultures, and to the ever present hope of "whitening" the race through
marriage with a lighter-skinned person; which, as has been suggested above,
is exactly what happened in the Fanon family. The elder dark-skinned Fanon
married a mulatto woman of Alsatian heritage, and Fanon married a French
woman. Fanon seemed defensive about his own attempt to "whiten the race."
In *Black Skin White Masks* he wrote that "when I marry a white woman, I
marry white culture, white beauty, the ultimate whiteness . . . . I am making
. . . white dignity mine . . . . But I don't think," he added later, "that I am
abdicating my personality by marrying a European women . . . . If my
children are suspected, if the crescents in their fingernails are inspected, it will
be simply because society will not have changed."[30]

   "Whitening" the race was also an historical phenomenon. Although the
courts made numerous attempts to block intermarriage throughout the French
Antilles, extra-conjugal relations nonetheless persisted. With or without
benefit of clergy, people did "magically turn white," either by having
children with lighter-skinned persons through association and co-habitation,
or through education and cultural transfusions. A case in point was that of
one Magdeleine Roblat. When she baptized her son from a white planter in
1751, she was designated as "nominally" free, and in another connection ten
years later, she was referred to as a "free mulatto." Yet on her marriage in
1768 to Sieur Marcher, an upper class white, there was no mention either to
her color, or to her social station. She had "magically turned white."
Historically free men of color alienated from black cultures, also "whitened"
themselves by their political behavior where, with a few notable exceptions,
they strove for identification with the politics of the white power structure.
With the aid of these social safety valves, which by the twentieth century
were embedded in the culture and social fabric, Martinicans had adjusted to,
were attached to, were even blind to the inner rigidities of their society. Small
wonder that the young Fanon seemed ambivalent towards the racism in his
own society. This kind of uncertainty, the mature Fanon now argued, guaranteed the continuation of non-recognition which always found ways of avoiding
creative conflict. Historically, freed blacks, mulattoes and later bourgeois
Antilleans were prone to ambivalence and avoidance. Believing in their
historic roles as intermediaries between white and blacks, their faith in
French assimilation policies seldom wavered.[31]

   Not so working class blacks, Fanon countered. Like their remote
ancestors the field slave, they were less alienated from indigenous values
than their bourgeois counterpart. Elaborating on this argument which he was
later to apply to the Algerian peasantry, he remarked that working class
blacks seldom harbored vague hopes of transforming non-recognized

blackness into human dignity—without conflict. "For the black who works on a sugar plantation in Le Robert [in Martinique]," he continued, "there is but one solution: to fight. He will undertake this struggle and lead it, not because of any Marxist or idealist ideology, but because he can only perceive life in the form of conflict against exploitation, misery and hunger. It would never occur to me to ask these blacks to alter their idea of history," he concluded, "I believe that they agree with me," since they don't seem to be mesmerized by the past.[32]

Fanon's reference to the less alienated fighting underdog in Martinique was his first hint of the anti-colonial role which he perceived for the masses. It was also his first suggestion that violence comes "naturally as if by instinct" to the less alienated peasantry, and that violence can play a redemptive role. In 1946, his brother Joby had worked with Aimé Césaire's election campaign in Martinique, and had drawn his younger brother's attention to the importance of mobilizing the masses for a successful political campaign. When he returned to the theme in 1961, he had already left Martinique for good, and was in Algeria. The underdogs in the anti-colonial war against the French (1954-1962) were the peasants. Like Martinican sugar-cane workers, Algerian peasants responded "instinctively" in an anti-colonial posture because they had always perceived life as Struggle against poverty, misery, famine, depredations, enemies and natural disasters. After the French occupation of Algeria in 1830, they never "resolved" non-recognition and conflict by identifying with the colonizer. Not having bourgeois pretensions, "they knew they were black," or Arab or peasant, or whatever the case might be. Moreover, not standing around waiting for recognition from the colonial "lord"—they knew they would not get it—they "instinctively" extended their age-long struggle against opposing forces, to include the colonizing "lord." Moreover, morality for them was something concrete: if the colonizer took their land, then clearly and simply he was the enemy. In effect, therefore, Fanon was saying that fighting underdogs understand the feeling and behavior (if not the concept) of creative conflict better than their bourgeois counterparts. They came from traditions where conflict struggle and violence were respected. The "lord" used it effectively against them, and when in their interest, they turned it against him. That generations of Antilleans slaves rose up against their masters, is testimony of this. Similarly, resistance traditions among the Algerian peasantry sang the glorious praises of a "war of one hundred and thirty years" (1830-1962) against the French. The latter part of this conflict (1954-1962) was to bring victory against the oppressor.[33]

Violence worked. Masters forced slaves to create value by means of violence, and slaves turned it against masters in order to prevent annihilation. The Algerian colonizer coerced the masses to create a colonial state, and the masses turned violence against the colonial "lord" in order to preserve their nation from destruction.

This is exactly what Hegel, and later Fanon had said: in matters of self-defense in order to avoid annihilation, the bondsman must match the lord's opposition with his own. If the bondsman failed to resist his lord, the latter's opposition would annihilate him. Through matching opposition, the Algerian masses recovered their nation. Through mutual resistance on slave plantations, the master got his value, and field slaves avoided annihilation.

The wheel had come full cycle. In his quest for the background to creative conflict, Fanon found it at home, among the same earthy people with whom he had brushed shoulders as a child in the Martinican countryside. Ironically the background to creative conflict was in the non-recognized Martinican, and his devalued culture. Had Fanon developed the idea, relating it empirically to the Martinican peasant and unrecognized masses, his concept of creative conflict would have been more suitably developed. But he did not. Instead, influenced by Cartesian logical abstractions, which dominate some aspects of French thought, he related creative conflict to the abstract "primitive" of the theoretical world arguing, as was discussed in the previous chapter, that the abstract "primitive" and the non-recognized bondsman had internalized the Other's image of himself. This association deprived creative conflict of an empirical dimension, and probably postponed the development of the concept of violence and holy violence. In fact, the latter emerged only after he had gathered empirical data from his experiences in Algeria, which were still years away.

## III

## The Makings of Violence Part I: Conflict in the Antillean and Algerian Social Structures

*"The violence which presided in the structure of the colonial world, which has destroyed the native social forms with a tireless rhythm, and demolished without reserve the system or reference points in the economy, the manner of appearance and of dress, that same violence will be claimed and assumed by the colonized people at the moment when, deciding to be a part of history, they storm the forbidden quarters."*

Fanon

Fanon had developed the concept of creative conflict from the Hegelian paradigm and from combative "instincts" of Martinican peasants. But it was leading him nowhere—not in 1952 at any rate when *Black Skin White Masks* was published. Although taking shape, the concept lacked empirical data, and still had little in common with his later theory of violence and holy violence. Groping for substance, Fanon later found supporting data in two areas: in colonial social structures; and in the history of colonial violence in Algeria. Both of these, especially the latter he argued, engendered conflict and threatened societal counter-violence against the colonial state. These insights did not come easily. In fact, it was only after he had left Martinique for the last time in 1953, and was working in Algeria (1953-1957), a war-torn country in the midst of an anti-colonial conflict (1954-1962) against France, that these ideas began to crystalize. Working at the Blida-Joinville psychiatric hospital, since renamed L'Hôpital Psychiatrique Frantz Fanon, Fanon saw at first hand the roots of violence in the Algerian social structure. Earlier he had uncovered avenues for potential conflict in the Martinican social structure (i.e., sugar workers). On recognizing parallels in the Algerian social structure, he could no longer avoid conclusions that seemed to beg: both in Martinique and Algeria, French policies had created conflict and violent-prone environments which, in the case of Algeria, could flare into a revolutionary conflagration simply by "lighting a match." Thus if it was "too late" to apply the Hegelian paradigm to Antillean societies, this was probably not going to be the case in Algeria.

Fanon's intellectual odyssey began shortly after leaving the Caribbean for the first time in 1944, during World War II, when he served with the Free French armies in Guercif in Morocco, and Bougie in Algeria.[1] He was nineteen years of age. From the colonial bourgeois perspective, it seemed "normal" and "right" to fight for France which had been subject to German occupation since 1940; and there is no evidence that Fanon believed he was performing other than a "natural" duty. After all, France was the mother country; and although the colonial world was undergoing rapid changes during the 1930s and the 1940s, ultimately leading to independence in the fifties and sixties,[2] Martinican events were actually moving in the opposite direction. In fact, Martinicans—together with the people of Guadeloupe and Guyáne—were reinforcing old ties with France. By acquiesing to the act of union (Union Française) in 1946 Guadeloupe, Guyane and Réunion (a small island in the Indian Ocean), became overseas *départements* of France.[3] Like Normandy, Provençe or Alsace, they were legally and administratively a part of France. It is hardly surprising, therefore, that Fanon volunteered to serve in the ranks of the Free French armies. Commenting later on his status, he reminded readers: "I am a Frenchman." "I am personally interested in the French destiny, in French values, and the French nation . . . . The Martinican is a Frenchman [who] wishes to remain within the French Union.[4]

During his North African tour of duty Fanon, the patriotic Frenchman, met north and sub-Saharan Africans for the first time. He noted that while French officers encouraged the West Indians to keep their distance from the African troops, who were known as "Senegalese," the Arabs and whites, in turn, disdained both West Indians and "Senegalese" alike. All this was very confusing, and small wonder Fanon recognized the contradictions in this range of prejudices. On the one hand, he said, the French told Antilleans that they were neither "black" nor "uncivilized." It was the "Senegalese" who were black and uncivilized; and well disposed Frenchmen never confused the two, allowing the Antilleans to rule "the black roost as its unchallenged master." On the other hand, "North Africans despised men of color." To complicate matters, he further recognized the obfuscations in this absurdity, because "the Frenchman does not like the Jew, who does not like the Arab, who does not like the Black." In short, nobody liked the black. But were not Antilleans black? French assimilationist values always provided the much sought-after negative reassurances. The Antillean was an Antillean. The *African* was the black.[5] Had Fanon been seeking reinforcement of his cultural "whitewashing," which is possible given his Martinican racial attitudes, the North African experience could only have confused and exaggerated his conflicts, and rendered his situation *vis à vis* the French more ambiguous.

He was soon in France, fighting in the valley of Doebs, where he was wounded at Besançon on the Swiss frontier. The citation for bravery which he received was from the hands of none other than Colonel Raoul Salan, who ironically became Commander-in-Chief of the French army during the Algerian war of liberation.[6] Other than the bravery citation, little else is known of Fanon's first European experience. Apparently he spoke rarely of this period of his life, except to admit shock at confronting the double racism of European and Arab alike. Yet in 1953 he returned to Algeria, an Arab country, to find "roots," and proclaimed at the top of his voice for the world to hear that the Algerian war was his, and the Algerian people his people.[7] Simone de Beauvoir has two possible explanations for this adopted identity, explaining first that he had a "passionate" need for roots. If such is the case, it is curious that coming from one part of the world where he was not recognized, he should have identified with another where he was also to be denied recognition. Thus de Beauvoir's second explanation seems more feasible: that in the last analysis "all colonized people were his brothers; and that in the Algerian cause he recognized his own."[8] One of the male nurses at the psychiatric hospital at Blida-Joinville confirmed this assertion by adding that "as a man at the crossroads between the strong and the weak, he chose to identify with the weak."[9]

After a brief return to Martinique, where he worked for Aimé Césaire's political campaign, in 1947 he was once again in France, where he later enrolled in the dental faculty in Paris. But dentistry was not his calling; and ironically he complained that "there are just too many niggers in Paris."[10] Within a few months he moved to Lyon, where he began training as a medical student. There, in a less distracting environment, his intellectual development began in earnest.

In addition to medical literature, he read widely in the philosophical and existentialist *genre,* including the works of Sartre, Nietzsche, Marx, Lenin and Hegel. In between, he also read Kierkegaard, Karl Jaspers, Heideggar, together with the writings of Jean Lacroix, Merleau Ponty, Husserl and Emile Durkheim. It is likely that many of these not only shaped his concept of creative conflict, but also his future theory of violence. *Black Skin White Masks* was his first attempt at an intellectual synthesis, which combined this range of ideas with his life experiences and clinical observations.[11]

As part of this synthesis, he developed the idea first mentioned in his thesis, of conflict within the colonial social structure. By the latter he meant that in wholesome societies, mentally healthy people interacted effectively with their social environments. Where structural obstacles to interaction had developed, however, this was not the case; because in these societies—especially where blockages occurred systematically throughout the social structure—conflict, potential or actual, interrupted lines of communication. Confusion and frustration frequently followed. For example, Fanon cited the case of Martinique where social conventions encouraged education and achievement, but simultaneously fuzzed over opportunities for upward social mobility by interjecting discriminatory racial attitudes. Similarly he cited the case of Algeria where under earlier regulations subsequently removed,

abandonment of Islamic law—a retrograde step in the eyes of a believer—
was one of the conditions for French citizenship. In both cases, structural
obstacles in the society were likely sources of conflict, confusion and
frustration. In other words, although the societies seemed "open" in some
respects—seeming to offer even-handed opportunities and a reasonably just
distribution of resources—they were in other respects "closed." The catch
was that the "closed," non-recognizing elements in the social structure were
not always apparent until one was already in the system.[12] Blockages inherent
to the social structure were likely to cause conflict, Fanon urged. And if no
satisfactory means for conflict resolution existed, the social climate could
deteriorate, ultimately inducing chronic anxieties, depression and even
madness. Under these circumstances, creative conflict would, and did give
way to violence, as structural or institutional rigidities hindered the struggle
for recognition.

Focussing on conflict in the Antillean social structure, Fanon found West
Indian societies less rigid than their counterparts in Algeria, although
nonetheless ambivalent and lacking in satisfactory means for peaceful
conflict resolution. Seemingly open—giving rise to one set of expectations—
they were in reality *partially* closed, thereby leading to unexpected
consequences. Colonial society and social structure in Martinique, therefore,
mocked individual and collective self-improvement efforts to the point where
Fanon found the irony unbearable. Mockery in the social structure was
deliberately fostered, he charged, especially since French assimilation
policies *seemed* to favor real opportunities for upwardly mobile blacks by
*appearing* to prohibit racial barriers to advancement. Barriers nonetheless
existed in masked form, and were the hidden agenda in social conventions
which resorted to discrete shade references—linguistically differentiated—
such as "white," "creole white," "mulatto," "mixed," "colored," "quadroon,"
"octaroon" "black," etc. It was, as Fanon said, "tacity assumed" that
values such as "good" and "bad," "nice" and "decent" were discreetly
applied to each distinguishing shade, beginning with "white" and "good" at
the top of the social scale.

In those instances where aspiring well-to-do and light-skinned bourgeoisies were accepted by the "white/good" power structure, it would *seem*
as if conflict was peacefully resolved by consensus within the social structure.
It was, however, another matter on the "black/bad" side of the social scale.
Here Antillean societies were closed as the ruling consensus "tacitly" refused
to recognize the achievements of dark-skinned, upwardly mobile achievers.
The consensus was less tacit if the achiever's blackness was combined with
other "bad" attributes, such as a limited education and a modest socio-
economic background; or if the achiever originated from the bottom end of the
social order. Accordingly, Antillean masses, including peasants and

agricultural laborers, were excluded from the social consensus and from peaceful conflict resolution. Their options for individual and collective social change were systematically blocked by ambivalence in the social classes, and by conflict-producing obstacles within the social structure.[13]

Hence, Fanon argued, if the masses were deliberately placed in conflict-ridden situations, and systematically denied satisfactory means of peaceful conflict resolution, they would abandon hope of recognition from the ruling consensus. Seeking alternative, they would return to sub-group norms, such as the use of conflict, counter-conflict, and violence.[14]

On arriving in Algeria in 1953, Fanon found a different situation within the social structure which, from the outset, was explicitly conflict-ridden and violence-prone. Here, covert racial classes based on ancestry, appearance or association—as in the case of Martinique—gave way to overt and complex plural societies based on distinct ethnic, religious and cultural differentiations; and far from discreetly covering racial differences with linguistic mumbo jumbo, ethnicity and culture were the hall marks of almost all social, political and economic transactions. Accordingly, if the Antillean social structure was ambivalent and nuanced on the one hand: tacitly permitting some types of discretionary consensus decisions within the social structure; denying other opportunities while *seeming* not to; or openly rejecting assimilation and peaceful conflict resolution for black "unredeemables"; on the other hand Algerian societies seemed structured for violence.[15]

Divided, as Fanon said, into "separate species": Berber, Arab and European, each community preserved its language, its social and political institutions, together with corresponding values. Unlike Martinican societies where peoples of African and European descent had been settling and intermarrying since the seventeenth century, followed in the nineteenth and twentieth centuries by immigrants from the Middle East and East Asia; the peopling of Algeria first occurred in great antiquity, when Berber communities appeared in North Africa well before the Christian year. By the eleventh century, Arab conquerors introduced a new ethnic and cultural element when they established hegemony over the region. The French conquest of 1830 provided the dominant element in the Algerian colonial social structure. Collecting in separate cultural segments, speaking different mother tongues, occupied for the most part in separate economic sectors, Algerian subgroups kept their distance: an Arab was an Arab; a Berber was a Berber; and a European was a European.[16] Observing this phenomena, Fanon concluded that but for the dominant European presence, Algerian colonial societies lacked an overall collective consensus or common will. For example, while the colonizer's language and norms dominated in public, in official exchange, or at the work place; in private family situations, people reverted to sub-group norms. The languages, behavior and customs observed in sub-groups were different from those used when in the presence of the colonizer.

Given this cultural diversity and overall lack of consensus, Fanon wondered how conflict in the Algerian social structure was resolved, and how and by what means Algerians linked up with the overall social environment. As in the Antilles, ability and achievement played a role. With promises and rewards offered by French assimilation policies, some upwardly mobile Algerians could and did interact successfully with the colonial community. By cutting across sub-group loyalties, these évolués, as they came to be known, established linkages within varying Algerian social structures.

But, Fanon countered, this linkage process created two problems. First, the desire on the part of évolués to obtain a European education, a job in the modern economic sector, and a European life style etc., led to competition and more social divisiveness. The social cohesion which *should* have followed was fragmented by competition. Hence, Fanon concluded, the collective consensus really was the desire to compete, which in turn aggravated conflict. The second problem which developed from this linkage process within the social structure was more threatening than the first, Fanon warned. As in the Antilles, linkages failed to reach the Algerian masses who were as remote from the dominant European consensus as the vast Saharan steppes were from the colonial cities. What place did these Algerian masses have in the colonial elite consensus? Not much, Fanon concluded. How then did they interact or link with the colonial social structure? Social elements cohered by means of the colonizer's coercion and violence, Fanon warned.

Recognizing then that linkages within the social structure created conflict for Algerian évolués, and that the masses had interacted with the social environment primarily through the colonizer's violence, Fanon concluded that from the European prespective—violence worked. Not only had violence worked, but the oppressive role of certain public institutions—such as the French army in Algeria—was frequently justified on grounds that "they [the Algerians] only understand the language of force." Furthermore, in European eyes, the Algerian submission to one hundred and thirty years of coercion "proved," among other things, the success of violence.

But by its very success, Fanon argued, conflict and violence had turned Algeria into a "breeding ground for madness."[17] According to de Beauvoir, the pressures might even have been too great for Fanon himself. Recounting an intolerable situation, she showed that frequently in clinical work at Blida-Joinville, Fanon would one minute be called upon to administer to the victims of French torture, and the next to prescribe for the nervous exhaustion of the over-zealous torturer![18]

Fanon's own nausea apart, madness was clearly occurring at points where whole cultures—in this case Muslim and Christian—came into conflict, giving rise to chronic anxiety, ambiguities, a vague sense of being threatened and, as in the Martinican case, no clearly defined "enemy." For example, as shown above, French adminstrators tried to alter the Algerian female dress code by subjecting bourgeois women to "civilizing" pressures. The real objective was to "modernize" their social attitudes. Far from "modernizing" these women, however, colonial pressures produced emotional turmoil both for the women and their husbands torn as they were between loyalties to religious beliefs, and obligations to civic and social duties.[19] The medical profession was another area where whole cultures came into conflict. While Algerian patients mistrusted the colonial practitioner and his medical science, they questioned the loyalties of western trained Algerian doctors.[20] Finally, in one of his most revealing studies of whole cultures in conflict (discussed above) Fanon showed that on administering the western designed Thematic Aperception Test to hospitalized Algerian women, they responded with confusion, which was *not necessarily* related to their disorder.[21]

Once Fanon had determined that causal links existed between cultures in conflict on the one hand, and oppression and madness on the other hand; once he recognized that from the European perspective violence worked, his earlier concept of creative conflict and the Hegelian paradigm—based on Antillean data—began to give way to a theory of violence. Now relegating the Antillean material to the side, he turned to Algeria where massive structural obstacles kept the society in turmoil. Because he saw that while sub-groups related to each other mainly through competition, conflict, oppression and violence, the colonizer in turn successfully played the role of violent moderator.

Although Fanon's analysis of conflict and violence in the social structure drew heavily on Algeria at war, we know that even in pre-war Algeria, conflict and violence had been widely used by the colonial state.[22] Oral traditions of the 1830 French conquest, followed by approximately forty years of "pacification" were reminders of this violent past. His shift from the Hegelian paradigm to the theory of violence was not therefore based exclusively on the twentieth century war of liberation data which he assiduously gathered. War-time relationships were merely a continuation of conflict and violence which had been developing since the 1830's in the Algerian social structure.

But if Fanon found the genesis of his concept of violence in the colonial state's coercion, he found its further manifestation in societies' response to French assimilation policies. In theory, French assimilation policies were predicated on the principal that peoples in tropical dependencies could profit from a close association with the French language, culture and civilization. The formula for this close association was "assimilation," whereby appropriately tutored and eligible members of the colonial society could be assimilated into the French social and cultural matrix. Accordingly, assimilation could occur on several levels simultaneously, including the economic, political and cultural. Where appropriate, it even included rights to French citizenship. One of the hidden agendas in the policy was that the more assimilated were "whiter" and more "civilized" than the less assimilated, where "whiter" and "civilized" referred to a cultural, rather than to a genetic "whitewashing." Not surprisingly, many assimilated people were left with the impression, as Fanon admitted, that they had "magically turned white."

There were, however, obstacles in this seemingly "open-ended" assimilation policies. Ironically, structural obstacles existed *even* in those social conduits ostensibly designed to assist social integration and linkages in a plural society. Thus, Fanon argued, if assimilation policies were really unjust principles, unjustly, half-heartedly or inefficiently applied—which apparently was the case in Algeria—this mismanagement could provoke resentment, resistance and violence on the part of those who qualified, but whose expectations were left unmet. Fanon was not the first to identify this unexpected correlation between the misapplication of French assimilation policies, and violence. A generation before at the International Colonial Congress in Paris (1889), another Antillean, Alexander Isaac, senator from Guadeloupe and one of the vice-presidents of the Congress, revealed the unexpected correlation between misapplied and misguided assimilation policies, and violence. Defining assimilation as a program of social integration and adherence to common values, he warned that if policies were half-heartedly implemented, blunted expectations could erupt into violence, provoking counter-violence on the part of the colonial power.[23] Violence did not erupt as frequently as Isaac had warned. Yet continuous frustrations and a sense of betrayal did develop as expectations conflicted with the colonizer's unwillingness to fulfill promises. By 1903, Arthur Girault, (1865-1931) assimilationist and colonial administrator, was admitting that assimilation was nothing but a "safety valve" which kept a man from being first in his own country, because it was a colony.[24] Few had suspected that the "safety valve" could become a "bottleneck"; or that colonized people would lose faith in the mother country, enough to question colonial legitimacy—by force if necessary—if institutional provisions failed to regulate the orderly integration of those who qualified.

This is exactly what happened in Algeria. Between the 1930's and the 1950's when it was apparent that integrative mechanisms had failed to meet bourgeois expectations, moderates began to open a dialogue with those recommending organized anti-colonial violence.[25] Most noticeable was the failure of, and the moderates' response to, the Blum-Violette proposal. Introduced in 1937, the proposal would have admitted 20,000 Muslims to full French citizenship within the first year of its application. Maurice Violette, who served as governor-general of Algeria (1925-1927), and Léon

Blum, Popular Front premier, expected to conciliate Algerian revolutionary moderates. The proposal foundered, however, on the shoals of white settler opposition, whose spokesman claimed that "since 1919 we have extended maximum concessions. We should not be asked to go further because it is impossible." After the failure of the Blum proposal, Algerian opposition to French rule, which had existed in organized form in Paris since 1925, began to crystalize around the *Ulama,* and Muslim nationalists elements.

Half-hearted implementation of misguided assimilation policies in Algeria *had been* a prelude to violence. Like Martinicans, Algerians had " . . . been told that they were French. They learned it at school. In the street. In the barracks . . . . On the battle fields. They . . . had French squeezed into them . . . in their bodies and in their souls." Then one day, they realized that they had been siphoned off into a "safety valve," and were told to "go back to the Casbah."[26] Many did, figuratively speaking. But not the political dissidents, especially those who were to become tomorrow's revolutionaries. Recognizing structural blocks and incompatibilities in French assimilation policies—for example cultural and educational policies which offended traditional Muslims, or the growing awareness that reform and assimilation were illusory promises in the face of white settler opposition—many dissidents turned to non-negotiable demands and violence against the colonial state.[27] As an anonymous writer in *El-Moudjahid*, the revolutionary journal of the Front de Libération Nationale (F.L.N.), was later to observe: "The historical importance of the armed struggle did not only reside in the possiblity that the people had to use military force against the colonial forces. It resides also in the fact that the struggle aggravated contradictions in the colonial society, and led to escalating outbursts."[28]

Among the dissidents ready to explode were those who, on challenging the assimilation "contract" and finding it wanting, decided to transform chronic discontent into violent political action. Breaking with moderate, reformist bourgeois traditions, many sought to establish revolutionary links with the peasantry. Referring to the many missed opportunities which could have resolved conflict peacefully in Algeria, Fanon observed that "by an ironic twist of events the argument for violence which the colonizer chose and which he showed to the colonized, has been taken over by him. Now it is the colonized who assert that the colonizer only understands force."[29]

The road to revolutionary violence lay open.

Incubating ideas in the heat of war, Fanon turned his back on the Hegelian paradigm. Like negritude, which he had earlier espoused, it was too mild a "therapy" for the malignant conflict in the Algerian social structures where "colonialism will only give way when the knife is at its throat." Building on creative conflict, which permitted struggle as defense against annihilation, the concept took on proportions pertaining to violence. He now had four components for his theory of violence: first, planned systematic obstruction in one group of public institutions which aborted the rewards and promises offered by another group; second, the frustrations, blunted expectations, and divisiveness in colonial societies resulting from chronic competition for resources which *seemed* to be, but were not always available; third, the colonizer's successful role-play as a moderator of violence; and fourth, the nay-saying political dissident who decided to challenge the system with counter-violence. In the Hegelian world of lord and bondsman, components one and three were the lord's "opposition," his "absolute negation," and "abstract negation." Components two and four were the bondsman's struggle, resistance—and violence, in the face of annihilation. Confronting intransigent and permanent opposition which was driving him to madness, the Algerian "bondsman" was deciding to resist his colonial "lord"—with murder.

It is unlikely that Fanon reached these conclusions after systematic research. His ragged methodology, the immediacy with which he seized on otherwise obscure relationships, and his impatience suggest otherwise: that as a keen observer, his unsorted perceptions and insights simply tumbled out of his head, and that he wrote them down without careful selection, much as he seemed to have done with parts of his doctoral thesis in 1951.

Thus, although creative conflict was conceived from Fanon's Martinican material, revolutionary violence was the product of his Algerian experiences. On the one hand, he filtered ideas through the theories of Hegel, Marx and Lenin, as well as the vast range of existentialist literature which Fanon had read during his student days, not the least of which were the works of Merleau-Ponty and Sartre. On the other hand, he enriched his psychological perceptions with clinical data. As a result, his concept of violence began to develop psychological proportions to which he added sociological observations, especially those pertaining to the peasantry, hastily jotted down in note form as he travelled over what had become "his" Algerian mountains, steppes and desert. Could it be that as he observed peasants and nomads— "his people"—he was reminded of Lévy-Brühl's "primitive." Did not "his people" live in "essential homogeneity" with their natural environment. Could they possibly be the custodians of Jung's archetypal forms? And what about their myths, their symbols, and imagery. How were their belief systems structured, and to what extent did projection reflect the collective inner mind? Come to think of it, what *was* their inner state of mind? Could it be reached, and by what means—"bogged down" as they were in "fruitless inertia" and "rural obscurantism." Was it by "touching their feelings," and "warming them up" before going away?

Fanon was well on his way to developing a theory of revolutionary violence. But holy violence? That was something else. It was sometime before he evolved that concept, and not before he had probed the "primitive" Algerian mind, discovered its *modus operandi*, and understood how it interacted with the spiritual universe in which it was embedded; and certainly not before he had discovered the "primitive's" use of myths, symbols, imagery and religious doctrine which permeated his spiritual environment. It was like searching for the key that opened the door to other levels of awareness and comprehension—the key to the subconscious and non-rational areas of the mind. As a psychiatrist, Fanon would have understood that.

It goes without saying that Fanon's understanding of the background to Algerian conflict and violence in the social structure was less than his understanding of Martinique. His adopted identity, notwithstanding, he *was* a stranger in Algeria, and never spoke the indigenous dialects, although reportedly he was learning Arabic. However, despite the fact that he had amassed quantities of undigested data during his work and travels in Algeria, his knowledge of the country and its people was for the most part impressionistic, although uncannily correct. Nevertheless, Fanon's analysis of conflict and violence in the social structure must therefore be considered as incomplete. Accordingly, a critical inventory of his sociological analysis and clinical data would necessarily be helpful—and, in fact, has been done.[30]

Apropos of his analysis of violence, he has been commonly accused, for instance, of basing far-reaching conclusions on a too narrow empirical base, and of universalizing observations, when in fact he should have stuck with Martinique and Algeria. He has also been criticized for yielding to the seductions of logic and abstract propositions at the expense of empirical data. All of which is true. It is not, however, my objective to discard Fanon's essentially correct insights into violence for want of a sound empirical base. Rather, the concern is to show the continuity and coherence in his concept as it evolved from creative conflict through violence and holy violence; and despite the discontinuities, to show that Fanon's concepts of violence and beyond were demonstrable in his Martinican and Algerian data.

It is this impressionistic coherence which has earned Fanon's writings a place in the literature on conflict and conflict resolution in the tropical colonial scenario. J. S. Furvinall's study on *Colonial Policy and Practice* (1948) was one of the earliest of this genre.[31] In his analysis of tropical dependencies, Furnivall, a British colonial officer, showed that colonial plural societies were fraught with potential conflict because the only axis for communication was an economic one. When the cultural-ethnic plural elements failed to "combine" beyond the common experience of the market where "each section in the plural society is a crowd and not a community," he argued, the society was in danger of being transformed "more or less completely into an economic system organized like a factory of production," where corporate integrity was in danger of destruction. Since democratic

forms of government were unsuitable under these circumstances, he
continued, colonial plural societies were ultimately held together by force.[32]
Furnivall's model was later modified by M.G. Smith who, quite
independently, was critiquing the former about the same time that Fanon was
developing his concept of conflict and violence in colonial social structures.
Smith modified the Furnivall thesis by developing analytical categories for
investigative purposes, and by giving the model universal significance as a
general theory of society.[33]

Since Fanon's death in 1961, and the independence of most former
colonial territories, there have been other attempts to understand and explain
conflict in colonial social structures, such as the study of pluralism within the
context of nation-building. Now there is less focus on institutional and
cultural exclusivity—analytical categories which were developed in M.G.
Smith's early work—and more on the structure of power in plural societies.
With few notable exceptions, such as South Africa, sharp ethnic and cultural
cleavages have ceased to dominate in institutionalized forms, although they
still exist in one form or another in various parts of the former colonial world
where ethnic and cultural pluralism have influenced the direction of change.
Categories which apply exclusively to rigid relationships, as was the case in
Fanon's study of Algeria, no longer have general application. Other recent
concepts deal with: "pluralism as a continuum" which "relates to the mode of
political incorporation of diverse groups;" with "segregation-assimilation;"
as well as with "cultural-diversity-homogeneity;" and "inequality-equality."
They also deal with "cultural pluralism" as institutional diversity, with
"social pluralism" as institutional diversity accompanied by group exclusivity,
and with "structural pluralism" as group stratification in relation to economic
and political power. In other words, the "scientific" study of the ancient
phenomenon of unequal distribution of resources along group lines suggests
that the social sciences have caught up with the study of invisible sources of
conflict in colonial plural societies.[34]

Moreover, Marxist analysis is also being applied to structure of power
studies in former colonial plural societies, and the re-emergence of the
particularistic minority identities, both of which Fanon anticipated. Finally,
the concept of "internationalization of race" has re-emerged as an extension
of domestic race issues into the international arena, and the intrusion of
international influences on domestic race relations. Despite these newer
approaches, it is interesting to note that the general framework for these
discussions is still a dominant-subordinate one. The Hegelian lord and
bondsman—albeit modified—are still alive and well. They now have a new
nomenclature, not least of which is that of "neo-colonialism," "dependency,"
and the new "interdependence." Similarly, as during the colonial era, a
correlation between race and economic status prevails on an international

scale—although perspectives have altered somewhat—a phenomenon which Fanon also anticipated.

Thus, although the immediacy of Fanon's analytical categories recede with passing years, his contribution, nonetheless, to the colonial sociology, and to conflict and potential violence in tropical plural dependencies has earned its place in the historiography of colonial sociology.

# The Making of Violence Part II:
# Algeria 1830-1954

*"The colonial regime derives its legitimacy from force and no time tries to hide it. Each statue, that of Faidherbe, or of Lyautey, of Bugeaud or of Sergeant Blandon, all these conquistadors who have alighted on the colonial soil never cease to signify one and the same thing: 'We are here by the force of bayonets . . .".*

Fanon

*"The war of Algerian Liberation started on . . . 21 November 1832 . . . [when] abd-al-Qadir . . . entered Mascara . . . ; the first of November 1954 which is the more modern date is only the contemporary version of that armed uprising."*

Jamal M. Ahmed.

By the time Fanon arrived in Algeria in November 1953, he was twenty-eight years old. Most of his life was already behind him. He had only eight more years to live, dying of leukemia in Washington D.C. on 6 December 1961, where he had gone for treatment.[1]

It is not really clear why Fanon went to Algeria. Mme Josie Fanon believes that he was politically motivated, and wanted to participate in what was obviously an impending struggle. Both Hansen and Beauvoir support this view.[2] Renate Zahar, one of Fanon's biographers, suggests, however, that Fanon regarded the work-period in Algeria as an interim before returning to Martinique. As a third possibility, both Geismar and Gendzier think that his decision was based on purely personal and professional interests. Simone de Beauvoir's conversations with Fanon likewise point to this direction: that seeking to integrate himself into a suitable social environment, he performed what he perceived as the required "social rituals," such as marrying a French woman and receiving a good professional appointment. Like Geismar and Gendzier, de Beauvoir therefore suggests that his revolutionary politicization followed the outbreak of the war.[3]

Whatever his motives, up to the time of his arrival in Algeria, Fanon's life had been full and rich. His most important contribution was still in the future. Graduating in 1952 from the medical faculty at Lyon, he returned to Martinique, where he practiced medicine in Vauclin, his mother's ancestral home in the southern part of the island. But Martinique had lost its hold on him. Few changes of social significance had occurred, and the prospects of radical change in the foreseeable future seemed remote. In any event, he was already assessing his native land with that critical mind which later produced the devastating insights known as *Black Skin White Masks.*

Aware of his own sense of alienation—no doubt reflected in discussions in *Black Skin White Masks*—he returned to France in 1952; and by the summer was working at the hospital of Saint Alban-de-Lozere, near Mende in Central France. There he worked with the Spanish social psychiatrist François Tosquelles. By focussing on the importance of social psychiatry and holistic medicine, Tosquelles—as was suggested above—had a profound influence on Fanon's intellectual and professional development, especially since—judging from his earlier interest in Lévy-Brühl's "essential homogeneity"— he was already moving in this direction. Working with Tosquelles on clinical and professional pursuits, Fanon learned that medical specialization was in danger of compartmentalizing and atomizing the life of the sick and disabled; and that the psychiatrist's function was to help people to integrate their lives into society—a sort of socio-psychiatric version of Lévy-Brühl's "essential homogeneity." The recommended method for achieving these objectives was to de-emphasize childhood traumas, and to focus instead on medical and psychiatric histories—not only of the sick, but also of those who shared their lives, such as family and community members.[4] That Fanon learned these lessons well is not in doubt. Between 1952 and 1961, the thrust of his work was to relate feelings and behavior to action in concrete social situations. By these means, patients were required to liberate themselves from a sense of isolation; to see themselves as part of a larger social unit; and to resolve personal conflicts within a wider social environment. We know that Fanon later added the idea of integration into a larger social unit to his concept of holy violence. But in the early 1950's, he was not yet ready for holy violence. He was still interested in socio-analysis and criticism of colonial societies, arguing, analyzing, testing hypotheses, but always recommending the destruction of colonialism; because he had found that obstacles and deformities in the concrete scenario had reached levels where the same syndrome of mental disorders kept recurring on a large scale. He concluded that the fault lay with the social structure which had ceased to be viable. It had to be destroyed.

Sometime between 1950 and 1953, he married Marie-Josephe Dublé, a young Frenchwoman whom he had met in Lyon.[5] By the time their only child Olivier—who looks very much like his father—was born, Fanon and Josie were already in Algeria.[6] There Fanon became one of six divisional directors of the French psychiatric hospital at Blida-Joinville. Situated about thirty five kilometers from the capital city of Algiers, the hospital, now named for him,—a large picture of Fanon hangs in the main reception hall—lies in a spacious walled compound where trees provide occasional shade.[7] The hospital was really a self-contained unit, housing about two thousand patients, less than half of whom were Algerians. The rest were Europeans.

The six divisional directors shared the management of the hospital which was subject to a central administration. Male nurses and interns completed the medical staff. (Some of the nursing staff who had known Fanon were still in residence in 1972, and many had warm memories of him.)

During his Algerian years (November 1953-January 1957), Fanon's work output was phenomenal. There are repeated references to his commitment to the Algerian cause, and his professional devotion. Rising early in the mornings, he worked feverishly throughout the day with few breaks, freqently returning to his office or clinic at nights. It was not unusual for him to spend the night fully clothed on a couch or chair. He provided medical assistance to all who found their way to the clinic, whether they were ordinary civilians, or from the armies of the Front de Libération Nationale (FLN).[8] Before long, the hospital acquired the reputation of being a "nest of *fallagha,*" and of *"feda'iyin,"* or those who sacrifice themselves. Of necessity, his treatment of the latter two was covert, as freedom fighters seeking medical aid were sometimes on the French Commander-in-Chief's most-wanted list. At the same time, he was also treating men, including torturers, from the French Commander's combat troops. When not providing direct assistance, whether in the form of work therapy, simply talking to people, or administering drug and sleep therapy—a treatment which apparently worked with the war weary and the traumatized—he travelled to the *maquis,* or freedom fighters' stations, to counsel soldiers on how best to handle combat-fear and torture. Sometimes suggesting the organization of supportive groups among freedom fighters, he was really transferring the clinical group therapy (which incidentally had not worked well at the Blida hospital) to the *maquis.*

In Algeria, Fanon saw the violence at first hand about which he later wrote in *The Wretched of the Earth.* After spring 1957, when the Resident Minister of Algeria Robert Lacoste confirmed the existence of petroleum deposits in the Sahara, fighting was intensified to protect not only potential oil reserves, but also France's strategic interests in Bizerte and Mers el Kebir, part of the NATO complex. The Armée de la Libération Nationale (ALN), or the FLN armies pushed south in an attempt to protect the mineral deposits thereby seizing control of large areas of the Algerian countryside. At the same time, the city of Algiers was targetted for an urban guerrilla dog-fight which lasted from December 1956 to the fall of 1957. Terrorism and counter terrorism followed, and after General Massu and the Tenth Parachute Division were allowed to increase their influence on the police and security in general, violence and counter-violence in Algeria assumed terrible proportions.

Watching this fire-eating scenario unfold, Fanon found empirical data for the violence which he knew to exist in Algerian colonial society and history.

He found them in the violence on the colonial frontier; and in the long history of Franco-Algerian conflict which had not only shaped Algeria's development, but had left a stench of violence and counter-violence "in the atmosphere." The 1954 war of liberation was accordingly seen as simply another incident—albeit a successful one—in the century-long record.

The major contact zone between the Europeans and Algerians, the colonial frontier, the line between the "civilized" French areas  and the "uncivilized" Algerian counterparts, was particularly volatile and potentially explosive. Diverse populations met there, all with historical claims and strong cultural identities operating from corporate bases. Among the oldest were the Berber-speaking populations, who, as noted, migrated into North Africa before the Christian era—possibly from an easterly direction.[9] They were followed, between the seventh and eleventh centuries by Arab migrants and conquerors, whose groups were so large and influential that their language and religion came to dominate throughout all North Africa.[10] By the sixteenth century, significant numbers of Jews from the Iberian Penninsular had moved to North Africa, followed finally by the Ottoman Turkish hegemony, which created a fourth group, or cultural component in Algerian plural societies. In 1830, this cultural and ethnic matrix known as Algeria fell to the French conquest.[11]

Not long after the French presence was established, conflict and violence came to dominate relationships between the conquered and conqueror alike. "The first confrontation took place under the mark of violence—bayonets and cannons," Fanon snarled.[12] And it took nearly a century of intermittent warfare (1830-1922), 40,000 bayonets and the loss of thousands of lives before Algeria was "pacified."[13] Moreover between the 1920's, when the south Saharan Tuareg were finally subdued, and 1954 when the war of liberation broke out, this "thirty year peace" was punctuated by frequent uprisings. Between 1954 and 1962, Algeria was once again at war with France. Hence, although fighting was intermittent, for approximately one hundred and thirty years, Franco-Algerian relations were marred by threats of violence and the tensions of living in such a society. This violence on the colonial frontier, Fanon insisted, was made possible by barracks and police posts, policemen and soldiers who were by and large the only links between the French and Algerians. Behold, he cried, "has not the skin of Algeria, for the last one hundred and thirty years, been subject to wounds which gape ever larger?"[14]

Fanon identified three "zones" in Algeria most susceptible to conflict and violence. The first was the land question, characterized by settler ownership of the most arable lands. Settlers acquired land by just about any means available; and in 1954 when the war broke out European settlers and administrators either owned or controlled close to forty per cent of the arable land, although they only made up about ten per cent of the total population.[15] For appropriation purposes, the French divided land into four legal categories. The first—conquered lands—included those originally under Turkish suzerainty, and lands belonging to Muslim populations which resisted the French. Appropriated between 1830 and the 1920's they included some of the best lands in the Mitidja coastal plains, together with good lands in the Kabylia mountains and the High Plateaux. The second— habus—were inalienable lands held in pious trusts and used sometimes for charitable purposes. In 1843, they were placed under the control of the Domaine or land department; and by the following year habus lands became available for settler occupancy. The third—collectively owned tribal lands— were subject to equally arbitrary measures. By decrees of 1844 and 1846, tribal lands also became available for settler occupancy. Finally, in 1846, the French adopted the "vacant land" policy which permitted settler occupancy of privately and collectively owned agricultural and grazing land.

By the end of the nineteenth century, the emergence of the "landless Algerian" about whom Fanon spoke had already become a reality. Deprived of land for pasturage and for tillage, some entered the French economy as share-croppers and as day laborers. Land subdivisions into small holdings— in order to meet the needs of rising generations—left the remaining population with even less land to work.[16] Many migrated to the cities where they formed the nucleus of the lumpenproletariat whom Fanon called "the horde of starving men uprooted from the tribe . . . and clan," who go around in "circles between suicide and madness." Others later migrated to France in search of a livelihood.

By the 1920's and the early 1930's they were grouping around exiled political activists such as Massali al-Hajj, founder of the Etoile Nord-Africain (The North African Star), one of the first Algerian groups to think in Islamic nationalist, and reformist terms.

The second conflict zone on the French frontier which Fanon identified was the European town. From the European perspective, towns were central as they separated the "civilized" from the "barbarian." For landed settlers in rural areas, towns were places to escape, from the "inert, passive and sterilizing pressure of the 'native' environment." In Fanon's analysis, however, towns became symbols for the division of the "manichean" colonial world into "two different species," and centers from which "native" populations were decided for, acted upon, manipulated, controlled, coerced and heavily taxed. Outside THE TOWN was the native town which Fanon called "reservations." Here the colonial "species" moved around like crouching animals, daring only to cross into THE TOWN when required by economic necessity.[17]

European urban development began shortly after the conquest. Towns most affected by the expanding frontier were Algiers, the capital city, Oran in the west which came under French administration in 1831, as well as Bougie and Bône (Annaba) in central and eastern Algeria respectively, which were occupied by September 1833. Before long the French were in Arzew (1834) and Mostaganem (1834) in the west, as well as Blida—where Fanon was to take up residence at the psychiatric hospital. By 1837, they had captured Constantine, and within the decade, Mascara in the west had come under their control. By 1847, outlines of the French urban frontier were stabilized from Tlemcen, Oran and Mostaganem in the west, through central area towns such as Orleansville (Al Asnam) and Algiers, to eastern towns such as Constantine, Philippeville (Skikda) and Bône. Rarely did the Franco-Algerian urban frontier extend beyond one hundred kilometers from the coast, and as was invariably the case in colonial situations, the Europeans in a small urban frontier exercised disproportionate power over the majority of the Algerian people.

As Fanon observed, rural masses remained relatively aloof.[18] Until the 1930's, the majority of the Muslim population remained in the country-side: approximately ninety-three per cent in 1885; ninety-two per cent in 1906; and nearly ninety per cent in 1931. Impoverished, landless and demoralized by French "pacification," many seemed—as Fanon said—to be "retrograde," "obscuranist," "petrified," and "bogged down in fruitless inertia." By the 1920's and 1930's, however, the situation began to change. Driven by rising birth rates, persistent rural penury, epidemics and famines, land-hungry Muslim masses began converging on the cities.[19]

After about the 1930's, the "manichean" or the urban-rural dichotomy, which had "mercifully" separated Europeans from the mass of the population—began to close. By the 1940's the shanty towns about which Fanon spoke were already in existence; and by the 1950's, both the people of the country-side and the shanty towns—had declared war on the cities. Invading the European town with bombs and timed explosives, urban guerrillas transformed main streets and stylish European cafés into battlefields. The Battle of Algiers (Dec. 1956-Fall 1957) dramatized this frontier conflict on a grand scale, confronting Europeans with the inescapable reality that the urban frontier, behind which they had sought protection for over one hundred years—had ceased to be a barrier.

For those rural masses who, however, remained in smaller towns and in the country side, the administrative and military frontier—Fanon's third colonial frontier—was undisguised violence. As with the urban frontier, administrative and military frontiers served different ends in this diverse society. While for white settlers the lines of demarcation guaranteed political and legal separation, for Algerians it was sometimes a form of apartheid:

complete with unequal civil and political liberties; together with highly visible institutions of coercion and oppression. In his analysis of violence, Fanon discussed the effects of this institutionalized and violent apartheid on administrative and military frontiers, where "the geographical layout"—as suggested above—was marked by barracks and police stations, and where "the official liaison or representative of the settlers and of the oppressive regime is the policeman and the soldier." It is they, he continued, who control civil populations in their "reservations" with force, and with threats of violence.[20]

Administrative centers were complex structures designed to divide plural populations according to ethnic and religious identities. For example in arid southern regions occupied almost entirely by Muslims, the French presence was primarily a military one. Operating through various administrative instruments, military personnel, specialists in Arabic dialects and cultures, administered these southern departments either directly, or through local dignitaries, such as *bachaghas, aghas, qadis* and *shaikhs*. By 1900 there were about twelve of these *communes indigènes*, or administrative units made up exclusively of "natives."

In areas where European populations existed to some degree but in a small minority, the administrative formula was different. Here a type of administration known as the mixed commune (*commune mixte*) was applied, where official policies ensured the submission of Muslim populations by permitting limited participation in municipal elections, and by leaving local affairs in the hands of *qadis* or local officials who administered according to Muslim law. Departmental matters, however, were handled by French authorities. Of the seventy-nine mixed communes in 1900, seventy-three were ruled by civilians, which ensured certain civil liberties for the European minority, while the remaining six were in military jurisdictions.

Finally, in areas where European populations dominated, self-governing communes (*communes de plein exercise*) prevailed. Here, as in France, an elected mayor administered according to French laws customs and municipal traditions. During the latter part of the nineteenth century, numbers of self-governing communes increased rapidly: ninety-six in 1869; one hundred and twenty-six in 1879; two hundred and nine in 1884; and two hundred and sixty in 1900.[21]

The administrative and military "frontier" was therefore the product of a combination of policies which separated the plural elements within the Algerian society. These policies favored settlers who, for the most part, lived in jurisdictions separated from the rest of the Algerian populations. Although there were of course some exceptions, all too frequently settler attitudes encouraged these discriminatory and authoritarian practices. Seeking to ensure supremacy at the price of separation, many settlers preferred plural institutions which restricted representation, to unitary ones with wider representation, as was the case in more homogeneous societies. Thus, except in those urban areas where assimilation policies were implemented, the administrative and military frontier became a barrier of increasingly violent proportions, especially when, in the 1930's and 1940's, social unrest increased, and urban migration became a matter for serious concern.

But if Fanon found empirical data for the background to violence in administrative and military policies on the colonial frontier, the historical evidence left little doubt—as noted—that massive violence had occurred intermittently in Algeria throughout the nineteenth and twentieth centuries. Although the decision to expand conquered territory was not officially made until 1834, *de facto* frontier expansion began almost immediately in the east; and in the west, General Bertrand Clauzel's war plan (*systéme guerroyant*) went into effect during 1835-36. But the real military offensive did not come until 1841 with General Thomas-Robert Bugeaud's policy of total occupation (*un systéme de domination absolue*). For approximately six years, Bugeaud pursued a policy of destruction and mass killings, razing whole villages, burning crops, destroying and removing animals. "It is not necessary to chase Arabs," he is reported to have said. "It is only necessary to prevent them from planting seeds, harvesting and pasturing their animals." In the west he raided rebel country and pursued resistence to the Tafna valley. By mid-June 1847, he launched pitiless campaigns against communities in the Grand Kabylia, where troops vandalized terrifed populations. Although Bugeaud left office in 1847, the *razzia* method was continued by his successors until 1857, when demoralized and exhausted populations of the Grand Kabylia finally began to submit to the French yoke. Fanon recalled that Budgeaud's atrocities were still alive in folk memories. No wonder, he observed, that adults, especially those in Kabylia, frightened naughty children with his bogey-man image.

Muslim populations resisted the colonial expansion with a total war effort, and their uprisings are enshrined in popular verses of the nineteenth and twentieth centuries.[22] Members of Sufi orders (religious brotherhoods), especially the Tijaniyya, and later the Qadiriyya, the most influential Sufi order in Algeria, swelled the ranks of resisters. But the name which still stirs fervor in the hearts of many, is that of 'Abdul Qadir, Sultan of the western Awal Sidi al-Shaikh, and leader of the Qadiryya. Between 1832 and 1847, when he was finally defeated, 'Abdul Qadir harassed the French from Mascara, Tittari and Tagdempt in the west, to Bougie, Dellys and Hamza in the center and east. He fought them in the mountains, in the valleys and in the plains. He cut communication lines, and threatened cities. Marching his armies to the outskirts of Algiers, he proudly claimed responsibility for mass murders, including those of one hundred and eight settlers in the Mitidja plains in 1839. He was involved in the "grand insurrection" of 1845, and the western uprising. Only in December 1847 when surrounded by enemies, broken lines, and diminishing supplies, was he forced to surrender.[23]

By 1871 there was the "great uprising." Smoldering resentment against French "pacification," land seizures and forced relocations, together with heavy taxes, destruction of villages, crops and animals, prompted large sections of the population to rise. The official inauguration of a civil administration (9 March, 1870) triggered the uprising. Fearing settler domination and the imposition of Christian law, as well as European land and labor policies, some powerful local dignitaries began to organize. But it was the fall of France in the Franco-Prussian war (1870), which determined the mood. Sustained by rumors that the "Sultan of France" had been imprisoned, the "French tribe" defeated, and the "nation" about to be dismembered, hope swelled that deliverance was at hand. On 14 March, 1871, the *mujahidins*—or those who fight in holy wars—gathered under the leadership of Muhammad Mukrani. By April the uprising had spread to the Grand and Little Kabylia. Before long, communities in the eastern and western Sahara were in revolt.

Uprisings continued. But the revolt was virtually over by September 1871—although the Tuareg of the Sahara did not submit until 1882. The conquest of what is known today as Algeria was not completed until after 1900. Probably about 800,000 rebels were involved in the uprising at one time or another, and Muslim losses were high. French casualities, which totalled 2,686 men, were small by comparison. Yet although broken, Algerian masses were not convinced of their defeat, as Fanon later reminded his readers. Anti-colonial warrior traditions remained alive, as the name of Abdul Qadir passed into folklore. In the villages, women murmured songs of heroes in their childrens' ears, and young teenagers were captivated by anti-colonial tales of heroes and their exploits in "the last great insurrection." With such traditions of resistance and heroism, Fanon urged, Algerians would hardly submit to the colonial "lord," neither would they be passive observers of his non-recognition. The "bondsman" would surely fight against this oppression.[24]

In civilian affairs, no less than war, Algerians girded for the fray. Even before the eleventh century Arab occupation of the Mediterranean lands, Mosque and Church had become macro symbols of whole cultures in conflict during the medieval Crusades. In the nineteenth century, Muslim-Christian confrontation in the Mediterranean basin was sharpened by the French presence in Algeria. As the two societies became increasingly polarized, reciprocal and unflattering stereotypes came to dominate. Eventually, most members of these polarized cultures related to each other mainly through conflict, the threat of violence, and violence.

French assimilation policies hardly bridged the gap between people in polarized plural societies and their conflicting cultures. As in the Antilles, assimilation policies were intended to create cohesion among assimilated elites of diverse backgrounds. But these policies met with limited success. Few Muslims adopted French citizenship, and only a minority submitted wholeheartedly to French cultural influences. Algerian attachment to Islamic law was too strong, and few were prepared to substitute an alien for an indigenous culture. [25] Settler racism did not help. Only a small proportion was prepared to concede French citizenship to large segments of the Muslim population. The majority preferred authoritarian rule and legal systems which guaranteed their privileges. Hence, whether by indifference, or by deliberation, French assimilation policies hardly bridged the gap between the polarized plural societies; neither did they diffuse the conflict. By the late 1930's when settler opposition was closing off remaining avenues of communication, societal conflict and violence re-emerged on a large scale.[26]

French assimilation policies in Algeria began officially in 1848, much later than in Martinique. Although these rights were temporarily withdrawn by Napoleon III's administration (1852-70), the idea of political assimilation had taken root; and in October 1870, Algeria was formally annexed to France. Assimilation in Algeria and Martinique were of course different. While in the latter it had been the culmination of nearly three hundred years of close association and inter-marriage, Algerian assimilation was imposed in conjunction with the French frontier. True there was a non-French European population which benefitted immediately as assimilation policies encouraged settler migrations. Yet there was little opportunity for Algerians and French to get to know each other; and with the exception of some European settlers and Algerian évolués who formed a small but influential proportion of the population, strong attachments were slow to develop between French and Algerian communities—quite the opposite from Martinique. Consequently by 1870, there were only 393 évolués of a estimated total Muslim population of over two million; and by 1900, fewer than a thousand Muslims were French citizens.

But those aspects of French assimilation which most angered Fanon were the legal and educational policies. In the case of the latter, the French urged "francization" among Algerians in the modern sector, encouraging urban elites to be French-speaking and French educated. But reminiscent of his own experience, Fanon noticed that even although some évolués followed the letter of the law, even converting to Christianity, the French never ceased to remind them of their "muslim origins." The latter usually connoted something perjorative: that the "muslim" was an oversexed predator; or lazy; or that he had "criminal instincts"; or that in biological terms he was not far removed from the reptile world.[27] Turning to assimilation policies affecting the legal status of Muslims, Fanon noted that the French had extended the area of French civil territories into predominately Muslim zones. As a result, Muslims were subject to—what was for them—heavy taxation, a special penal system, and French justice. In some parts of the country, French administrators had replaced the *qadis* or Muslim jurists in local courts, while in others, the numbers of Muslim courts were reduced. In other words, the same mind-set, which in the Antilles had by implication devalued traditional laws and folk cultures, was once again devaluing North African law and normative structure. As the colonial "lord" had refused to recognize Antillean blacks and their achievements, so was he now denying recognition to North African "bondsmen." Simone de Beauvoir was, after all, right in perceiving that Fanon saw himself in the struggle for liberation. On discovering the social proportions of his own psychological struggles for recognition in the colonial world, Fanon saw himself in the cause for which he fought.[28]

It came as no surprise to Fanon to learn, therefore, that although French assimilation policies seemed liberal in Algeria, as in Martinique, they were hedged with ambiguities, ambivalence and concealed limits. According to Fanon, many Algerian *évolués* failed to discern these limits. Many more seemed unable to cope with the ambivalence and ambiguities—believing that the "fault" lay exclusively with themselves. Most understood, however, that only a small percentage of Algerians were profitting even partially from assimilation, and that the majority suffered either from discrimination—which in some instances resembled apartheid policies—or, at the least, from neglect. Still, hoping that one day the more liberal "metropolitan mind" would prevail, a minority continued to attribute obstacles to their successful assimilation "merely" to the defensive settler mentality. But as settler demands for limited assimilation re-emerged, hope gave way to the harsh political realities. After October 1870 when they were granted elected representation in the Chamber of Deputies, settlers actively campaigned to discourage the extension of assimilation.

As has been suggested above, large-scale conflict seemed unaviodable after 1938 with the failure of the Blum-Violette Bill which would have offered citizenship rights to some 20,000 Muslims. Proposed by Popular Front Leaders Léon Blum and Maurice Violette (who had been governor of Algeria between 1925-27), the bill was first introduced in December 1926. It never reached the floor of the Chamber, and was killed in the committee on Universal Suffrage in 1938. Upset by the failure of the legislation, Blum was later to disavow colonialism in language more associated with revolutionaries like Fanon, than the statesman that he was. Criticizing "colonialism" as "the appropriation of [territory] by the chance of discovery or by conquest," he rejected it on grounds that it was the forceful domination and exploitation of natural resources in a way which was "disavowed by the law, by modern standards of morality, and by all that belongs to the history of humanity."[29]

It is impossible to state what might have been the outcome in Algeria had the bill succeeded. Its failure, however, heralded one of the last turning points in the struggle for Muslim recognition. Angered by repeated frustrations, abortive appeals for recognition, discrimination, and lost opportunities, moderate *évolués* such as Farhat Abbas, Abdelkrim Bendjelloun and R. Zenati, leaders of the Party of Young Algeria, became disenchanted. About the same time (1931), Muslim revivalists, such as Abdul-Hamid ben Badis, Al-Uqbi, and al-Ibrihimi who had been influenced by the Salafiyya movement in Egypt, founded the Association of the *Ulama*, an Islamic party for the development of a Muslim Algeria. Six years later, Massali al-Hajj, leader of the earlier (1925) nationalist party Etoile Nord-Africain (North African Star) formed a new nationalist Muslim part, the Parti du Peuple Algérian: P.P.A. *(Algerian Peoples Party)* dedicated to an Islamic and independent Algeria.

In other words, if Muslim opposition had begun to organize from 1926, by 1938 even the moderate *évolués* had lost faith in French good will. "For a long time," said one of the Algerian delegates to the Conference for Solidarity between the Afro-Asiatique Peoples (Conférence de Solidarité des peuples afro-asiatiques) which convened in Cairo (Dec. 1957), "the Algerian people believed that by peaceful means, they would be able to convince the French of the need to annul the 'colonial pact.' " But what were the results of peaceful endeavors? Nothing but "imprisonment, torture, assassinations and deportations. Having no alternative," he concluded, "we felt constrained to rise against oppression . . ."[30]

By 1947, hopes of reconciling plural elements were still foundering on settler intransigence and metropolitan sluggishness. Virtual architects of the "Algerian Statute" of September 1947, the settlers put their *imprimateur* on the provisions of a new constitution guaranteeing them political and economic supremacy. The constitution provided for two electoral colleges in the Algerian assembly of 120 members; and by giving the French college supremacy with an electorate of only 50,000, as opposed to the Muslim college with an electorate of 1,300,000 (slightly more than one tenth the total Muslim population) the administration virtually closed channels for peaceful negotiation. It can be argued that the assembly's limited powers over the budget and legislation could reduce settler influence on public policy. Events, however, proved otherwise. As the societies became polarized by conflict and the threats of organized violence, administration policies came more and more to resemble settler recommendations. With the Army's increased role in responding to rising violence, many settlers now came to regard the military as new allies.

Although the French seemed unaware, the increase in political crimes suggests that conflict lines had hardened by 1949. With the creation of the *Organization Secrète*, a group which functioned within the structure of Massali al-Hajj's movement, which was committed to Algerian independence and to a Muslim identity, the road to decolonization by revolutionary violence was open.

# The Birth of Holy Violence Part I: The Social Infrastructure

*"For the colonized person, life can only emerge from the decomposing corpse of the colonizer . . . . The practice of violence is all-embracing, since each forms a violent link in the great chain, a part of the great organism of violence which has surged forward and which has come as a reaction to the colonizer's first violence . . . . Violence invests the character of the colonized people with positive and creative policies."*

Fanon

*"Violence alone, violence committed by the people, violence organized and educated by its leaders, makes it possible for the masses to understand social truths and gives the key to them.*

Fanon

Colonialism *"is violence in its natural state, and it will only yield when confronted with greater violence."*

Fanon

By the end of the 1950's, Fanon's concept of violence had already taken shape. There were numerous components, each of which played a role. On the historical level, there was indisputable evidence that violence in Franco-Algerian history—what the French called "pacification of the natives"—had been longstanding, organized and systematic. For over a hundred years, the colonizer had played a successful, if intermittent role as a perpetrator and moderator of violence. On the sociological and cultural levels, violence had also been structured into the system, in the form of competition for scarce material resources, inter-group conflicts, social unrest, and planned obstruction in social institutions which blocked on one level the rewards which seem to be offered on another. A dominant white minority—who owned the major means of production, who discriminated against Arabs and Muslims on racial and cultural grounds, and who seemed from outward appearances to be corrupt and ineffective parasites—provided a continuing source of aggravation and resentment in the society. The military presence, especially in outlying districts, was a constant reminder that the state's coercive means were always close at hand.

Developing and changing with new experiences, by the late 1950's Fanon's concept of violence had also come to include something which he called "violence in the international context," by which he meant unequal trade exchanges between European and Africans since the fifteenth century, including the slave trade as well as the longstanding accumulation of profits based on price and wage systems discriminating against African producers and exporters.[1] All these had, in one way or another, done "violence" to African economies and social structures. "Violence in the international context" also referred to global political tensions created during the Cold War, such as the Americo-Cuban confrontation; as well as social unrest of the sort which occurred in Sharpeville (South Africa in 1960). By 1960, therefore, Fanon's concept of violence came to include just about everything which was a threat to the Third World. It goes without saying that as its meaning expanded, his concept of violence was becoming more and more difficult to understand, perhaps even meaningless. By using "violence" to explain everything,"violence" was explaining nothing.

And there the matter might have rested—an ardent revolutionary's overblown concept of violence—had Fanon not added the "sacred" and psychological dimensions in his developing theory of violence. By incorporating the idea of the sacred myth, religious symbols and millenarian concepts which he had seen at work in Antillean and Algerian peasant cultures; and by combining these with what he knew of human behavior, Fanon transformed an exaggerated *analysis* of violence—which was sadly deficient methodologically—into a dynamic *doctrine* for social change.[2]

Because essentially he was pointing to rising levels of frustration and blunted expectations on the part of those *évolués* who resented non-recognition: their political rights did not correspond to their value in society as they perceived it. On becoming political dissidents who despaired of gradual political change, they decided to meet violence with counter-violence. As Fanon observed, their national power base grew out of the alliance between urban dissidents, who had decided to cut down the colonial system by violence, and the Algerian peasantry, whose norms had amply demonstrated (as suggested above) the effectiveness of violence. Fanon apparently seemed genuinely surprised by this alliance, and was equally incredulous on learning that from the 1920's, the Third International (1919) had generated the idea that tropical dependencies would be the "proletarian nations" in the global anti-colonial struggle. His own theory of the "spontaneously revolutionary peasantry" may therefore owe nothing to the Third International, and it is likely that his theory of violence and holy violence developed uniquely from the Algerian experiences.[3]

By following his agenda, both before and after his expulsion from Algeria in January 1957 by the French Authorities, one can trace the development of the concept of violence as it began to take shape, until its eventual "blossoming" towards the end of his life, into holy violence.[4] Although now well beyond the idea of lord, bondsman and creative conflict, Fanon structured his concept of violence within the dialectic of French violence and Algerian counter-violence, a "Hegelian" idea which had been modified by Sartre.[5] An early form of the "thesis" appeared in the letter of resignation from Blida which he wrote to the Resident Minister, Robert Lacost, in 1956. In that communication, an obviously shocked and angry Fanon informed the minister that the ruling class's social structure of Algeria was hostile to the emotional survival of the Algerian people, and that he could no longer work in an environment where "the lawlessness, the inequality [and] the multi-daily murder of [men] were raised to the status of legislative principles," or where the establishment seemed indifferent to "the present-day events that are steeping Algeria in blood." He seemed scandalized by the fact that the present "happenings" were "neither the result of an accident or of a breakdown in the system . . . [but] the logical consequence of an . . . attempt to decerebralize" the Algerians.[6]

His address to the First Congress of Black Writers and Artists in Paris in September 1956, revealed Fanon's search for the suitable "anti-thesis" or basis for counter-violence against the destructive effects of a mismanaged colonial state. He spoke about "Racism and Culture" and, far from fostering the comfortable myth of his Martinican years: that assimilation policies were blind to racial difference, and that "one only needed to have children by someone less black than oneself" in order to correct permanently the chromosome chart, he condemned racism, describing it as a psychological and cultural aberration. Speaking now as the bondsman who was not just resisting, but who had declared war on the lord, Fanon charged that cultural racism was particularly dangerous, as by declaring its superiority, other cultures were *ipso facto* relegated to inferiority. Not surprisingly—since we have now come to recognize his style—Fanon's conclusions were ambivalent. On the one hand, he called on colonized people "to revalue" their cultures, "to fight all forms of exploitation," and develop a "will to struggle [for] the total liberation of the national territory." In the course of the discussion he even spoke of "insurrectional armed struggle." But on the other hand, he turned away from violence to seek solutions in "universality" and recognition of "reciprocal relativism of different cultures."[7] At this conference, Fanon was confronted (probably for the first time) with the divisions in the black world, between the anglophone and francophone Africans and Black Americans, which may explain this double-talk about "universality" and "relativisim"—both of which are mutually exclusive, and neither of which makes a useful contribution to his concept of violence.[8]

This confusion, therefore, suggests that in September 1956, he was still searching for a suitable formula for the anti-thetical concept of counter-violence. And holy violence was still three or four years away.

By December 1958, when he was a member of the Algerian delegation at the African Peoples' conference in Accra, Fanon was emboldened. Reporting the proceedings of the conference in *El-Moudjahid*, the journal of the Front de Libération Nationale on 24 December 1958, he charged that "no colonialist nation is willing to withdraw without having exhausted all its possibilities of maintaining itself." Debating the merits of decolonization by violent or non-violent means, he conceded that the latter could work under certain types of national and international pressures. But in the case of settler colonies, such as Algeria, Kenya, Angola and South Africa, where settlers will go to great lengths to preserve their "rights" by means of a "police regime, . . . [or through] discriminatory and inhuman measures,"[9] only "armed struggle will bring about the defeat of the occupying nation." Fanon had found the antithetical argument. The logical and historical responsibility for counter-violence rested with the colonizing "lord." His intransigence would respond only when "the knife was at his throat."

The next time Fanon publicly raised the subject, it was March 1959 in Rome, at the Second Congress of Black Writers and Artists, where he was a member of the West Indian delegation. His text on "National Culture and the War of Liberation" contained the kernel of ideas which he later developed in *The Wretched of the Earth* (1961), especially chapter four, which deals with an emerging national culture.[10] Thus by 1959, Fanon's position on counter-violence was becoming clear: and as he had in the past sought justification for creative conflict on sociological and psychological grounds, he now claimed a cultural justification for counter-violence.

Returning to earlier discussions of "dead," "dying" and devalued" cultures, first raised in *Black Skin White Masks*, Fanon asked by what means were cultures revived. Rejecting bourgeois remedies, he now openly advocated struggle—and revolutionary violence. Simply to revalue devalued cultures was futile, he snapped. It was the equivalent of putting old wine into new skins. Likewise, nothing dynamic or creative came from the emergence of compensatory cultures: they simply distracted colonized people from the real struggle. Forever trying to "prove" something—the old search for recognition—compensatory cultures were always addressed to the colonizer, thereby involving colonized people in an endless and futile dialogue. A narcisstic culture was crippling and counterproductive, so were imitative cultures. Now modifying his quest for a universal culture, as Sartre had done earlier, he argued that the latter lost sight of the fact that there was no such thing as CULTURE. Only national and particular cultures could claim legitimacy. Negritude, alas, was at best nothing but the racialization of European thought, and at worst a "blind alley." But a fighting culture—that was the way to revalue devalued cultures, and to create a legitimate national culture. Because, Fanon observed, a culture galvanized for struggle was one that was interacting with fighting people. As a consequence, both people and culture found new meaning and value in the heart of struggle. A fighting culture was not therefore a dynamic, revolutionary and national culture which simply transformed the masses into fighters, thereby "proving" the nation's existence. Rather, a fighting culture revalued and proved its existence by forging a dynamic and revolutionary nation from its violent struggle against the oppressor. A fighting culture created the nation and its people—and not the other way around. Fanon had found the cultural justification for counter-violence.[11] Violence revived and revalued cultures.

Once Fanon had established that organized counter-violence could revalue or recreate cultures, the way to holy violence lay open.

Not surprisingly, during the years when Fanon struggled with the concepts of counter-violence, he was also involved in the revolutionary praxis. After his expulsion from Algeria in January 1957, he made his way to Europe, where he and Josie were received both by her family in Lyon, and in Paris by Francis Jeanson, Professor of Philosophy who had written the preface to *Black Skin White Masks* in 1952. But wanting to be closer to the struggle, he returned to North Africa, to Tunisia in fact, which was home for many Algerian militants, revolutionaries and exiles. Working under the assumed name of Dr. Fares, Tunisia became his base until March 1960, when he left for Ghana. In 1959, his second book, *A Dying Colonialism* was published while Fanon was still in Tunisia.[12] Based on fieldwork in Algeria—compiled hastily as Fanon traveled the Algerian countryside for the F.L.N.—it is the most empirical of his books. Examining social, political and psychological changes which occurred during the war, it shows how collective behavior changed for the better when people were subject to "positive stress." He was later to refer to this as the creation of "new men" under the stress of war, a fairly common phenomenon familiar to those who have observed group action and heightened altruism during time of public stress.

As his commitment to the revolution deepened, Fanon thrived. In a sense, he too was becoming a "new man," as the Hegelian paradigm was slowly but surely transformed into revolutionary counter-violence. In addition to some innovative work based on the ideas of Tosquelles—at the government Psychiatric Hospital at Manouba in Tunis—he worked at the Centre Neuropsychiatrique de Jour (a day care psychiatric center), with the Front de Libération Nationale: F.L.N., and with the Armée de Libération Nationale: A.L.N. At Manouba, he held the post of *Chef de Service* and was accountable to the Tunisian Ministry of Health. Later he was involved in the work of the seven F.L.N. Health Centers in Tunis, and also taught at the University of Tunis. It is likely, as he taught courses for hospital interns, for psychiatrists of the Maghrib, and for political cadres of Africans under colonial domination, that he sharpened the focus on the theme of counter-violence. His course material must, however, have brought cold comfort to the French, as they were later dropped at the request of the Tunisian government, which according to Gendzier, was being pressured by the French.[13] In addition, he contributed to the revolutionary publications such as *Résistance Algérienne;* and between September 1957 to January 1960, to *El-Moudjahid,* the revolutionary journal of the F.L.N.[14] He was also writing about Algeria and decolonization in liberal metropolitan journals such as *l'Esprit,* of which Jean-Marie Domenach was director, and *Présence Africaine* which the Senegalese Alioune Diop first published in 1947. His articles also appeared in *Les Temps Modernes,* a literary-political journal greatly influenced by Sartre, which first appeared in 1945.[15]

Officially a member of the F.L.N. (he had joined in 1957), and with ambivalent attitudes towards violence out of the way, it is clear that his revolutionary work was obsessing him. It is also clear that war-time experiences were providing data for the developing concept of counter-violence about which he now had little hesitation to speak, and which were still to take on sacred and holy proportions. That his involvement was profound, was apparent to all who knew him. After September 1958, he worked in conjunction with the Provisional Government of Algeria (Gouvernement Provisoire de la République Algérienne: G.P.R.A.) Founded on 19 September 1958 in Tunisia by Algerian revolutionaries, the G.P.R.A. was accountable to the National Committee of the Algerian Revolution (Comité National de la Révolution Algérienne : C.N.R.A.), a parlimentary-like body which was formed in 1956. Fanon became a spokesman, and later a kind of traveling ambassador for the G.P.R.A. and the F.L.N.; and it was under their auspices that he attended the All-African Peoples' Conference in Accra in December 1958 (discussed above), where his fledging concept of violence made its debut. Obviously in a ferocious mood, it was here that conference participants heard his assertion that the colonial "lord" would extract his tentacles from the Algerian body politic only after he was convinced that there would be "sufficient pressures of the new ratio of forces" trained like a loaded pistol at his head.

It is likely also that he sharpened his focus on violence in conversations with friends and colleagues at the Accra conference, for he met President Kwame Nkrumah, who at the time was shaping his own ideas on consciencism and Pan-Africanism, and Patrice Lumumba, who was to become embroiled in the liberation struggles and civil war in the former Belgian Congo (now Zaïre). Lumumba and Fanon struck up an immediate friendship, and for the remainder of their short lives (both Fanon and Lumumba were born in 1925; Lumumba was assassinated in 1961, and Fanon died in 1961), a warm relationship existed between them. He also met Ngaloula of the Mouvement National Congolaise, Felix Moumié, Chief of

the Union Populaire de Cameroun (U.P.C.) who was himself wrestling with
the concept of violence (and who was later poisoned), and the syndicalist
Tom M'Boya of the Kenya Independence Movement, who was later
assassinated. In Accra, he met Holden Roberto, future head of the União das
População de Angola (U.P.A.) and eventually the Frente Nacional de
Libertação de Angola (F.L.N.A.). Although Roberto eventually eschewed
violence, in 1959 he was talking of organized resistance against the
Portuguese in Angola, which in fact occurred three years later in conjunction
with Agosthino Neto and the Movimento Popular de Liberação de Angola
(M.P.L.A.).

As part of his revolutionary work, Fanon went to Rome in March 1959,
where he attended the Second Congress of Black Writers and Artists. His
revolutionary profile must have, by 1959, been highly visible, as in that year,
he was the target of an assassination attempt in a Rome hospital where he was
recovering from injuries sustained in what may have been an earlier
assassination attempt on the Moroccan-Algerian border when his jeep was
unaccountably blown up by a land mine. The Roman assassination attempt
was attributed to Le Main Rouge (The Red Hand), an organization of right-
wing settlers who had mounted their own counter-revolutionary vanguard. It
later evolved into the Organization Armée Secrète (The Secret Army
Organization) a quasi official terrorist group headed by French army officers
and former members of the Bureau of Psychological Warfare.

Surviving the Rome incident, within a few weeks, he was in Cairo with the
G.P.R.A. He traveled as their spokesman to international conferences: the
Positive Action Conference for Peace and Security in Africa, and the Afro-
Asian Solidarity Conference in Conakry (Guinea) in April 1959 and Addis
Abbaba (Ethiopia), respectively; and two months later to The Third
Conference of Independent African States. The following year he was back
again in Ghana, where he was a member of the Algerian delegation to the
Second All-African Peoples' Congress. In his text, he analysed prescriptive
revolutionary theories that were emerging from the on-going Algerian
struggle, and agonized over the suffering of the Algerians whom he now
regarded as "brothers."[16] Assigned in March 1960 to the post of permanent
representative for the G.P.R.A. in Accra, Fanon hurriedly pushed for arms
and volunteers from the south. There was also the incredible undertaking of
opening a new front in the south; and to that end, Fanon and a team of six
undertook the perilous journey through Mali and the Sahara, north to Algeria.
Their objective was to survey infiltration routes, to open new lines of
communication, and to raise volunteer armies by radicalizing Africans in the
Sahel and Sahara. He drew up specific war plans addressed to commandos,
advocating how to draw on recruits, how to gather information, how to
develop strategies and how to deploy troops and weapons.[17] He was even

beginning to see links between the Algerian struggle, and those in Angola and the Congo (Zaîre).

But there was something amiss in all of this. Feeling remote from the struggle, he had been ill at ease in Ghana in a culture which he could not really understand. The fact that his English left something to be desired, aggravated his growing sense of "deprivation." He abandoned plans to write a book on Pan-Africanism and theories of violence—which he intended to call *Algiers—the Cape,*—and undertook instead a "revolutionary" journey through francophone Africa, calling for volunteers, and propagandizing for the newly formed African Legion and the Pan-Africanist revolutionary struggle. But the anticipated support from the north never came. The G.P.R.A. in Tunis was enthusiastic about southern arms, but hardly over-joyed at the prospect of sub-Saharan volunteers. The F.L.N. froze at the promise of some eight-hundred volunteers from Ghana and Egypt. The nationalists and moderates in the party warmed to the idea of receiving skilled technicians, but chilled at the prospects of Pan-African unity, or at Fanon's idea of universalizing the struggle on a continental scale.

In 1961, he let it be known that he was interested in the position of F.L.N. ambassador to Cuba. His feelers were left dangling. There was a sense that after the enormous efforts to reach the eye of the revolutionary storm, his enemies of the F.L.N. had succeeded in neutralizing and "exiling" him to the periphery. It is not clear why this happened. The F.L.N. leadership eschewed the development of the personality cult—favoring instead the collective image—which may explain their lukewarm attitudes to Fanon's activities and requests.[18] Moreover as a close friend of Abane Ramdan, who eventually came into conflict with the F.L.N. over ideology and revolutionary goals, and who died under mysterious circumstances in 1958, Fanon himself may also have been under a cloud of suspicion for wanting to "pollute" revolutionary goals.[19]

F.L.N. motives notwithstanding, it is without question that Fanon found the cultural, sociological and psychological infrastructure for the concept of counter-violence in his Algerian and sub-Saharan work. More importantly, this "fieldwork" provided empirical data which Fanon later applied to the "sacred" elements, as counter-violence "blossomed" into holy violence. For example, when he talked of violence "detoxifying" people, "opening minds and hearts," and creating "new men," he was clearly no longer referring to the bondsman's brute force. Rather, he was speaking of changed behavior, norms, and attitudes which he had observed under war-time conditions. Similarly, in advocating the politicization of "the people" by first working through traditional leaders—those "old men who are greatly respected and who generally possess an indisputable moral authority",—he had gone beyond violence and was dealing with ways in which societies change or can be changed during times of great public stress, such as war-time. Not only was he reporting empirical observations, seen many times over throughout the Algerian country-side, but he was also affirming that a traditional society is best mobilized from within, through traditional leaders and institutions. Viewing outside leaders as "foreigners," country people responded reluctantly to the leadership of townspeople. They "have no morals," Fanon quoted them as saying, and besides, townspeople could not be trusted. Finally, when he recorded the "early signs" of people who were "ready for violence," such as "refurbishing their culture," reviving anti-colonial stories "which women softly hum in their childrens' ears," or exchanging stories of ancient warriors and kings, the savagery of peasant violence was remote from his mind. Now beyond violence, he was referring to nationalism and patriotism, still held by some to be among the few remaining noble sentiments, along with religious beliefs.

Turning particularly to those aspects of Fanon's thought which were now clearly beyond violence, and which later formed the infrastructure of holy violence—that violence can alter peoples' behavior and provide new attitudes and psychological perspectives—his critics have never ceased to cry shame. For example, Caute implied that perhaps not even Fanon himself believed in the "detoxifying" power of violence. His own admission of the deleterious effects of violence on victims and perpetrators alike denied any salutory consequences.[20] Additionally, Hannah Arendt considered Fanon's links between biological, organic, and psychological forces, on the one hand, and power and violence, on the other hand, as "dangerous." If societal health depended on prescriptive violence, she countered, the next step would be to identify destruction and creativity as "two sides of the natural process." Collective violence would then appear as the natural "prerequisite for the collective life of mankind." And far from detoxifying, society would instead be poisoned, returning mankind to the pre-Hobbesian state of nature.[21] Gendzier has also scolded Fanon for his creative violence, arguing "that it is doubtful that the violence which Fanon advocated for the individual could possibly fulfill the psychological functions which he claimed." She concluded by regretting "publicly" his fusion of existential and political recommendations, which, given his tattered methodolgy, seems to be asking for too much.[22] Moreover, While Eli-Kedouri remarked that Fanon was a "panegyrist . . . of violence" who celebrated its virtues with "savage lyricism," Lewis Coser appropriately suggested an underanalysis of the concept, and like Arendt denied it had any therapeutic value.[23]

As suggested above, a closer look at the Algerian data which Fanon collected—and which incidentally are widely known—suggest, however, that violence under very special circumstances (i.e. the war of liberation) did produce the social, psychological and cultural changes of the sort which he recounted. Delegates to the Soumman Congress in the summer of 1956, where the F.L.N. defined its objectives, methods and future programs, announced that:

> *it is an undeniable fact that the A.L.N. has radically altered the political climate of Algeria. It has been the catalyst for a psychological shock which has liberated the people from their stupor, fear and scepticism. It has caused the Algerian people to have a new awareness and a national pride. It has also brought about a psychological and political conjunction of the feelings of all the Algerian people, this national unanimity which nourishes the armed struggle, and makes victory and liberty inevitable.*[24]

Although these psycho-political effects were not always lasting—and Algerians were also aware of this—they were significant enough to provide an empirical base for claims that Fanon was going beyond violence, and that heightened courage, bravery and altruism, even on the part of the cowardly and mean, were significant enough to inject a sacred and holy element into day to day war-time violence. Making these kinds of claims is not unusual. Few would deny that war-time conditions can and do change norms and behavior—temporarily or otherwise. And it is well to remember that Fanon never claimed permanence for the war-time normative and behavioral changes which he recounted, although he never concealed his aspirations.

Accordingly, turning first to the cultural revival as part of the social infrastructure of holy violence (not to be confused with Fanon's methodological use of cultural revival and revaluation as the justification for counter-violence discussed above), Algerians did insert their struggle within the infrastructure of a "fighting culture," which had a historical dimension and religious overtones. Calling themselves *moudjahidin:* those who fight in holy wars, *mousseblin:* those who fight God's battle, and *fida'iyin:* those who make sacrifices, they identified their war with the nineteenth century resistance wars against the "infidel" which followed the French conquest in 1830. Chanting the names of great and glorious heroes who had fought the French throughout the greater part of the last century, their joyous strains "moved the mountains," and stirred the "idle country-side." They did revive praise songs about the still-revered 'Abdul Qadir, Sultan of the Western Awal Sidi al-Shaikh and leader of the Qadiriyya sufi order, who for fifteen years (1832-47) fought the French in the mountains, in the valleys, and in the plains; as well as stories of the "Grand Insurrection" of 1845, and the "Western Uprising" two years later, when the blood of heroes stained the land. But most importantly, they retold narratives of the anti-French "great Uprising" of 1871—which still excites wonder (1972)—under the leadership of the exalted Muhammad Mukrani, when martyrs died and mothers wept as the bravest sons of Algeria were trodden underfoot. There was, for example, the nineteenth century lament of the lone and unveiled woman wandering the Algerian desert, weeping for the loss of her people who, "since time immemorial had known how to create and how to destroy," but "whose sky is now darkened with clouds, while shadows envelope" the land, obscuring even the fires of young men. Then there was the satirical tale told of Blida, the town where Fanon later resided, of "a dog (which God burnt in his tomb; yes God had to burn him as he himself had burned his Muslim brothers) which mounted to the top of the minaret" of the Sidi Belkassim mosque and cried: " 'Listen, oh ye Believers of God: God is communicating this to you for your well-being! You are saved! The Roumi [French] have fallen back in retreat.' " Not to mention the many curses heaped on Christian "idolatry" which polluted the land, and the cries of God beseeching salvation from the "miscreants."[25]

South of the Sahara, oral traditions recounted the deeds of Sundjata, the "Lion King," the mighty Manding King who in the fourteenth century smote his enemies, while the last battles against the French, of King Behanzin of Dahomey and Samoury Touré in the Ivory Coast were recounted with swelling pride. Additionally, stories of the "great past of the Arab civilization" were also revived, and the exploits of conquerors told *as if* people were once again putting the "infidel" to the fiery sword. All these things "happened long ago," the narrator would say, but "might they not happen again tomorrow?" To which Fanon added that if violence had not been the catalyst behind this cultural revival; if violence had not recreated this "fighting culture," to what then might one attribute this rhythmic outpouring which had "moved the mountains" and stirred the "idle countryside?"

Data for Fanon's second claim that there was a social infrastructure to holy violence were also drawn from his wartime experiences. Working both north and south of the Sahara, he noticed that in lineage-based, traditional societies, corporate responses frequently took precedence over individual ones. He seemed fascinated by this phenomena, which he called "solidarity," and on closer examination found that when a clan respected its leader, its members faithfully followed. In other words, uniting lineage-based groups for revolutionary action was easier if the leadership worked through existing social linkages; and radicalizing a community was more likely if traditional leaders were in favor of the revolutionary political objectives. Under these circumstances, people did act with speed as if "lit by a match." Furthermore, when "the countryside [was] discontented, the Arab telephone" immediately came into existence, as if from nowhere, spreading news "like a wild fire." From the mountains and vast steppes, angry peasants "with the dirt still between their toes" rose to the call, such as the Aurès peasants, who in 1954 covered themselves with glory by being the first to rise.

Few would claim that peasants are revolutionary. In fact the weight of evidence is to the contrary, beginning with Marx who dismissed them as a "sack of potatoes," and who later drew his famous analogy between agrarian life and "rural idiocy."[27] Yet Fanon was right. When mobilized from within, traditional lineage-based societies did for the most part follow *en masse* the leadership of their elders. Clan and lineage ties were stronger than ideology, as was demonstrated, for example, by the Aurès peasants who later turned against their revolutionary leaders because they were "foreigners." Village councils and assemblies, which were really clan and lineage corporations, were transformed into revolutionary tribunals and political and military committees. Although membership in the political party, the Front de Libération Nationale, cut across clan and lineage ties, people drawn into revolutionary conflict were more often than not initiated into the struggle by virtue of blood and marriage ties.[28] Not only were adult men and women involved, but also the young and old, who for the most part remained in the villages "to pray." These popular assemblies, according to an article in *El-Moudjahid*, the revolutionary journal of the F.L.N., "organized welcoming groups for the freedom fighters, took the census in the community, raised taxes, attended to security matters, and collected information on the enemies' movements." Moreover, "popular assemblies took responsibility for the enactment of justice . . . and exercised all the functions for which a municipality is responsible."[29]

There was therefore a dimension to this violence which transcended coercion and brute force. By integrating this violent phenomenon into existing social and politcal infrastructures, which in turn mobilized and politicized people through traditional channels of authority and command, revolutionary violence was becoming a creative force. For example, without this sociological infrastructure, divisions of the fighting regions into *wilayas* (military districts) may never have been possible; and cell-group organizations in the *maquis* and beyond, might well have lacked their now legendary cohesiveness—internal conflicts notwithstanding. Moreover, creative violence was also minimizing deep-seated inter-ethnic rivalries dating back, in some instances to the eleventh century, which if allowed to persist, could easily have thwarted war efforts by keeping people permanently divided. But deciding to cast aside rivalries in the interest of the collective war effort, Fanon reported that their reconciliation produced a "collective ecstasy," which may or may not have been the case. It is important, however, to notice that the reconciliation could only have occurred after an act of forgiveness. Traditional enemies with "long-buried" [but] not forgottten hatreds" forgave each other —for the hatreds of their fathers, and their fathers' fathers. It is difficult to believe that this could have occurred without a sense of relief; and it is easy to see why Fanon the psychiatrist called it "purification"—even if some of the ethnic groups participated only temporarily in the collective "love-in." And while some communities aborted revolutionary endeavors by later collaborating with the French, most did not. Fanon waxed eloquent about people forgiving and forgetting, and rhapsodized about the joys of "numerous reconciliations." He talked about the sense of relief which comes from forgiveness as a sort of mystical experience, which few can deny. As a psychiatrist he would have known that long-standing hatreds between ethnic groups can "poison" the cultural environment. Watching this unexpected cooperation between old enemies, he compared it to a congregation, or to Islamic brotherhoods in the height of religious passion.

Closely studying the metamorphosis of these "born-again" men, Fanon recognized that he was in the presence of something mysterious and perhaps even holy. Had he been religious, he might have attributed these changes to some kind of spiritual force. But since he was a psychiatrist and revolutionary, he probably thought instead of a kind of holy violence.

On turning to the psychological data, it is apparent that here, also, Fanon found a third inner rationale for holy violence when he claimed that violence "detoxifies" the individual, restores a man's self-respect—while preparing him for change—and makes him fearless. Violence, he said, is also a "royal pardon," whatever that means, through which "the colonized man finds his freedom." Finally, violence creates a "new man."[30] Social scientists don't usually talk this way. This type of poetic language and imagery confuse everything and explain nothing. Small wonder the critics cited above have never ceased to say that this is nonsense. Not even Marx, the father of "scientific violence" approached these extremes; and Sydney Hook's rebuttal: that it was "worse than false" to claim that violence "prepared the minds of men for change" seems reasonable. So does his subsequent condemnation of violence as "foolish," and "criminally irresponsible."[31] Leftists and Marxists have not fallen over themselves to come to Fanon's aid. Renate Zahar and Vietnamese Communist Nguyen Nghe have also faulted his judgment. While Zahar observed that violence was an ineffectual instrument of social change if unaccompanied by radical socio-political restructuring; citing empirical evidence, Nguyen Nghe remarked that far from "detoxifying" men, after participation in the national struggles, Vietnamese peasants resumed their slothful pre-revolutionary ways.[32]

Yet probing beyond Fanon's "poetry-talk" and the criticism which it has provoked, it is possible that Fanon, the medical man, deliberately used the term "detoxify" to describe cleansing in a personality which had been "poisoned" by "toxins" in the colonial syndrome, such as an inferiority complex, self-hatred, guilt, lethargy, depression, despair and suicide.[33] A "royal pardon" suggests something more specific: that one who was outlawed for a political crime against the French, would find a "home" and "royal pardon" in the ranks of freedom fighters where, instead of being treated like a common criminal, he would be hailed a hero. Shaking off his fear, and recovering his self-respect, a "new man" would be born.

Can violence accomplish all of this? Can acts of violence eliminate "feelings of inferiority" and free men "from inaction and despair?" Can violence educate or raise levels of political awareness while relieving psychic suffering? Can it create what Fanon called the "new man?" Alienated from their cultures, or from traditional lands, many Algerians subsisted in a state of cultural *anomie.* On the one hand, for culturally assimilated Algerians, like Ferhat 'Abbas, Ahmed Boumendjel, Ben Youssef Benkhedda and Ahmed Francis, who in a sense were neither French nor Arab, the agony of cultural *anomie* induced a sense of deprived identity. If, in addition, there were constant reminders of the inferiority of "the Muslim race," the chances of a damaged self-esteem were greater. On the other hand, for economically assimilated Algerians, such as wage-laborers whose contact with the modern European sector was restricted to wage-labor exchange, the situation was equally unbearable. Landless and deprived of a viable economic base as well as a corporate identity, landless laborers lived with a smoldering rage—like "sores under their skin," Fanon said. Among these, for example, were the Massada, who in 1880 had their good Rio-Salada lands appropriated, and were forced to seek a penurious livelihood in the southern mountains. Revolutionary leaders, such as Mohammad Boudiaf, Abdallhafid Boussouf, Abdelkader Guerroudy, and Brahim Mezhoudi came from families whose lands had been appropriated by the French. Thus by "stealing" the identities of the culturally assimilated, and by alienating hereditary tribal lands, the French had acted out the role of Hegel's lord: by their "absolute opposition" and non-recognition, they had reduced the Algerians to an "absolute negation."

Remembering that the Hegelian slave survived through conflict, and had realized himself through work, Fanon was now prescribing a similar work-conflict therapy, not only for himself, but also for the negated Algerians. Arguing that "revolution is work," that "the revolutionary is one who works," and that "to work means to work for the death of the white settler," Fanon urged that alienated people recover their material and spiritual losses through violence. In many ways this is exactly what happened in Algeria.

In his empirical studies, published as essays in a *Dying Colonialism,* Fanon accurately described the emergence of the "new man" in association with revolutionary work. Because, in effect, he was observing "before" and "after" scenarios of people and their behavior changes as politicization and commitment to the revolution deepened. There was, for example, the "before" resistance of colonial Algerians to the French radio and press as something "foreign," and the "after" integration of these communication media into the war effort. By 1956, the once-shunned radio was playing such an important role in the war effort, that a set could only be obtained with difficulty. Informing news of victories and defeats, recruiting and mobilizing people, the radio became *the* means for diffusing revolutionary ideologies and war-time propaganda, as well as putting one end of the nation in touch with the other. From a broader perspective, Fanon's data showed that when integrated into a familiar cultural framework, traditional people will accept "foreign things," including a foreign technology.[34] He revealed similar changes in attitudes towards western medicine—which before 1954 many Algerians had shunned—when the *maquisards* "learned" that the "lord's" medicine possessed healing properties quite distinct from the "lord" himself.[35] His remarks on the relaxation of family relationships, including the abandoning of women's *haik* or Muslim dress after 1954—is a fascinating account of how institutionalized role-play changes radically during periods of "positive stress."[36] His data were substantiated by the publications of the F.L.N., as well as by the delegates to the Soumman Congress in the summer of 1956, who hailed female freedom fighters, *"moudjahidates"* (*moudjahidin*: masc.) for their courage, bravery and willingness to make personal sacrifices. They also applauded them for the creation of a "Womens Committee" of the F.L.N., which trained the *maquisardes* (*maquisards: masc.*)and contributed in many ways to the on-going struggle.[37]

If the published documents of the revolution are any indication, Fanon was not alone in hoping that the war-time changes would inject new elements into the society for the future. In some instances, events proved otherwise, especially where women and peasants were concerned. Underestimating the role of Islam-in-society, the "liberation of the Algerian woman," which his Western mind-set had hoped for, never occurred. Similarly, the peasants whose violent "instincts" he once compared to "rising gusts of wind," and "impetuous wolves leaping on their prey," showed long ago that pragmatism outweighed revolutionary ideology.[38] His remarks, notwithstanding, in his "before" and "after" scenarios, Fanon's data confirmed that under the stress of war and the hope of victory, some norms and types of behavior could and did change. And if not all Algerians became "new men," and not all peasants were transformed into "impetuous wolves leaping on their prey," revolutionary violence did change some people—if only temporarily—and did create new normative options for the post-revolutionary generation.

These mixed results, despite expectations *apropos* of the society at large, Fanon's data drawn from the *maquis* and military sub-groups scattered throughout Algeria also demonstrated the emergence of the "new man" in association with revolutionary work. Studying the supportive environments and networks which freedom fighters had developed for them-

selves, Fanon recognized a group therapy format with which he had
been familiar. While engaging in similar pursuits—drawing up strategic
blueprints for the struggle to which they were committed and for the
"glorious" post-colonial hereafter—members performed a group therapy
familiar to all who have participated in the dynamics of shared goals, actions
and commitments. Fanon had administered group and work therapy in his
clinical undertakings at the Blida psychiatric hospital, and was familiar with
some of its consequences.[39] He had seen where under certain circumstances,
collective labor and commitment to common ideals sometimes produced
salutory, even creative effects. It is, therefore, hardly surprising that he
should have recognized similar dynamics at work within tightly knit
supportive circles of fugitive militants where revolutionary "workers" were
committed to a "higher cause." Because while the colonial state condemned
militants as wild-eyed criminals, group members, perceiving themselves as
"servants of a holy cause," provided supportive environments for themselves
in the name of the "higher cause."[40]

Therapeutic consequences generated within tightly knit groups resisting
outside pressures are not uncommon. Citing empirical data, Bernard J. Siegal
suggested that certain types of groups whose identities were threatened,
tended to develop defensive patterns of cultural adaptation which were ego
supportive. For example, group sanctions discourage potentially destructive
behavior, preferring to minimize group confrontations and violence.
Moreover, strong disciplinary measures subordinated the individual will to
that of the larger entity. Ralph H. Turner substantiated Siegal's argument by
suggesting that group members who were committed to common identities
and interdependencies tended to limit intra-group "antagonistic-cooperation"
to the "point at which group members [saw] the group bonds in danger of
immanent dissolution." Recognizing the dangers which they faced individu-
ally, and the collective benefits likely to accrue, group members tended to
retain strong group identity and collaborative bonds.[41] Finally, in Durkheim's
study on *Suicide*, which Fanon may have read (he made references to
Durkheim), the former inferred causal linkages between heightened group
integration and falling suicided rates. Moreover, Durkheim showed that
community disasters frequently were followed by temporary periods of
heightened altruism, warmth, generosity, like-mindedness and a desire for
unity,—all qualities to which Fanon referred. *Anomie*, or a sense of
normlessness, including social and personal disorganization and demoraliza-
tion, decreased when meaning was restored to existence.[42]

Evidence suggests, therefore, that group activity among members subject
to external pressures can produce supportive and creative behavior. Internal
group pressures, control mechanisms and commitment to "group survival,"
"group integrity," a "higher cause," a "noble ideal," an "ultimate reality,"

can temporarily enoble mens' minds, causing them to behave *as if* they were "new men." In effect Fanon seems to have been saying that tightly knit militant groups committed to the destruction of the colonial state by violence, and to the emergence of a national integrity, can temporarily solicit heroic purposeful and dynamic responses from members. Brute force alone or violence could not have achieved this, and it is clear that Fanon was no longer talking about violence *per se*.

Two "therapeutic" consequences could result from life in a supportive environment of the sort just described. First, alienated colonial man could disalienate himself through collective commitment to something other than that which the colonial "lord" had created. The colonial "lord" had alienated the Algerian "bondsman" from his indigenous cultures. Adoption into the "lord's" cultures was an inadequate substitute: the new culture was totally alien. Cultural and psychological "homelessness" expressed itself in anxieties, neuroses, and sometimes even as psychoses. In the last analysis, alienation disintegrated inner communication channels which had previously favored self-awareness. And while self-alienation distorted internal realities, cultural alienation disorganized external realities, disabling judgement, wisdom and perception.

Within anti-colonial militant groups, which by their very nature provided supportive group "therapy," colonial man could "go back home." Ambivalent up to now about the colonial world—which was equally ambivalent about him—he could disalienate himself through collective commitment to a "higher cause." It was his very own, forged from his mind and body, and sealed with his life and death. It is debatable whether or not this type of commitment could permanently alter the fundamental structure of any personality type. The variables are too numerous. Yet, the spell-binding euphoria of closely knit groups bound by trusts, confidences, friendships, (including life and death itself, to the same "higher cause") could temporarily assauge feelings of anger, guilt, inferiority, ambivalence and insecurity by providing a specific focal point for alienated psyches, diffused restlessness and an ill-defined anger. Conceivably, commitment also could heighten self-awareness, together with a collective reappraisal of social realities, and turn despairing cowards into courageous activists. Participation in this type of committed group activity could temporarily, at least, drain away feelings of guilt, insecurity, and ambivalence, and direct them into constructive, focussed activities. This seems to be what Fanon was saying: that in supportive environments, "going back home," even *via* commitment to violence, could make the militant feel as if he had received a "royal pardon" for "crimes" against himself, committed in the name of the conqueror's morality.

Second, if Fanon recognized equivalencies between the cleansing force of group therapy at the Blida psychiatric hospital, and the "royal pardon" of "good" violence in supportive environments where confidences, trusts and friendships were exchanged, he also realized that the process of anti-colonial action decolonized the mind. "To decolonize the mind is to show that it can work against the other fellow," an interlocutor at Blida remarked, adding that "when he [i.e. the militant] sees that it [i.e. the mind] works against the Other, then that is decolonization of the mind."[43] Evidently, Fanon encouraged people, anybody, not necessarily active militants, to work for the destruction of the colonial state, in order to initiate mental decolonial processes. He neither intended that violence *per se* should instruct, nor that it was intrinsically capable of revealing social realities, while raising levels of political awareness. Rather he believed that like Hegel's bondsman colonial man should generate a new self-image by developing his own abilities to act against his master. So long as he did not, he would think that he could not. Acting caused him to recognize the possible, thereby marking the beginning of mental decolonization and politicization. Once politicized, the decolonized man developed the concept of a general organized struggle; and in so doing, another militant or "new man" was born. In this instance, Fanon concluded, armed combat "really exorcised" the sense of inferiority, which affected even the most aware.[44]

Once again Fanon waxed eloquent about the birth of the "new man." "Let us go forward brothers," he cried, "we must leave our dreams and abandon our old beliefs . . . . The dark night in which we have been plunged" is behind us . . . . We have work to do . . . and nothing more to fear."[45]

Having shown that certain types of violent circumstances can revalue "devalued" cultures as well as alter individual and group behavior, Fanon now urged friends and colleagues alike to "abandon . . . old beliefs," as has been suggested previously. In effect he was developing a morality of oppression which sanctioned change, telling people that it was alright to modify their behavior and attitudes, because change was dedicated to a "higher cause." Granting permission to change was an important element in Fanon's holy violence. It mitigated the sense of guilt which frequently comes to those who "break the moulds," or "disobey the gods." By "absolving" their "sin" in advance, Fanon's morality of oppression paved the way for violence with a clear conscience.

Arguing that European concepts of good and evil were for conquerors, and therefore unsuitable for colonial peoples, he reversed them, showing that if Europeans had profitted from their morality in the colonies, their presence had brought only servitude to colonial peoples. With such contrasting consequences, morality could hardly be the same on both sides of the colonial experience. That which was "good" on one side, clearly was "evil" on the other. European morality should be inverted in the colonies where a new morality was called for. Hence, the "good" was a concrete anti-colonial thought-act, such as thinking about the equality of Man in an unequal power relationship (as in the case of lord and bondsman), and simultaneously putting that equality into effect. More specifically, if exploitation and oppression of the "native" were "good" for the colonizer, resistance to these was equally "good" for the colonized, even if resistance required counter-violence. Similarly, if the colonizer had created a "good" immoral economic and political order, its destruction by equivalent means was also "good."[46]

Fanon's break with conventional European morality was deliberate. He was developing a morality for the oppressed, together with survival strategies. Harbingers of a new morality tend to question the old moral order in times of rapid social and political change, when new values are called for, when legitimacy is doubted or undermined, or when state institutions and goals are in systematic conflict with those of society.[47] Machiavelli's response to modern state exigencies was to permit the "good" immoral act in the name of the state. Marx permitted the "good" revolution as a means of establishing a higher moral order. Nietzsche rejected Christian morality on the grounds that it was for slaves, and developed instead a morality for the strong or would-be masters of the post-Christian era. And now the man from Martinique was permitting oppressed colonial people to perform outlawed, even criminal acts against the colonizing "lord," because in his morality of oppression, these acts were "good."

Fanon demonstrated the morality of oppression at work in the society by correctly observing that in Algeria, a colonized person would frequently begin his career as a militant by submitting to the "sacrifice trap." He would commit a "good" crime.[48] Having performed what many militants regarded as a *rite de passage*, the colonized man, now a criminal, was unable to re-enter colonial society, save as an outlaw. The murderous ritual had "irrevocably" altered his relationship to colonial society. Regardless of previous levels of political awareness, the fugitive was now confronted with the new political realities, and a new political morality. His act forced him into an either/or situation: either remain in hiding, an isolated fugitive with a price on his head; or join a band of anti-colonial militants, thus becoming politicized in the process.

Assuming he chose the latter, the more remote the outlaw's chances of re-entering society, the deeper his commitment to anti-colonial militancy. The more he was sought by the French police, the greater his stature within the militant community. Indeed the enormity of his "good" crime against colonial society was regarded as a measure of his courage and heroism. According to the morality of oppression, the criminal was becoming a hero—and a "new man" was being born out of violence.[49] His personality had not altered fundamentally—apart from his deepening commitment and its consequences to a "higher cause." But changing societal attitudes, especially those of militant communities, now considered his violence against colonial society as "good." The perpetrator of a "good" crime was becoming a hero. In effect, Fanon was showing that a society in the process of changing itself, also redefined its values and the role its members played. He was also demonstrating that in a war-time situation which called for shifting normative scales, the morality of oppression differentiated the criminal from the hero, even when both were commiting murder.

Fanon's holy violence, as distinct from counter-violence, coercion or brute force *per se* was now almost complete. While the latter simply meant ridding oneself of the colonizing "lord" by "putting the knife to his throat," the former suggested a renaissance, something creative, such as a revival of murdered cultures, transfusing dynamism into anaemic traditional norms, and modifying dysfunctional behavior with functional transplants. Aligning all of these with the political exigences of a modern revolutionary situation and with a new morality to the point where lethargy became action, muddleheadedness a focussed politicization, and despair became hope, was the penultimate of holy violence. Empirical data revealed that all these occurred in war-time Algeria. That some virtues of the collective euphoria slipped away with the conclusion of hostilities, is not surprising. Moreover, as evidence cited above shows, a heightened collective euphoria which creates a "new man" is at best a temporary phenomenon.

Thus the man from Martinique proved to be a shrewd observer of human behavior under great stress, and a perceptive analyst of the psyche. What he still lacked was the "soul" and "spirit" of holy violence, as well as its "vision." He was to find these in his Martinican memories, as well as in the cultural and religious backwaters of the Algerian peasants' collective psyche. He was about to discover another dimension to his much criticized theory of the "revolutionary peasantry": the holy violence long embedded in the "primitive" minds and cultures of "his" Algerian peasants.

# VI

# Holy Violence Part II: The Philosophical Script and the Vision

*"Now the problem is to seize this violence that is in the process of changing direction. When formerly it took pleasure in myths and went out of its way to find new ways to commit collective suicide, notice how these new conditions will cause them to change their orientation."*

Fanon

Fanon's concept of holy violence was now almost complete. Beginning in 1952 with the simple concept of creative conflict in the Hegelian lord-bondsman relationship—which Fanon had extrapolated from Martinican social data—by 1957 it had developed into revolutionary counter-violence against the collossal intransigency of the French presence in Algeria. Between 1957 when he left Algeria, and his visit to the Soviet Union in 1961 for medical treatment—he first noticed the leukemia symptoms while in Ghana—the war-time empirical data, gathered both from north and south of the Sahara, had added three-dimensional aspects to counter-violence: revolutionary counter-violence was becoming the catalyst for a cultural revival; a new social cohesion; and an individual and collective psycho-political rebirth. Now a dynamic force capable of positive (as well as negative) change, it is clear that Fanon's concept of violence was beyond mere brute force. It was entering a new creative realm where, like a revitalizing spirit, violence was animating Algerian societies—from within. Violence had taken on hidden proportions. While its overall effects were visible, its invisible process in the societies' inner and undersides were defying rational explanation. Its impact was also escaping rational control. But although working mysteriously like a revitalizing ferment in old social wineskins, this dynamic act was still only profane. Having come thus far, it still lacked the truly sacred and holy elements. Fanon was to find these in the "vision" of holy violence embedded in the "primitive" minds of the Martinican and Algerian peasantry.

When discussing Fanon's intellectual development, it is customary to relate his thinking to Cartesian and Hegelian influences, and his concept of violence to Marx, Sartre and Merleau Ponty etc. Many of Fanon's biographers including Zahar, Caute and Gendzier have done this. Gendzier added a new dimension when she revealed Tosquelles' influence on Fanon's view of psychiatry. All this is of course true, especially since they partially explain the "European part" of Fanon's intellectual development. Few, however, have attached serious importance to those free-flowing areas of Fanon's thought which slip imperceptibly, from psychiatric to existentialist analysis, or from the rational world of the Hegelian dialectic to those non-rational dimensions in the "primitive" mind of Third World peasants. Instead most critics fault him for these methodological heresies which have flawed his work, while missing the garbled "truths" which he was trying to reveal. Yet these analytical delinquencies were once more demonstrating an earlier claim made in *Black Skin White Masks*: that "the blackman lives in two dimensions—one with his fellows, the other with the white man." Thus there were two Frantz Fanons who ultimately completed the concept of holy violence. While the "Antillean" Fanon—the man from Martinique—flushed out and decoded the sacred elements of violence from "primitive" symbolism in Algerian peasant cultures and beliefs-systems; the "European" Fanon, philospher and political activist—wrote the philosophical script for this non-rational phenomena. His ragged methodology was therefore touching two bases simultaneously. And while the man from Martinique probed Algerian peasant belief-systems, which were adding sacred dimensions to the violent ferment possessing Algerian peasants, Dr. Frantz Fanon developed the philosophical underpinnings for the holy violence which was claiming the Algerian people. It isn't that Fanon was schizoid. It is, rather, that his dual intellectual heritage was simultaneously analyzing, and becoming possessed by, the mysteries of holy violence.

## The Philosophical Script

The European Fanon's debt to Hegel, Marx and Sartre is well known.[1] For his philosophical script, it is also known that he adapted Marx, arguing that "in the colonies, the economic infrastructure is the same as the superstructure . . . . Which is why a Marxist analysis must always be slightly adjusted each time one approaches the colonial problem. Everything in Marx's thought," he continued, "including his concept of the precapitalist society, . . . needs to be thought through again" when applied to the colonies.[2] From Marx and Sartre he took the humanist ideal, and the whole radical criticism of history and social knowledge since Aristotle—although he narrowed the empirical base to the European presence in tropical dependencies. He also accepted the anthropomorphism of Feurbach which he found in their thought, as well as the democratic ideals, propaganda and sloganism which came out of the French Revolution. From Marx particularly, he inherited the ambivalence of the Romantics towards past and present institutions, which he combined with ideologies established by workers' protest movements and pre-scientific socialism. In effect, the intellectual framework which Marx, and later Sartre developed, provided Fanon with the basic philosophical script for holy violence.[3]

From Marx, specifically, he borrowed the concept of "historical materialism" which looked for all causation in matter, as opposed to metaphysical or "primary causes." Similarly, he adapted the master's mode of production analysis, thereby recognizing that material life determined social relationships of production, as well as the political and spiritual processes of life. In his economic analysis—such as it was—he applied Marx's theory of surplus value to the colonies. All of which provided the philosophical justification for change by violence. Without waiting for metaphysical interventions, material change could result from material action in the material world. As to methodology—despite his scorn that such things were for"mathematicians and botanists"—he produced a poor adaptation of Marx's systems analysis: that society was an interrelated whole which changes as a result of internal contradictions and conflicts. Finally, he accepted Marx's "historical necessity" by claiming the conjunction of the "inveitable revolutionary process in history" with the confirmation of it by the revolutionary elect. Claiming the peasants as his revolutionnary elect, he never tired of re-assuring them that at last, "in the full glare of history," they were finally on the winning side.[4]

But although his indebtedness to Marx was great, it was Sartre who ultimately shaped the philosophical script, especially the latter's *Being and Nothingness*, and *Critique of Dialectical Reason*. Consequently, Fanon never abandoned the existentialist insights which both enhanced and confused his psychological perspectives. Similarly, Sartre's concept of universalism never ceased to fascinate him. In fact, Caute's assertion to the contrary, universalism dominated the philosophical script for holy violence to the end, especially when he appealed for the spread of the Algerian revolution to sub-Sahara Africa, and that all former colonized men should "go forward in the company of Man" by applying humanist and universal values.[5] He was also inspired by the master's sense of responsible commitment, even in the face of chaos, which Sartre had talked about in *Being and Nothingness*, as well as the latter's crisis of an alienated consciousness. On the revolutionary role of the proletariat, both the mature Sartre and the later Fanon came to deny their role as torch bearers of the "historic mission" on grounds that wrapped in "an obscene narcism," they had ceased to be revolutionary. Fanon went further by arguing that because of differences in the colonial environment, the colonial proletariat had never "developed a consciousness in the class struggle." Finally, under the master's influence—after reading his preface to Léopold Senghor's *Anthologie de la Nouvelle Poésie Nègre et Malgache*—Fanon tearfully abandoned the concept of negritude. By relegating it to a "transition"—a "minor term in a dialectical progression"—

instead of a "conclusion" he sobbed, Sartre had "destroyed black zeal." By challenging the black's "unreflected positions" and "unhappy romanticism," he removed the ground from under their feet. Besides, as Fanon was to learn later, negritude could not do for social change what violence could achieve in the colonial syndrome.[6]

But if Fanon's philosophical script for holy violence was influenced by Marx and Sartre, it was also shaped by the revisionists, beginning with Engels, whose *Anti-Dühring* (1878) Fanon took issue with in his *The Wretched of the Earth*.[7] From Lenin he adopted the idea of materialism as ideology or doctrine—something which Marx seemed reluctant to do—and the concept of "imperialism" as the export of capital and of capitalism into tropical dependencies. Similarly, like Lenin and the Third International (1919), he questioned the effectiveness of spontaneous revolutionary activity on the part of the producing class, favoring instead the bureaucratization, or rationalization of the political party under the direction of revolutionary elites. In its mature form, his theory of the "spontaneously revolutionary peasantry" was really only a slogan for the revolutionary uprising of the Algerian peasantry under the leadership of the Front de Libération Nationale. The extent to which he was consciously influenced by the global analysis of the Bolsheviks is not clear. Yet like them, he associated the colonial world with the industrial proletariat, and invested the Third World peasantry with the "historic mission" of the "proletariat revolution" on a global scale.[8]

It has been suggested that two other Marxist revisionists were also written into the philosophical script for holy violence. According to Hannah Arendt, Fanon was influenced by George Sorel (1847-1922).[9] Friends and associates however, deny, this, arguing instead that he was especially impressed with the revolutionary categories of Rosa Luxemburg (1870-1919). From her, he borrowed the theory that if or when capitalist modes of production were introduced into pre-capitalist economies, the difference between the two (which were now sharing the same economic environment) would be so great that their conjunction would disrupt not only economic forces, but also create social unrest and violence. Tension, inter-group conflict and even international war would accrue. The striking parallels between his and Sorel's thought are therefore coincidental, despite the fact that like Sorel, Fanon had a "myth" of action, and a concept of "creative violence." In his *Reflections on Violence* (1908), Sorel developed the "myth" of revolutionary syndicalism which—as a tool of indoctrination based on non-rational beliefs—could evoke action and a moral commitment to destroy the oppressor. He also talked of the creative role of violence which reveals itself above all in the type of class struggle that makes no concessions to non-violence. But according to Fanon's friends, he was influenced by none of this. Similarities in their thought are therefore coincidental.[10]

Although Fanon drew heavily on Marx, the revisionists and especially Sartre for the philosophical script for holy violence, he, nonetheless, modified their views. First, he adapted Marx's concept of alienation. By his later years Marx's alienation was primarily an economic and social experience: the alienation of the producer from the means of production. The latter determined working relationships and dominated the intellectual and moral environment. Fanon modified this alienation to mean two things: the alienation of colonial people from their material resources, and from their national and cultural identity; and the alienation of individuals from themselves as a consequence of French assimilation policies. Disalienation in both cases was however possible through revolutionary violence. Thus although the cause and content of alienation differed, the means to disalienation were identical. Second, Fanon modified the Marxist historical *schema* which interpreted history in relation to conflicting production modes ranging from primitive communism to capitalism. Marx had discussed colonialism in some of his work. But he knew little about it, and his criticisms focused mainly on the expansionist capitalism of the bloated and "greedy" bourgeoisie. He had practically nothing to say about the "immorality" of colonialism as perceived by Fanon. In fact, his comments suggest that he accepted the nineteenth-century conventions that inferred the European superiority and their right to impose themselves on "barbarian" (Marx's term) people. Fanon modified this *schema*; and in his historical interpretations, naïvely situated anthropological man "in the beginning," in a blissful pre-colonial state of nature, marked by sovereignty and collective control over material resources, and where there was an absence of conflict. This cooperative production mode existing in the state of nature was disrupted by the introduction of capitalism and the colonizing presence, resulting in the manifestation of "evil," in the form of capitalist exploitation, and above all, racism and "colonialism."[11]

Thus by focussing on colonialism and racism—more so than on capitalist production modes and exploitation—Fanon de-emphasized the concept of class struggle, which was central to Marxist and revsionist thought. Marxists had defined class in relation to production means; and the ruling class was the one which owned them. As their production modes became out-moded, the ruling class was replaced—after a violent struggle—by the most productive class. Ultimately, according to Marx, the industrial proletariat of Western Europe was invested with the "historical mission" of liberating the society from the bourgeoisie, their exploitative capitalism and oppression. Fanon's de-emphasis of class and class struggle has radically separated him from mainstream Marxist thought. And nowhere is there a serious discussion of class conflict in his philosophical script for holy violence. Of course his critics Marxist or otherwise, have been dismayed. Trying to make sense out of his methodological nonsense, Vietnamese communist Nguyen Nghe rightly criticized him for not differentiating between the real proletariat and the *petite bourgeoisie* in colonial class structures. Similarly Hansen argued that his unwillingness to define social class hampered a serious criticism of his analysis. Likewise Caute regreted that Fanon made no distinction between the "hard-core corrupted lumpenproletariat, and the immigrant peasants who move back and forth between town and village, and who are more capable of the revolutionary activity he describes."[12]

Although all the above criticisms are valid, they seem unnecessary, because Fanon never wrote class struggle into his philosophical script for holy violence. In fact, he even wondered if Africans had any sense of class struggle at all. Instead, he offered an ill-defined class analysis which included: the white colonizers who comprised the dominant political class by virtue of the near monopoly of production means; the colonized *bourgeoisie* and the proletariat—quantitatively too small, too poor and too assimilated to spearhead a violent anti-colonial revolution; and the decadent lumpenproletariat and the peasantry, who were outside this class analysis.[13]

In effect, therefore, Fanon's class analysis had less to do with ownership of production means, than with "ownership" of the decision making process. Because in addition to the former, class in the colonial society was also determined by race—about which Marx had practically nothing to say—and only those of European origins could aspire to membership in the ruling class.[14] Among the colonized people, the majority of whom were non-European, class was frequently determined by skin color, the degree of assimilation, and wealth—not to be confused with ownership of production means. Conflict, when it occurred, was not really between the colonizer and the colonial bourgeoisie—which should have been the case had he followed the Marxist model— but between racial classes whose members competed for recognition by the colonizer. This class conflict therefore was more like a competition for scarce resources in a racial class struggle, and less like a conflict between workers and owners of production means. To this extent his "class struggle" was more like a "collective auto-destruction." (Fanon's term), and less influenced by Sartre than Caute suggests.[15]

All of which left him with the peasantry and the lumpenproletariat. Outside the class structure, and the least assimilated of the colonial peoples, they manifested traditional peasant virtues, not least of which was readiness to use violence as a means of solving problems. In Fanon's class analysis, therefore, there were two types of conflict occurring at different times: first, the inside conflict between members of the colonial bourgeois racial classes; and later the conflict between the colonizing group—who were the only ones to meet the Marxist class criteria—and the peasantry-lumpenproletariat who, as a non-class, fought to seize control of the state. In the last analysis, therefore, Fanon's "class conflict" was a national struggle for economic and political power; which is exactly what happened in the Algerian revolution.

*The Vision*

Having written an elaborate philosophical script for his concept of holy violence, the "European" Dr. Frantz Fanon began to phase out, giving way to the "Antillean" Fanon. Now on center stage, the man from Martinique with a revolutionary vocation, who saw the "vision" of holy violence embedded in "primitive" peasant minds, who knew how to decode Algerian peasant imagery and symbolism, proclaimed aloud to the world that Algerian violence was sacred and holy. It is not unreasonable to assume that he drew on memories, perceptions and experiences of the Antillean world which had produced him; and it is likely that his abilities to understand and interpret non-rational mental processes embedded in Algerian peasant cultures were enhanced by first hand experiences of the Antillean "primitive" world.

It may no longer be possible to reconstruct Fanon's Antillean intellectual development, especially since much of it has gone unrecorded. His Antillean heritage is, however, another matter; and it seems safe to assume that as a child growing up in pre-World War II Martinique, Fanon was exposed to thought-categories of pre-literate people. He spoke of Antilleans prior 1939 passing their time "drinking rum and dancing the beguine." What he did not say is that prior to 1939, Martinique was a poor, underdeveloped island, populated mainly by pre-literate peasants of African descent, many of whom were steeped in superstitutions and creole peasant cultures. He talked about the rich and varied canvas of Algerian folk cultures, but although he must have been aware, he was silent on the Martinican counterparts.

Hence Fanon probably knew that the "theology" of pre-literate peasant cultures, including those of the Antilles, tends to be dominated by shakers and movers of the spirit world whose immediacy is understood by fear and faith. From his comments on Algeria, it is clear that he also understood the peasant's belief in the fluidity of movement between the spiritual and material world: how spirits communicated with earthlings; how they "fly into your mouth when you yawn"; the spiritual visitations of ghosts, *djinns* and other restless out-of-body-creatures. The man from Martinique must have known also that in some peasant cultures, spirits communcate through unknown tongues which only the faithful understand, and that pre-literate "theology" attaches causal importance to movements in the spirit world, which also control the moral environment, including good and evil. In Martinique he would have seen how spirits "affect" crops, "influence" rainfall, "avert" sterility, or "punish" evil doers, and that the spirit world was also "protective" even to the point of surrounding believers with impregnable magical superstructures.

He certainly knew about projection discussed in chapter one, because he used the concept in his doctoral thesis (1951), and knew that through projection, spirits take many forms, and that symbols, images, metaphors and

myths comprise an important element in spiritual super-structures. Among
the Algerian peasantry he found some truly bizarre projections, such as
"leopard-men, serpent-men, six legged dogs, zombies [and] a series of tiny
animals or giants."[16] He also knew of the ritual through which peasant
cultures communicate with the spirit world, and that through appropriate
rituals, spirits can "transform" lives in accordance with peoples' wishes.
Although he was aware of these phenomena—he referred to them in his
dissertation—Fanon never commented on a corresponding superstructure in
Martinican peasant cultures. But they were surely there. When André
Malraux, Minister of the Fifth Republic, left-wing novelist and hero of the
Spanish Civil War, visited Martinique in 1958, he was entertained by folk
dancers dressed as devils. Related symbols and images were also widespread
throughout the Caribbean islands, and are still found, for example, in the
Jamaican Pocomania, the Trinidad Shango, and the Haitian Voodoo, about
which Fanon knew.

Not surprisingly, the man from Martinique never admitted to this part of
his heritage. But it may partially explain his intellectual development, in the
sense that he had a profound understanding of non-rational experiences,
especially as they were perceived in "primitive" peasant cultures. He may
not have participated in folk rituals—that would have been unthinkable for an
aspiring Martinican bourgeois family. But he was aware of their existence,
and must have grown up with people in Martinique who regulated their lives
according to these beliefs. In a poor underdeveloped country, this would have
been unavoidable.

Hence, although it was the "European" Dr. Frantz Fanon who wrote the
philosophical script for holy violence, it was the man from Martinique, with a
revolutionary vocation, who understood the dark stirrings of the Algerian
peasant mind. And if the philosophical script legitimized the Algerian
peasants' will to fight, it was probably because the "Antillean" Fanon
decided that it was worth legitimizing. Where was the "I am a Frenchman"
Fanon now? Where was he who in 1952 "imagined himself submerged in a
white flood composed of men like Sartre or Aragon," and "would have liked
nothing better"?[17] He had been replaced by the man from Martinique,
"integrated" and "entangled" into "the atmosphere of myth and magic,"
which was "frightening" him, "as it behaves so much like the real thing." "By
terrifying me," he continued while identifying with the Algerian peasantry, "it
. . . integrates me into the traditions of my region and tribe, and at the same
time it reassures me. It gives me status, as if it were an identity card from the
state. In underdeveloped countries, the occult sphere belongs . . . exclusively
to the magical realm," he concluded. "By entangling me in this inextricable
network—the infinite qualities of my world are thus confirmed."[18] Had
Fanon taken leave of his senses? Probably not. He had entered into non-

rational levels of perception and awareness, from which minds and personalities are profoundly and silently influenced.

Returning now to earlier forays into the "primitive mind"—obtrusively attached to a conventional doctoral thesis—Fanon ignited his earlier insights into a revolutionary blaze. In the white heat of war and passion, he learned that the sacred dimensions to holy violence were embedded, and had always been embedded in the "primitive mind!" In 1951 he had talked about Lucien Lévy-Brühl, and Marcel Mauss, discussing the use of myth and imagery in primitive religious beliefs, and had raised the issue of "essential homogenity," or oneness of primitive man with nature. Similarly, he spoke about projection and collective representation—where the collective mind projects its inner meaning on to objective reality—which he also found in Mauss and Lévy-Brühl. By 1952, there were hints of Jung's "analytical psychology," his libido theory, and his self-regulating system, which explained how the conscious and unconscious minds relate to each other through compensation. But above all there were Jung's archetypes and the archetypal use of the myth. In his writings, Jung had claimed that myths were psychic manifestations reflecting the state of the psyche more than the state of nature. By projecting this inner sense on to reality, the unconscious became "visible" and accessible to new ideas communicated to it through symbols or coded language. In this way, the rational and non-rational co-existed in the mind. At first these unconscious manifestations were without specific meaning. But as they survived cultural change, from one generation to the next, they acquired special meanings given to them by the culture. The projection process therefore never ceased, and myths had a continuing dynamic potential. Having read Jung, Fanon would have known all this, although in 1952, he made little use of the information.

Armed now in 1961 with empirical data on the Algerian peasant, the man from Martinique with a revolutionary vocation chiselled away at earlier insights until he had a phenomenology of the workings of the "primitive mind," or how a non-rational and tradition-bound mind that knows neither modern science nor logical reasoning moves from one level of awareness to another. Empirical and clinical data had shown that once the "primitive mind" identified with an idea or object, it was thereafter seldom aware of its own separate identity—and incidentally this does not apply only to the "primitive mind." Following, therefore, Jung's archetypes and the archetypal use of myth, the man from Martinique confirmed that the "primitive's" mind did impose (or project) its inner meaning on to external realities. "Reality" was the uncritical fusion of both the external and internal worlds. This being the case, he thought, might not Algerian peasant myths, symbols, images and dreams be therefore important. Were they not coded communications that "bounced back" from Jung's projections; and were they not the collective psyche made "visible!"? Now separated from the unconscious through the unrelenting process of cultural change, could they not be decoded, and the stylized and ritualized "language" understood. Once decoded, could their substance not be politicized? By becoming conduits of revolutionary change that communicated directly with the unconscious, might not myths, symbols, images and dreams be transformed into revolutionary tools, indoctrinating "primitives" with ideologies otherwise escaping them?

I suggest that the man from Martinique developed the myth of violence and revolution—as a means of indoctrinating the "primitive" peasant mind—and incorporated it into his concept of violence. This idea has already drawn criticism. Discussing the problems posed by analysing Fanon's concept of violence, Hansen rejected the mythic notion, asserting that "although no serious critic would deny the presence of certain myth making in Fanon, it would be wrong to dismiss the entire argument as a myth." Equally critical of the notion, Richard Ralston rejected it as "questionable" and "unspectacular," and called into question alleged assumptions that Fanon did not really know very much about the peasantry.[19] Although both criticisms were directed against the present author, my argument was the exact opposite: that Fanon developed the mythic notion *because* he knew the peasantry so well. Perhaps those critics who dismiss the myth as a mere unsubstantiated idea have failed to grasp what a myth really is, or what many a successful politician knows: that the myth can be a powerful tool of indoctrination. The man from Martinique obviously knew this, which explains his fascination with Algerian peasant myths, symbols, images and dreams. Moreover, as a psychiatrist, he would have understood the full import of the myth as a belief or tenet which orginated in the unconscious mind. To denigrate the role of myth, therefore, is to misunderstand it, to underestimate its silent power over the collective unconscious, and to ignore psychogenic factors derived from dominant archetypes in any culture. The man from Martinique was only saying that while myths lie "dormant" in every culture, relevant ones can be activated, or created anew during times of stress, transition or modernization, especially when an old order is giving way, but the new has not yet taken its place. In the case of Algeria, the myth of holy violence was intended for "transitional" people, such as the lumpenproletariat and the peasantry, who had "seen the modern world penetrate into the most remote corners of the bush, and who developed an acute sense of all the things he does not have. By a sort of childish reasoning," Fanon continued, "these people convince themselves that they have been robbed of these things."[20] What fertile ground from which to reap a mythic harvest! The myth of violence—which is used in "primitive" cultures along with symbols and images—was a way therefore of "talking" to "transitional" people in their "language," and on their terms.

Because the myth communicates by association directly with the subconscious, and since the "primitive" views the world as "a more or less fluid phenomen" interacting with his fantasy in a way where subject and object are not differentiated, the myth becomes a "fact," and the fact becomes a myth.[21] Accepted by intuition, and by faith, as if sacred or from the spirit world, the coded myth is conveyed directly to the non-rational processes of the mind. A rational comprehension of the myth would destroy its mythic qualities; and once a myth has been implanted in the mind— usually by indoctrination or by penetrating the "sedimentary" structures of the mind—it becomes *gnosis*, or a higher form of knowledge. Pertaining to sacred and spiritual truths, Fanon claimed that the "primitive" mind seized these truths, "as if by instinct." Illustrating the power of the myth, he showed how Algerian peasants "resolved" their conflicts on the "phantasmic plane," which is another way of saying "fantasy world." Their mythical-magical world was peopled with fierce evil spirits, and as mentioned above, with the leopard-men, serpent-men, six legged dogs, zombies, *djinns*, and monsters. What did this mythical-magical "therapy" achieve? It informed believers that they shared an environment not only with the devil-colonizer, but also with hosts of truly evil spirits whose proximity was much more immediate and unbearable. And since the devil-colonizer was the lesser known of the evils, submission to his oppression was preferable to the immediate terrors of the spirit world.[22]

What has this to do with holy violence and the creation of the "new man"? The man from Martinique was simply saying that a myth accepted by faith and understood as *gnosis* can re-create or transform the individual as well as the group; and that at a deep spiritual level the believer *believes* that he can transcend himself. In his mythical-magical world controlled by the imagination, he *could* become a leopard-man, a serpent-man, or a six-legged dog; or prevent *djinns* from flying into his mouth when he yawned. If leopard-men myths could "re-create" or "transform" the believer, why couldn't the revival of archetypal resistance myths of great Algerian heroes and warriors rouse him from his "imaginary maze," and prepare him for the struggle? If he could confront "giants," "zombies" and terrifying "tiny animals," couldn't he face up to the devil-colonizer who was far less terrifying? Wouldn't it be possible, the man from Martinique asked, for all this "muscular orgy," "auto-destruction," and fear to be "channelled [and] transformed," to the extent that the devil-colonizer could be made to "disappear as if by magic"? Through the potency of this magic—after all it had been "proven" in the past—wouldn't it be easy for the believer to *believe* that he, the "new man" had emerged from this deep spiritual mystery? This kind of born-again mystery is not uncommon. In fact it frequently occurs, and it is surprising that both Hansen and Ralston missed the mythic potency that can cause a man to believe that he has transcended himself, or that he is in touch with some cosmic force. *How* the mind immediately grasps these "truths," and transfers them from one level of awareness to another is, however, another matter. Jung attributed this to an "intrapsychic fact" which defies explanation. The man from Martinique simply said that it happened like a "rising storm," like a "huge hurricane," or "as if by instinct."

Of course these wonderful changes could not occur without ramifications elsewhere. In the previous chapter, normative alterations, and the emergence of a morality of oppression were discussed in relation to the social infrastructure of holy violence. The myth was frequently the "higher authority" which sanctioned these normative changes, and gave the initiate "permission" to break the moulds, and challenge the gods—even the devil-colonizer—with impunity, and without guilt. In the Algerian case, the anti-colonial crime—any anticolonial crime—became the "good" crime authorized by the myth in the name of the "higher cause." The supreme crime, of course, was to be "personally responsible for the death of" a member of the "colonizing specie." Then naturally there was the bandit "who terrorizes the country-side for several days, while the police are after him . . . . He finally succumbs; or he commits suicide so as not to give away his accomplices . . . . If the act for which this man is pursued by the colonial authorities is exclusively directed against a person or a colonialist's property," the man from Martinique continued, "then the line between [a common thief and a hero] is clear . . . .Obviously there is no point in saying that such and such [a person] is a thief, a drunken fool, or a depraved person," he concluded, because to the people he has become a hero, "a beacon lighting their way . . . . They automatically identify with him."[23]

But if "mythic doctrine" "authorized" changes in the normative structure, such as transforming the bandit into a hero, it also implied that conventional norms should be re-imposed if or when there is a return to normalcy.[24] This little known aspect of mythic thinking has been overlooked by Fanon critics cited above, who charged him with erecting a "circle of hate," and a theory of "violence and counter-violence." Even the man from Martinique himself seemed unaware of this final "doctrine" in the myth, as he complained that without precautionary measures, international tensions, continuing conflict between "capitalism and socialism," and "violence triggered by minorities" could perpetuate the reign of terror.[24] As the whole world knows, his fears were unfounded in Algeria, and for that matter, in most African coutries which won their independence by violence. Although the war produced some permanent change in Algeria, the return of peace also signaled the re-emergence of many pre-war norms, not least of which were those affecting the role of women and the peasantry in peacetime.[26] As studies of societal conflict have shown, a group tends to limit intra-group "antagonistic-cooperation" at the point where group members fear that fundamental group integrity and inner unity is in danger of immanent dissolution.[27]

Once the myth of holy violence in the redemptive revolution had developed, the man from Martinique turned to the millenium. He still needed to identify the myth more closely with the mysterious spiritual world which swirled around the "primitive's" inner being and spilled into his universe. Once that was achieved, the revolution had a terrible instrument for change at its disposal. The myth directed at the individual, together with the millenium directed at the group, transformed a humdrum anti-colonial war into a passionate religious experience, offering a redemptive goal, a means of transcending the self, and above all, a glimpse of the glorious revolutionary hereafter.[28]

All revolutions contain mythic and millenarian elements, whether one refers to the seventeenth century English Puritan Revolution, the eighteenth century American and French Revolutions, the nineteenth century European Liberal revolutions, or the twentieth century Bolshevik, Chinese and anti-colonial peasant revolutions. The Algerian War was no exception, and in the millenarian euphoria, freedom fighters in the *maquis* became "religious brotherhoods," and a "church" wherein all worked for the fulfillment of the "Higher Cause." Hobsbawm referred to millenarian movements as pre-political "archaic forms" in social movements; and in his case studies of six twentieth century peasant wars, Eric R. Wolf found that when harnessed to "marginal men" such as alienated intellectuals who indoctrinated the masses with modern revolutionary theories; disgruntled landowning peasantry; disinherited rural and urban transients; or a politicized urban working force, still closely geared to life in the villages, Hobsbawm's "archaic forms" gave way to a modern peasant revolution.[29]

Not surprisingly a similar phenomenon occurred in Algeria. Extraordinary or perceptive skills were hardly needed to realize that many Algerian peasants, at least, were ready for a total rejection of the social and political order, and that they nourished vague millenarian hopes that deliverance from the "evils" visited upon them by the devil-colonizer would disappear "as if by magic," not in the remote future—but now![30] Thanks to pre-revolutionary indoctrination by the *Ulama* and the *Comité révolutionnaire pour l'unité et l'action*, millenarian vaporings in the "primitive" peasant minds were harnessed to organized revolutionary violence. Here we cite again the case of the Aurès peasantry who covered themselves with glory by being the first to rise on the morning of 1 November 1954, and whose political indoctrination began the previous year. In their pre-political phase, they were probably not looking for what Hobsbawm called "a new and perfect world," but simply a return to the justice and stability of the traditional world as it had been preserved in the collective unconscious.

It is hardly surprising that the man from Martinique should have played on the millenarian harps of Algerian peasant "theology." He would have known that millenium "theology" is associated with the apocalyptic tradition, together with the "doctrine" of the "end of history," and that it is a by-product of Zoroastrian, Judeo-Christian and Islamic thought. It is rare to find millenarian movements outside these great traditions; and Fanon would have known that millenarian "theology" not only promises an imminent salvation, but also that it would be irrevocable, predetermined, and full of crises. Thus harping on millenarian themes, his lyrical voice coaxed *mujahidin* and *feda'iyin* alike to enter the holy apocalypse, as "salvation" was achieved only by cooperating with the same sacred and pre-determined plan which incidentally some revolutionaries called "marxist," while others were claiming it for Islam. In the appropriate millenarian tradition, the man from Martinique reminded *mudjahidin* and *feda'iyin* alike that they lived in a "manichean" world—didn't every peasant "know" that the colonial world was a manichean world—which was divided between "the children of light," and the "sons of darkness."[31] "Caught in a veritable Apocalypse," they should rise from the European "abyss" of "spiritual disintegration," which had "justified . . . crimes and legitimized . . . slavery . . . racial hatreds and . . . exploitation," because "the new day" was "at hand." After all, he promised in his "slightly stretched" Marxist "theology," in the last analysis, "all decolonization is successful." Reassuringly, he announced that it would be "introduced by new men." Why? Simply because "decolonization is the veritable creation of new men," that's all; and because with decolonization, "the last shall be first and the first shall be last."

The dreams, he promised in his still "slightly stretched" Marxist millenarian reassurance, would become a reality. The "native" would have "all sorts of possessions"! He will "sit at the colonizer's table . . . sleep in his bed [perhaps even] with his wife." Finally, he urged, who can resist "remaking a history of Man," within the "grandiose glare of history," for which "all humanity was waiting." Preaching the word that we "are nothing on this earth if . . . not first slaves of a cause . . . the cause of justice, the cause of liberty," the man from Martinique urged *mudjahidin* and *feda'iyin* marching on to war, to stick with the "savage struggle," cautioning that "truces," "stalemates," and "defeats" were incompatible with the pre-determined plan; and always reminding listeners that there was the virtuous violence, the victory already assured, the "doomsday atmosphere," and the "veritable Apocalypse."[32]

Why would he speak like this? Because the man from Martinique would have known that millenarian movements occurred under circumstances similar to those which produced the myth: that they usually affected groups on the cutting edge of change and that these people were usually convinced that life's realities had failed to match misguided expectations. Powerless to achieve objectives through dominant institutions, and having themselves developed only archaic or primary political vehicles, their fantasy role-reversal—of the sort encouraged by mythic thinking—finally made it possible for them to approach the dream world, and the "close-at-hand paradise . . . guarded by terrible watchdogs." Living in an atmosphere dominated by religious beliefs, trances, visions and superstitions, together with the immediacy of magical and occult worlds, they could without difficulty convince themselves that their desires were predestined for success. Similarly, as with individuals inspired by the myth, groups could draw on "intellectual" reserves present in peasant cultures. Shared knowledge of the world around them—expressed through known symbols and futuristic images—could provide the "theoretical" framework. By these very acts, the man from Martinique saw Algerian "primitives" revitalize and internalize those familiar metaphors in their culture associated with sacred and pre-destined goals.

Thus, joining ecstatic choruses that *mudjahidin* and *feda'iyin* were cooperating with a divine plan for salvation, *was* the way to mobilize radical activity by contagion and by frenzy. No wonder, the man from Martinique spoke of violence festering "like a sore under the skin," spreading "like an epidemic," or running amok "like a wild fire." It was as if violence had taken on a separate autonomy, and was claiming the Algerian people. Why? Because millenarian "theology" justified non-cooperative and anti-establishment behavior. Like mythic thinking, it *temporarily* created a new morality, kept hope and inner spirits high, created a dominant mood of hope by contagion, and promised that as part of a divine plan—*mudjahidin* and *feda'iyin* were on the winning side. Fanon had watched "conversions" to millenarian "theology" (after all he was one of the high priests), and knew that this new elect, the born-again *mudjahidin* and *feda'iyin* committed to a glorious shared hope and the "veritable Apocalypse," were developing a new group identity. He had seen despair, depression and lethargy dissolve in the dizzy millenarian euphoria, and had witnessed the impossible become possible. Recognizing action replacing apathy, guilt and inferiority giving way to pride, he acknowledged that a collective, positive self-image was emerging. The collective personality was being revitalized, regenerated and rehabilitated, as the "children of light" in the manichean colonial world overcame the "sons of darkness." Collective creative forces were at work as "new men" were born. Holy violence was making men whole.

The transition from millenarian "theology" to the *jihad* or holy war, was easy. Beginning with Hegel, Marx and Sartre, the man from Martinique was ending with myth, millenarianism, and holy war. The fusion between a secular dialectic, anti-colonial revolutionary violence, and the sanctity of creative violence was complete. Holy violence was fully born. In Islamic Law, which divides the world into *dar-al-Islam* (the domain of Islam), and *dar-al-harb* (the domain of war),[33] Fanon's manichean world realized its sacred proportions. Islam had produced the *jihad*, a fundamental tenet, as a symbol of violent change which committed the participant to a cause greater than himself. As with the myth and millenarian "theology," it was a religious and cultural invention which precipitated subconscious and inarticulated collective reactions. It determined in advance good from evil, right from wrong. To die while engaged in such a holy war was to guarantee salvation in the after-life, and recognition on the right hand of God. As one *mujahidin* wrote before his death: "we must not think that this is finished, for to die for God's cause is to attain eternal life [while] to die for one's country is only a duty."[34] Although the man from Martinique had no deep knowledge of Islam, and misunderstood some of its precepts and social applications, it is nonetheless likely that he deliberately encouraged the idea that once again the "infidel" French were the *real* enemies, not only of the Algerian people, but also of God. In Islamic Law, violence (not only killed the French, but) guaranteed eternal salvation. Holy violence was real.

Addressing himself primarily to a Muslim peasantry, the lumpenproletariat and to their revolutionary leaders, it would have been silly to ignore the sacred role of *jihad* in the revolutionary war. Who else would have had a greater felt need for salvation than the oppressed or impoverished peasantry, and the derelict lumpenproletariat who "circled colonial towns," drifting "between suicide and madness."? Wouldn't the words from the Holy *Qur'an*, sura 11:186, which exhort believers to fight the infidel in God's way, not strike a deep resonance in the hearts of believers? Wouldn't the rousing cries, cheers, slogans and sermons associated with Holy War fill the *mudjadihins'* heart with joyful thoughts of violence? Despite his atheistic tendencies, the psychiatrist from Martinique was aware that the same categories in the "primitive" peasant mind which accepted by faith the myths and rituals, or the millenarian and apocalyptic "theology" in Algerian cultures, would also respond to the glorious call to *jihad.*

Some revolutionary leaders shared these cultural and religious insights. For example, the Marxist-Muslim Massali al-Hajj (b. 1898) and the Islamic nationalists associated with Abd-al-Hamid Ben Badis (1899-1940) were among the first to recognize the role of Islam in the nationalist struggle when they created the Association of *Ulama* (Ben Badis: 1931), and the Parti du Peuple Algérien: P.P.A. (Massali al-Hajj: 1937). These were political-religious organizations originally designed to counteract French and other western influences. Associated with the Egyptian Salafiyya movement, and growing out of the Islamic renaissance of Jamal al Din al-Afghani (1839-97), Muhammad Abdu (1849-1905) and al-Kawakibi (1854-1936), they were later joined by other Muslim nationalists, such as al-Ibrahimi (1889-1965), al-Tayyib al Ugbi (b. 1889), Mubarak al-Milli (1898-1945), and Ahmad Tawfiq al-Madani. The journal *al-Basair* became the chief vehicle for their ideas. Aiming at an independent Muslim Algeria, an Arabic and Islamic revival, as well as the purification of the faith, the movements operated out of mosques, religious orders and Koranic schools, especially in Tlemcen (in the west), and Setif and Constantine (in the east).[35] When the Organisation Secrète, a group committed to Algerian independence through violence was founded in 1947, it functioned under the organizational structure of Massali al-Hajj's Islamic nationalist group. It was this group, in conjunction with the Aurès peasants, known for their "banditry" and long-standing resistance to the French, which sparked the revolution on the morning of 1 November 1954.

It goes without saying that throughout Algeria, Islamic nationalist movements flourished best in rural *communes* especially those of fewer than 30,000 souls. Moreover, according to the *Shari'a*, or Islamic Law, the property of infidels, such as that of the colonial "lord" defeated in war, could legally be seized as booty. In the event of victory, Algerian peasants could seize settler land (or recovery of hereditary lands depending on the point of view), and be within the constraints of God's Law. Islam had not only rendered violence holy. It had raised holy violence from the mythic and millenarian dimensions in Algerian folk cultures and transformed it into God's Law. Holy violence was a legal obligation! As with mythic and millenarian thinking, holy violence as a legal obligation lost much to rational analysis. Its efficacy and mystery as the means to make men whole, however, remained as long as it was accepted by faith. Only then could "new men" be born.

However, while some were aware of the relevance of the Islamic component in this holy war, others were less so. For example believing that the *mujahidins'* "passion [for] Islam" was a substitute for a revolutionary ideology, Robert Lacoste, Resident Minister of Algeria to whom Fanon had submitted his letter of resignation from Blida in 1956, remarked that "they [mujahidin] are seeking to justify, on the grounds of religious kinship, the . . . interference of foreigners."[36] But it is no longer in doubt that the Algerian revolution was nationalist, and that Islam provided the dominant ideology. That Fanon seemed aware of this is clear. Even his detractors concede, not least of whom was Dr. Mohammad El-Mili whose criticisms of Fanon in *al-Thaqafa* (1972), the official journal of the Ministry of Information, acknowledged that the man from Martinique came to understand the revolution's Islamic underpinnings;[37] and that like thousands of Algerians, he perceived it as a continuation of the nineteenth century *jihads* against the French. To suggest that the war was wholly a religious endeavor would, however, be misleading. Fanon was also aware of this recognizing, as did the F.L.N. leadership, that the newer or secular meaning for the term *mujahidin*: a regular in the uniform of the Armée de Libération Nationale, was equally valid.

Thus a fretful idea no bigger than a man's hand on the Caribbean horizon mushroomed into a joyous Algerian theory of liberation which claimed universal application. After ten years of travail, creative conflict had become holy violence.

The birth of the idea coincided with the death of Fanon. Leukemia symptoms which had first appeared in 1960 were about to claim him. His death in Washington, D.C., where he had gone for medical care, was not apparently unnoticed. According to columnist Joseph Alsop, who was the first to report the alleged C.I.A. role in bringing him to Washington, Fanon died "almost literally in the arms of the C.I.A."[38] Fearful of Soviet interference, the C.I.A. had routinely monitored the Algerian war, keeping an eye on the F.L.N.'s known leftists such as Fanon, and possibly his close friend Abane Ramdan who died in 1958 under mysterious circumstances—although the latter's death has not been attributed to the C.I.A. Mme. Fanon and a close friend, who wishes to remain anonymous, have denied the C.I.A.'s alleged surveillance of Fanon. Yet according to Geismar, who still remains the main source for the events surrounding Fanon's last months, the F.L.N. Minister of Information M'Hammad Yazid, and others encouraged Fanon's voyage to the United States for medical treatment after unsuccessful attempts in the Soviet Union.

Departing from Tunis in late September, thanks to the assistance of the American Embassy in Tunis, Fanon was reportedly the guest of the C.I.A. at the Dupont Plaza Hotel (Washington, D.C.) from 3-10 October, where he alledgedly received no medical treatment, until his admittance to the National Institute of Health in Bethesda, a Washington suburb. Suspicions apart, there is no explanation for the delay in Fanon's admittance to the hospital, especially since hospital beds were not in short supply. In Bethesda he was treated by Dr. David Haywood, a hematologist from the Pacific Medical Center in San Francisco. Geismar reports that Ollie Iselin, the C.I.A. representative, was a regular visitor at the hospital.[39] So were Mme. Fanon, his son Olivier, and the close personal friend mentioned above, all of whom deny these visitations.[40]

But it was too late: "We did everything we could," Haywood reported eight years later. "In 1961, there wasn't much you could do about chronic granulocytic leukemia, especially since he came to us so late . . . . We talked a lot before he became too ill," he added "mainly on Africa."[41] On 6 December 1961, his pain-racked and weakened body succumbed to double pneumonia. With the assistance of the State Department, and the C.I.A. according to

Geismar, his remains were returned to Tunisia. On 12 December, twenty official cars accompanied the ambulance bearing his remains to Ghardimaou near the Algerian frontier where the A.L.N. General Staff had its headquarters. Accompanied by F.L.N. officials, a detachment of soldiers, and by Ollie Iselin to a point fifteen minutes inside the Algerian frontier, Fanon's remains were lowered into "his" Algerian earth.[42] "Frantz Fanon," promised Belkacem Krim, the Vice President of the Provisional Government of the Republic of Algeria who pronounced the eulogy, "your example will always remain with us. Rest in peace! Algeria will not forget you."[43]

At 12:00 noon on 19 March 1962, the Franco-Algerian cease-fire went into effect. The manuscript for *The Wretched of the Earth*, the "sacred" book of holy violence the proofs of which he had read while in the American hospital had arrived safely with Maspero, his Paris publisher. And, in America, the Fanon myth was about to begin.[44]

# Conclusion: Holy Violence as Metaphor

*A metaphor is the friendly ... borrowing of a word, to express a thing
with more light and better note, though not so directly and properly
as the naturall name of the thing meant, would signifie.*

Thomas Blount (1653)

*For* old things *being put away, all things will become new; we shall
be* new Men, *new* Creatures, *we shall have* new hearts, *and* new
*songs in our mouthes, be made partakeers of the* new Covenant, and
at last Inheritors of the New Jerusalem.

John Spencer (1658)

This indepth psycho-political and socio-psychological inquiry into
Fanon's concept of holy violence and his revolutionary theory suggests that it
is hardly as unusual as his critics suggest. Apart from the fact that there is not
much to set his theory apart from the revolutionary traditions of Marx, Lenin
and Luxemburg, even his specific claim that revolutionary violence can be a
uniting, binding and cleansing force—giving rise to a "new man"—has
precedents in seventeenth century revolutionary thought, in the theories of the
pre-Marxian utopian socialists, and Russian anarchists. This latter concept
even appears in the thought of Mao Tse-Tung. His concept of revolution and
holy violence therefore has many precedents, and is not as idiosyncratic as
his critics suggest. Not even Sartre acknowledged this in his preface to the
first edition of *Les Damnès de la terre.* Exhorting Europeans to "have the
courage to read this book," Sartre—whose influence on Fanon was
considerable—avoided drawing the reader's attention to the fact that Fanon's
concept of violence, including holy violence, owed much to his own *Critique
of Dialectical Reason.*

But if Fanon's revolutionary theory is specifically associated with the
traditions of Marx, Lenin and Luxemburg, even his more general
revolutionary goals were not without precedent in Western European
thought. With the notable exception of Thomas Hobbes, Edmund Burke and
analysts of that *genre*, many theorists have supported Fanon's claim of the
right to resist those who would abrogate personal or interest group freedoms,
including self-determination and the "Rights of Man." Indeed by 1159, when
John of Salisbury published his *Policratus*, and between 1254-1256, when
Saint Thomas Aquinas' *Summa Theologica* was written, the right to resist
the "tyrant" or prince who was "subject to the law" had crystalized. In
Northern Europe, the Protestant Reformation, harbinger of domestic

absolutism, institutionalized the right to resist both at home and abroad, thereby clarifying for the first time the minorities' right of resistance. Even Calvin, no lover of popular rights, referred in his *Institutes* to the magistrates' divinely derived duty to resist rulers who failed to govern according to God's law. Furthermore, drawing on natural law, the Scriptures and English common law, republicans such as Milton defended the "crime" of regicide in *Tenure of Kings and Magistrates*. And one need only be reminded that Lockes's moral right of revolution preceeded Marx's by over two hundred and fifty years.

In French seventeenth and eighteenth century thought, the writings of Montesquieu, Diderot and Voltaire, in particluar, reflected an admiration for English civil and political liberties. Accordingly, by promoting organized resistance-by-violence as a means of social change in defence of life, liberty and property, Fanon was not only recommending a method tried and true. He was also in line with medieval religious radicals, sixteenth century conservatives, seventeenth century republicans, eighteenth and nineteenth century secularists, as well as moralists, social revisionists and revolution-aries. The precedents were there. Moreover, by developing a morality of oppression, including "good" violence, for the recovery of political freedoms, and the right of self-determination, Fanon was hardly being innovative. Apparently when threatened with institutional inequality, a loss of life, liberty and property, as well as the right of self-determination, wide segments of Western humanity will fight, "as if by instinct"—but justify it with "reason"—for the restoration of their perceptions of "equality," and the "natural inalienable" "Rights of Man."[1]

With all these historical precedents, what *was* there about Frantz Fanon which disturbed his associates and critics, or which produced dis-ease with his more or less conventional ideas? Two possible reasons suggest themselves.

First, it is possible that Fanon disturbed associates and readers alike because he confronted them with the shrill psychology of a revolutionary personality. There is, of course, no fixed typology of the "revolutionary personality." What we find instead, are certain frequently recurring personality phenomena occurring—in one form or another—in a wide range of revolutionaries, which identify processes at work within a tentative paradigm that we call the "revolutionary personality." Mostly, these phenomena include profound anger, as well as *angst*. Additionally one usually finds an inner turmoil that expresses itself in mixed forms such as doubt, fear, ambivalence, insecurity, guilt, feelings of insecurity and anxiety, all of which fuel the so-called "revolutionary personality." Other expressed phenomena also include courage, an indomitable hope, charisma, blind devotion to a cause, the ability to generalize and relate a problem to its collectivity and, in the case of a revolutionary leader, the know-how of communicating with followers—potential or otherwise—on subliminal personality levels. Above all, that which distinguishes the so-called "revolutionary personality" from others who share these qualities to one degree or another, is that the latter eventually dominate the revolutionary's personality, and "control" his behavior to the extent that he functions most effectively when working exclusively towards revolutionary goals. In other words, as a self-selected highly specialized person with tunnel vision, the so-called "revolutionary personality" engaged in struggle usually ends up by subordinating most desires for satisfaction of basic needs, to The Revolution.

It is well to remember, however, that the turbulent psychology of these restless spirits has yet to be studied on a wide cross-cultural basis, which is really the only kind of typology that could appropriately include a "revolutionary personality" such as Fanon's.[2] By way of contrast, it is also well to remember that not all revolutionaries have shrill "revolutionary personalities," including some from the Third World. Neither Lenin nor Gandhi, for example, had strident personalities, and on the contrary were known for quiet leadership and low-profile-authoritarian styles.[3] However, although they too generated their share of denigrators, the latter hardly recoiled in horror—as was the case with some of Fanon's critics. Instead, sometimes eschewing a certain close-mindedness, many weighed arguments before advancing rebuttals, thereby leaving latitude for genuine dialogue—a "luxury" which many Fanon critics were later to deny him. Thus if some Fanon critics recoiled in horror, and others raised eyebrows in dismay, their actions may in part be attributed to the explosives in his "revolutionary personality."

Second, if Fanon's revolutionary stridency sometimes offended, there were also those who were surprised by his cross-cultural protests emanating from an unexpected quarter: i.e. from a black man—neither an Arab nor a Muslim—who was speaking on behalf of an Algerian nationalist revolution; who was a product of "one of our old[French Antillean] colonies"—and should therefore have known better—and who claimed (in French) to be speaking for the entire Third World! These cross-cultural protests may partly explain why Mohammad El-Mili, Algerian Director of Information in the Ministry of Information and Culture (1971), was uncomfortable with Fanon's role in the revolution, "because he was a European";[4] why Martinicans were embarrassed (1975) by some of his utterances including Joby Fanon, his brother, who cautioned Geismar (1970) "against exaggerating the unusual qualities of his younger brother";[5] why a Frenchmen such as Jean Lacouture later wailed that *Les damnés de la terre* was a "formidable and virulent pamphlet . . . a long cry of hate";[6] and why some Third World *bourgeoisie*, including some sub-Saharan elites, still frequently avoid discussions of Fanon's ideas. When viewed from these several points on the cultural spectrum which Fanon represented, his ability to transcend cultural boundaries was often unrecognized, unappreciated, misunderstood, and in some instances, even feared.

It seems, therefore, that the cross-cultural *angst*, or anger/anguish in Fanon's personality, combined with protests from an unexpected quarter— catching so many unawares—may have been responsible for the wide-ranging responses to his rather traditional revolutionary theory.

Speaking in a more general context, James Billington attributed this revolutionary *angst* to "fire in the minds of men," by which he meant that there was more to the "revolutionary personality" than a hungry belly—Aristotle and de Tocqueville had proclaimed this to previous ages. Instead, there was a screaming quest for power.[7] James C. Davies' "J-Curve" theory, and Abraham Maslow's hierarchically indexed list of "basic needs," provide substantiating data to support the Billington thesis: that revolutionaries fight to retain realized gains which they fear to lose (Davies);[8] that they escalate demands indexed to present levels of frustration in relation to future expectations (Maslow);[9] and that in the last analysis revolutionaries want to gain access to the types of power resources which they believe will minimize or remove inequalities. As Aristotle said in his fourth century B.C. study of the psychological roots of political violence: "discontented" men "enter on strife in order that they may be equal," and they continue in strife" in order that they may be greater" than the other.[10]

That Fanon was screaming for equality and power, (if not for himself—and this is open to question) for the wretched for the earth, is clear. That he was involved in the struggle is an understatement. Had Fanon been detached, critics might have tested his claims of self-determination for colonial peoples on its own merits, the more so since the 1960's *was* the era which saw the official end of empire. But because Fanon himself was part of that claim, they were confronted by a man with fire in his mind and acid on his pen, whose shrieking *angst* assaulted their sense of revolutionary propriety. Recoiling from his presence, Fanon's critics may have been more startled by the anger and anguish—of the sort which was evident in the moods of the 1960's—than by his somewhat conventional claims: that in Western European thought, it has been historically demonstrated that when confronted with the "tyrant" and his outmoded institutions, people who perceive themselves as oppressed, tend to reclaim sovereign rights over life, liberty and property—with violence if necessary. Which is what Thomas Jefferson, for example, did in 1776, when he proclaimed an eighteenth century self-evident truth: that "all men are created equal" (although his practice of "equality" differed somewhat from that of the latter twentieth century).

But despite the conventional nature of Fanon's revolutionary thought, and his cross-cultural *angst*—which is not really unusual—there *is* something about his prescriptive violence as a secular and rational category which disturbs. Associated with a religious doctrine, as is the case with Islam and aspects of medieval Christian doctrine, or presented as myth, as was the case in Fanon's revolutionary ideology, prescriptive holy violence can be integrated into religious beliefs and irrational thought-processes of the mind. But as a rational category with moral overtones, which is how modern scholarship perceives it, prescriptive holy violence *is* disturbing. Historically it has only been justified *ex post facto*, that is if or after its effectiveness has been demonstrated in relation to goals, as, for example was the case with the French and American Revolutions. What this suggests therefore is that while Western trained scholars nurtured in Judeo-Christian-Puritan traditions find an *a priori* justification of holy violence disturbing, the *ex post facto* acceptance of successful violence exists as a historical reality.

Not surprisingly, this ambivalence towards prescriptive holy violence in theory and in practice is apparent in the social science literature as, with the possible exception of Marxist and revisionist-Marxists, most social scientists reveal a certain fear of prescriptive holy violence. It is rare, however, that they admit to this dis-ease. Instead, they tend to "solve" the problem by relegating the study of violence to a "relatively unsuited [field] for contemporary social science research." For example, in his study of *Violence and Social Change* (1968), Henry Bienen showed that although violence as a form of social and political action is very old, there are by comparison few scholarly studies on the subject.[11] Citing Harry Eckstein (1964),[12] he argued that "there is nothing in the world of political events that can account for relative neglect of violence in social analysis in the past," and suggests that although the concept has long since been theoretically analysed, when faced with empirical data, historians and social scientists "have not been able to bridge the gulf between theoretical schema and empirical work." Instead, there appears to be some tacit assumption that violence and internal wars are "relatively unsuited [fields] for contemporary social science research."[13]

Bienen was, of course, referring to unauthorized violence; and despite the latter's increase—including internal wars—since the 1960's when his book appeared, there is still an unexplained neglect in the literature. For example, in Africa alone, since the Algerian war of liberation, four other African countries—Guinea Bissau (1962-1974), Angola (1961-1975), Mozambique (1964-1975), and Zimbabwe (1966-1980)—all gained their independence through violence and internal wars; and similar events are occurring (1982) in Namibia and South Africa. Moreover, internal wars and unauthorzied political violence of one sort or another have also occurred in Africa, either in the form of military *coups* and counter-*coups*, or as civil wars (e.g. Nigeria and Zaïre). Undeclared wars over disputed territories (e.g. Republic of the

Western Sahara and the Ethiopia-Somali war) have also become a feature of contemporary African politics, not to mention the unauthorized uprisings and unrests in other Third World countries. Yet there is still a surprising paucity in the scholarly literature on the theory and practice of unauthorized violence.[14] Too frequently this important area of legitimate research is still left, for the most part, to ideologues—avowed or otherwise—some of whom lack appropriate analytical skills and intellectual rigour.

In 1968, Bienen attributed this relative neglect to possible biases on the part of historians and social scientists, including their hidden assumptions that unauthorized violence is "destabilizing, leading to anarchy, and to incoherence." These possible biases could still be discouraging research in the growing area of unauthorized violence as a form of social action; which is curious especially since—the initial periods of uprisings apart—the data have not always borne this out. In fact the contrary seems to be the case. Some of the most stable nations today achieved their independence, modernity, and nationhood by means of unauthorized violence, as for example Great Britain, the United States, France, the Soviet Union and the Peoples Republic of China.[15] Admittedly each revolution or period of radical socio-political change by violence was accompanied by destabilization of one sort or another. But in none of the above was there permanent "anarchy" and "incoherence" as the hidden assumption suggests. This is not to argue in favor of radical socio-political change by unauthorized violence, especially since we know that modernity and nationhood were achieved elsewhere by other means, with the minimum amount of unauthorized violence. We simply suggest that the biases about unauthorized violence which influence historians' or social scientists' "legitimate field[s] of study" are sometimes misleading. Besides, once unauthorized violence succeeds or becomes legitimized, few scholars have problems identifying it as a "legitimate field of study." Neither have they difficulties identifying and studying authorized (as opposed to unauthorized) violence in society and state. Which for example accounts in part for the plethora of monographs on wars, successful revolutions and civil wars, not to mention violence authorized by legitimate social institutions, such as the church.

The problem, therefore, is not just with unauthorized violence, as Bienen suggests, but with unauthorized violence whose range, leverage and scope are such that they *do not* seriously threaten *the status quo*. A small band of terrorists or guerrillas, for example, may terrorize the citizens of a country. But since they lack the range, leverage and scope to achieve declared objectives on a national scale, their demands are likely to be narrowly defined, and of a specific nature, such as the release of political prisoners. In the process, the "destabilization" which their activities create can fuel the hidden assumptions that violence "destabilizes," and can foster fears of "anarchy" or "incoherence." But if the range of unauthorized violence is such that it reaches the masses—as for example the French Revolution; or if its scope is enhanced by linking it to a powerful ideology—as was the case with the Bolshevik and Chinese Revolutions; or if by "breaking with the past" with the help of unauthorized violence a new nation comes into being, as was the case with the American colonies, then this type of unauthorized violence is radically different from that of a band of terrorists. Because while the terrorists and guerrillas continue to lie outside the accepted framework of legitimate social action, successful revolutionaries ultimately legitimize themselves and their revolution. And "almost as if by magic," a successful revolution becomes a "legitimate field of study."

It may not always be possible to determine the precise point at which unauthorized violence—which has a mass range, leverage and scope— becomes authorized in the revolutionary process. However, one such study which attempts this precision is Crane Brinton's classic study on the anatomy of revolution.[16] In his discussion, Brinton traced the odyssey of violence in the revolutionary process from its outlawed unauthorized state, at the outset of the revolution, to its legitimization at the end by the winners. Focussing on what remains as "permanent" after the "revolutionary fever" has abated, Brinton argued that the "Thermidorean Reaction," or the swing to the right in the revolutionary process invariably incorporated some ill-gotten gains seized earlier by perpetrators of the unauthorized violence. Ironically, this period is seen as a return to *statis* or normalcy; and although there *is* no return to the *status quo ante*, the ill-gotten gains of unauthorized violence are factored into the new equilibrium, along with amnesty to former moderates of the Terror, or the repression of the White Terror against unrepentant revolutionaries etc. In the next stage, these ill-gotten gains (now in modified form) are also written into future governmental programs, along with others as basic as the return of some pre-revolutionary institutions, the transfer of property, the new government and the new ruling class. The loosening of moral restraints, and the return to pre-revolutionary leisure and pleasure all appear to obscure the fact that a successful revolution—i.e. one which ends for ever the abuses and excesses of the old regime—is legitimizing violence.

By the "formal restoration" and the acceptance of irrevocable change marking a "new era," some of the revolution's ill-gotten gains are legally recognized. Thereafter, the revolution is so respectable that it passes into history as a glorious moment. Societies, clubs, institutions and research groups come into existence to honor, respect, celebrate, commemorate and to study this great sequence of events. In America, Brinton notes, the Daughters of the American Revolution came into being; in France the Légion d'Honneur, and in the Soviet Union, the Istorik Markist. Finally the hitherto unauthorized violence and its ill-gotten gains are not only permanently protected from future detractors, but illegitimate violence has been given the *de facto* and *de jure* blessing of legitimization. According to Brinton, therefore, while the legitimization of violence appears sometime between the Thermidorean Reaction and the formal restoration, revolutionary lore and mythology are post-restoration phenomena.

Brinton's empirical data, therefore, supports the above argument that the problem is less with the *ex post facto* legitimization of revolutionary violence, than with its pre-revolutionary *a priori* justification. Because while the former is a recognition of an objective reality, the latter is an act of revolutionary faith. This observation may explain why Arendt, no proponent of violence, appropriately argued that a theory of revolution never justifies *a priori* violence.[17] Violence can only be legitimized historically, after the fact.

Because Fanon never lived to see the formal transfer of power after one hundred and thirty years of French rule in Algeria, his revolutionary theory is an *a priori* justification of unauthorized violence, which the soldiers and politicians subsequently legitimized. Without full assurance that the colonial "lord" would leave, Fanon justified holy violence on grounds of faith so that later generations of Algerians might profit. He did not commit himself to violence by faith because he was a "hothead," or because "an unhappy childhood had given him some uncommon taste for violence," Sartre explained. But because, given the circumstances and the kind of man he was, he believed that there was no other way. "Have the courage to read this book," urged Sartre in the preface to the first edition of *Les damnés de la terre*. Why? Because it was written by a rational man in a given situation, who was courageous enough to have faith in the hideous monstrosity of *a priori* violence as the only solution to an otherwise insoluble problem.

Yet as was discussed above, it is clear that Fanon was as uncomfortable with this monstrosity as Prometheus was with his rebellious act of daring. In the Promethean rebellion and the Fanon revolutionary myth, there is the compelling necessity to commit the uncommitable: to steal fire from the gods. As was shown above, when a body of knowledge becomes too complex, too unknowable and too terrible to handle rationally, such as resisting the colonial "lord," or stealing fire from the gods, processes in the mind transfer this knowledge to a level of comprehension where it becomes *gnosis*—or a higher form of knowledge beyond question—which is accordingly accepted by faith. *Gnosis* is, moreover, best understood indirectly through symbols, myths and metaphors. It was suggested above that Fanon used indirect means, i.e. myths, symbols and metaphors, to communicate with the Algerian "primitives," because knowledge of the terrible unknowable was best understood by faith. The suggestion now is that in order to understand holy violence, Fanon himself may also have transformed this terrible unknowable into *gnosis*, and dealt with it as metaphor. There would have been nothing unusual about this. Indeed the precedents are there. It seems that when faced with thinking the unthinkable and committing the uncommittable, revolutionaries tend to transform their struggle into a metaphor. Thus if holy violence began as a paradox in the mind of Fanon, it ended as a metaphor for a process in the terrible unknowable, within an unavoidable historical matrix. If this no longer seems to make rational sense, it is because it does not. In the mind of Fanon, holy violence had become a metaphor.

Originating from the Greek *metaphérein*, meaning to transfer or change, a metaphor is the language of the internal landscapes of the mind. As a figure of speech, it is capable of comprehending knowledge *beyond* rational perceptions. Like the myth, a metaphor is, therefore, transferred knowledge that has become transformed in the process. By definition, a metaphor becomes part of indirect knowledge. Accordingly, if through science and logic we can only know the material and rational world *directly*; through metaphor, we can "know" almost anything *indirectly*, including the unknowable. Moreover, we can talk about the unknowable—beyond science and logic— through the use of metaphor. This is easily done, and many people do it all the time, although poets are usually better at it than most. Because a metaphor permits us to say that "this" (the known) is equal to "that" (the unknown), whether the "this" and "that" are concrete substances, statements, or abstract ideas. A metaphor moreover suggests the identification of two ideas or objects with a third which is separate, but which shares qualities found in the first two. The more unknowable the unknown, the more indirect the metaphor. Or sometimes we use metaphors of metaphors to understand the unknown unknowable. Thus, for example, when Christian doctrine speaks of the Holy Trinity as Father, Son and Holy Spirit, it has transformed and transferred knowledge derived by faith of God and the Holy Spirit (the unknown unknowable) into a third knowledge (the known), which are the qualities associated with a father, a son, and a father-son relationship. The Holy Trinity is therefore a metaphor, as well as a metaphor of a metaphor.

Like the myth, the metaphor is, of course, very old; and in turning to the latter, Fanon was once again descending into the "archetypes of the primordial world." In his study of the use of metaphor in revolutionary theory, Melvin J. Lasky argued that revolution as metaphor originated in the "paradigmatic gestures of archaic humanity," and was related to the "archetypes of the primordial world." As an "episode in the ancient and familiar sacred dramas of the cosmos, [and] as . . . part of an inescapable ritualist process of legitimizing human acts through an extra-human model," he continued, the sky, old dwelling-place of the gods and "its world shaking signs" of "thunder, lightening and storm" provided these extra-human models. Thus, he concluded, revolution as metaphor originated in "the great mythological scenario, with its ritual role for hostilities, its states of sacred fury, its hopes of human redemption, its planetary certainty, and the coming of the Great and Golden time."[20]

Expanding the discussion, Lasky demonstrated that in its origins, revolution as metaphor was associated with the "older astrological fancy . . . of political mysticism which linked local political events with universal signs."[21] We recall that Shakespeare adopted similar devises, as for example prior to the death of Ceasar, Calpurnia, his wife, associated astral phenomena with political change. By the mid-seventeenth century, revolution as metaphor was identified in the minds of some with the Copernican "vertigo" and "delirium" that was turning the "sky" inside-out, and man's ideology upside-down. As knowledge of the "sky" became more "scientific," it was believed that terrestrial reflections of the Copernican "vertigo" and "delirium" were manifest in the political sphere, and accordingly subject to similar laws. Thus associating revolution with a delirious and vertiginous Utopia (i.e. the "sky"), the concept of a revolving Copernican universe persuaded men that "if one Utopia perishes [on earth] in the power struggles of a revolutionary situation, another Utopia is born in the compensatory dreams" associated with the "sky."[22] Thus revolution was equated with recurring political change, together with a longing for this change, similar to a desire for resurrection, reincarnation and redemption—all of which would occur according to some inner law or necessity. Additionally, a "Golden Age" was projected forward; and the concepts of Utopia, Paradise, Nirvana and Arcadia "intertwine [d] with the imagination at [a] . . . high-pitched transcendental level where the cosmic drama of imagined human destinies unfolds." The "absolute of future happiness" exists.[23] As rebirth and salvation became metaphors of revolution, the four R's (resurrection, reincarnation, redemption and revolution) drew closer together in meaning. In the hands of Milton, revolution struggled to find new metaphors, as the poet turned to "lingering implications of change and sin, revolt and repentance."[24] Note, however, that the scene was still set in "heaven," or the "sky," and the signs of revolution were still the stars, the thunder, light, lightning and the storm.

With these astrological and cosmological allusions, as well as Copernican and religious origins, it is hardly surprising that Fanon saw the revolution as a metaphorical imperative descending "like manna from above," and that his figures of speech should have come from light. For example, as "the match is lit," revolutionary demands "light up the sky." The revolution transforms itself into a "wild fire," and revolutionaries become "firebrands." It is also not surprising that his revolutionary metaphors should evoke earth-shaking events, such as "volcanic eruptions" where evil "humors flow away with the roar of molten lava," while "lids blow off." Likewise, there are "whirlwinds" and "whirlpools" in Fanon's revolution, as "torrents" rush and "rising gusts

of wind" whip up the fury of a "hurricane." Drawing on nature red in tooth
and claw, revolutionary peasants become "angry wolves leaping on their
prey." Turning sometimes to medical metaphors, revolution became a conta-
gious and uncontrollable "epidemic." Then associating revolution with religion—as the English Puritans did over three hundred years before—where an
"atmosphere of doomsday" prevailed, social relationships were transformed
as revolutionaries became "Brother, Sister or Friend." In this "Utopian
atmosphere," it was known in advance that "the last shall be first, and the
first shall be last." Then suddenly the nation-at-war becomes "a religious
confraternity, a church, a mystical body."[25]

Who can deny the volcano its force, and who can stop the whirlwind?
Who can tame the fury of a hurricane, or subdue wild wolves leaping on their
prey? All these uncontrollable and untamable forces, as frightening as the
Copernican "sky" in "vertigo," have leant their sacred fury to the members
of a mystical religious group, who are bound together by brother-love, and
whose collective struggles—on the brink of doomsday—are transforming
heavenly dreams into political realities. If the fire and the fury are frightening,
how reassuring to know that those heavenly laws which keep the "sky" in
motion, also have their earthy counterparts which guarantee political change
according to some mysterious order. Otherwise, how *could* one be sure, as it
was promised, that "the last shall be first and the first shall be last?"

When viewed from this perspective, Fanon's revolutionary theory
becomes a metaphor for the unbeatable combination of scientific law and
religious faith. It *was* alright to kill the colonial "lord" after all, as this act was
not only written in the heavens—and accordingly reflected here on earth, but
with faith and good revolutionary works, these things would come to pass, as
was promised by the great Creator of the "sky." His metaphor, moreover,
suggests that revolution was a sacred and invincible fury whose origins
descended into profound antiquity, and into archaic human behavior. In a
word, holy violence was born in a primordal world so remote from rational
perceptions that only the astronomical revolution could, as a metaphor of
thought and speech, depict its antique force and sacred fury. It mattered little
that Fanon exaggerated, or that he was up to his ears in playful
contraditions. Revolutionary militants enveloped in a political mysticism of
their own making, usually are.

Thus if Fanon transformed holy violence and his revolutionary theory
into a millenarian myth in order to communicate more effectively with those
whom he called the "masses"; in the last analysis, holy violence remained a
paradoxical metaphor for the unknown, unthinkable, yet necessarily
commitable act. Frightened by it, he nonetheless remained resolute. Then
permitting his political imagination to soar generously and permissively on
themes of change precious to the revolutionary's soul, he cried: "Come . . .

Comrades . . . it would be better to decide *now* to *change* our ways . . . . Today we are witnessing the *statis* of Europe. Let us flee, Comrades, from this *motionless movement* . . . . We must start *anew*, develop *new* concepts, and try to create a *new* man." Why? Because "we no longer have anything to fear."[26]

# Footnotes

## Preface

[1] For some examples of comparative and theoretical discussions of Fanon's revolutionary theory, see Paul A. Becket, "Algeria and Fanon: The Theory of Revolutionary Decolonization and the Algerian Experience." *Western Political Quarterly*, 26 (March 1973), 5-27; Lewis Coser, "Fanon and Debray: Theorists of the Third World," in Irving Howe, ed., *Beyond the Left* (New York: McCall Publishing Co., 1970), pp. 120-34; Robert Blackey, "Fanon and Cabral: A Contrast in Theories of Revolution for Africa," *Journal of Modern African Studies*, 12 (June 1974), 191-209; Denis Forsythe, "Frantz Fanon: Black Theoretician," *Black Scholar*, 1 (March, 1970), 3-10; Abiola Irele, "Literature and Ideology in Martinique: René Maran, Aimé Césaire, Frantz Fanon," *Research Review*, 5 (no. 3) Trinity Term (Ghana University: Institute of African Studies, 1969), 1-32; Jack Woddis, *New Theories of Revolution: A Commentary on the Views of Frantz Fanon, Régis Debray and Herbert Marcuse* (London and New York: International Publishers, 1972); Yoweri T. Museveni, "Fanon's Theory of Violence: Its Verification in Liberated Mozambique," in Nathan Shamuyarira, ed., *Essays on the Liberation of Southern Africa* (Dar-es-Salaam: Tanzania Publishing, 1971), pp. 1-24; Robert Smith, "Beyond Marx: Fanon and the Concept of Colonial Violence," *Black World* (May, 1973), 22-33; Peter Worsley, "Revolutionaries Theories," *Monthly Review*, 21 (May, 1969), 30-49.

[2] For example, many Algerians have been reluctant to discuss Fanon's role in the revolution. Explaining that the latter was a collective endeavor, they frown on attempts—on the part of Westerners—to pursue what they interpret as a Fanon personality cult. Not surprisingly, many of my informants requested anonymity. For what appears to be other reasons, including the possibility of disagreement between the Algerian Provisional Government (G.P.R.A.), and the Armée de Libération Nationale (A.L.N.), additional information on Fanon has been withheld. For example, in 1961, Fanon lectured to the exterior military of the A.L.N. at Ghardimaou (Tunisia) not far from the Algerian frontier, where the A.L.N. General Staff had its headquarters. To the best of my knowledge, neither the tapes of his lecture nor their content have been released. Obtaining information on Fanon in Martinique also, at times, proved difficult. Because his books are not widely read in Martinique, and because his family is not well known, some attempts to acquire information frequently evoked questions such as: "Who is his father?"; and "Frantz who?"

## Introduction

[1] For generally sympathetic monographs of Fanon, see David Caute, *Frantz Fanon* (New York: The Viking Press, 1970); Renate Zahar, *L'Oeuvre de Frantz Fanon: Colonialisme et aliénation dans l'oeuvre de Frantz Fanon*, trans. from the German by Roger Dangeville (Paris: François Maspero, 1970); Peter Geismar, *Fanon*, (New York: The Dial Press, 1971); Irene

Gendzier, *Frantz Fanon: A Critical Study* (New York: Pantheon Books, 1973); Emmanuel Hansen, *Frantz Fanon: Social and Political Thought* (Ohio State University Press, 1977). For some criticisms of Fanon's concept of violence, see W. W. Rostow, "Guerrilla Warfare in Underdeveloped Areas," in T. N. Greene, ed., *The Guerrilla and How to Fight Him* (New York: Praeger, 1962), p. 55; Nguyen Nghe, "Frantz Fanon," *La Pensée* (Paris, 1963), 23-36, see especially pp. 27-28; Louis Coser, "The Myth of the Peasant," *Dissent*, XIII, no. 3 (May-June, 1966), 298-303; Hannah Arendt, *On Violence* (New York: Harcourt Brace and World Inc., 1969), pp. 70-75; Caute, *Fanon*, p. 75; Elie Kedourie, *Nationalism in Asia and Africa* (New York: World Publishing, 1970), p. 139; Sydney Hook, "The Ideology of Violence," *Encounter* (April, 1970), 34-35; Zahar, *L'Oeuvre de Frantz Fanon*, pp. 97-98; Aristide R. Zolberg, "Frantz Fanon," in Maurice Cranston (ed.), *The New Left* (New York, 1971), 133-34.

[2]Geismar, *Fanon*, p. 17; Caute, *Frantz Fanon*, pp. 28, 32, 33; Gendzier, *Frantz Fanon*, p. 198.

[3]Paul Adams, "The Social Psychiatry of Frantz Fanon," *American Journal of Psychiatry*, vol. 127, no. 6 (Dec., 1970), 112. Frantz Fanon, *Black Skin White Masks*, trans. from the French by Charles Lam Markmann (New York: Grove Press, 1967). Originally published as *Peau noire, masques blancs* (Paris: Editions du Seuil, 1953); *The Wretched of the Earth*, trans. from the French by Constance Farrington (New York: Grove Press, 1963). Originally published as *Les Damnés de la terre* (Paris: François Maspero, 1961).

[4]See for example the speeches of Amilcar Cabral, in *LSM Guinea-Bissau: Toward the Final Victory—Selected Speeches and Documents from PAIGC* (Richmond, B.C., Canada: LSM Information Center, 1974); Robert Blackey, "Fanon and Cabral: A Contrast in Theories of Revolution for Africa," *Journal of Modern African Studies*. 12, no. 2 (1974), 191-209; Walter C. Opello, Jr., "Guerrilla War in Portuguese Africa: An Assessment of the Balance of Force in Mozambique," *Issue: A Quarterly Journal of Africanist Opinion*, IV, no. 2 (1974), 29-37; Colonel Donald H. Humphries, *The East African Liberation Movement*, Adelphi Papers, no. 16 (London: London Institute for Strategic Studies, 1965). Of the modern revolutionaries, Régis Debray's concept of violence most resembles Fanon's. See Régis Debray, *Revolution in the Revolution?* (New York: Grove Press, 1967); Jack Woddis, *New Theories of Revolution: A Commentary on the Views of Frantz Fanon*, Régis Debray and Herbert Marcuse (London and New York, 1972); Louis Coser, "Fanon and Debray: Theorists of the Third World," in Irving Howe (ed.), *Beyond the New Left* (New York, 1970); Paul L. Adams, "Dehumanization and the Legitimation of Violence," in Jules H. Masserman and John J. Schwab (eds.), *Man for Humanity: Concordance and Discord in Human Relations* (Charles C. Thomas, Springfield, Ill., 1972), pp. 162-70.

[5]*A Dying Colonialism*, trans. from the French by Haakon Chevalier with an Introduction by Adolfo Gilly (New York: Grove Press, 1965). Originally published as *L'An V de la révolution algérienne* (Paris: François Maspero, 1959); later published as *Sociologie d'une révolution*, (Paris, François Maspero, 1966): *Toward the African Revolution*, trans. from the French by Haakon Chevalier (New York: Grove Press 1967). Originally published as *Pour la révolution africaine* (Paris: François Maspero, 1964).

[6]*Les Damnés de la terre*, p. 9.

[7]*Ibid.*, p. 25.

[8]*Ibid.*, pp. 21-23, 33.

[9]*Ibid.*, pp. 33-34.

[10]*Ibid.*, p. 51.

[11]For an interesting study of the epic political theorist who derives his inspiration from the

moral order see Sheldon S. Wolin, "Political Theory as a Vocation," *American Political Science Review*, LXII, no. 4 (Dec., 1969), 1078-82, *et passim*.

[12]*Les Damnès de la terre*, pp. 44, 51.

[13]For accounts of these attitudes in the puritan revolt see J.E. Christopher Hill, *The World Turned Upside Down: Radical Ideas during the English Revolution* (London: Temple Smith, 1972); *Anti-Christ in Seventeenth Century England* (London and New York: Oxford University Press, 1971) and other monographs on the English puritan revolution by Christopher Hill.

[14]Alexis de Tocqueville, *The Old Regime and the French Revolution*, trans. from the French by Stuart Gilbert (New York: Anchor Books, 1955), pp. 205-208.

[15]John Shelton Curtis ed., *The Russian Revolution of 1917* (New York: Van Nostrand Co., 1957), pp. 116-20. See also J.E. Christopher Hill, *Lenin and the Russian Revolution* (Harmondsworth, England: Penguin Books, 1971).

[16]Gendzier, *Frantz Fanon*, p. 90.

[17]*Les Damnès de la terre*, pp. 20, 22, 24, 179. See also chapter 1.

[18]"Letter to the Resident Minister (1955)," *Toward the African Revolution*, pp. 52-53.

[19]*Les Damnès de la terre*, pp. 20, 22, 24, 178. See also chap. V, especially those disorders which Fanon called "reactionary psychoses." pp. 181-94.

[20]*Ibid*., pp. 11, 14, 43.

[21]*Ibid*., pp. 192-94.

[22]*Ibid*., pp. 189-92. For Algerian accounts of French torture, see Patrick Kessel and Giovanni Pirelli, *Le Peuple algérien et la guerre: Lettres et témoignages, 1954-1962* (Paris: François Maspero, 1962).

[23]*Les Damnès de la terre*, p. 47.

[24]*Ibid*., pp. 24, 54, 90.

[25]D. McKenzie Brown (ed.), *The White Umbrella: Indian Political Thought from Manu to Gandhi* (University of California Press: Berkeley, 1958), pp. 47, 142-43, 144, 146, 147, 152. For Gandhi's own works see Mohandas K. Gandhi, *An autobiography: The Story of My Experiments with Truth*, trans. Mahadav Dessai (Boston: Beacon Press, 1957); *Collected Works* (Delhi: Ministry of Information and Broadcasting, 1958- ), 55 vols. to date. For secondary studies see Erik H. Erikson, *Gandhi's Truth on the Origins of Militant non-Violence* (New York: Norton, 1969); Louis Fischer, *The Life of Mahatma Gandhi* (New Hork: Collier Books, 1973), first pub. in 1953; Louis Fischer (ed.), *The Essential Gandhi: His Life, Work and Ideas*, An Anthology (New York: Vintage Books, 1962); Martin Deming Lewis (ed), *Gandhi: Maker of Modern India?* (Boston: Heath, 1965). Finally for a personal, affectionate yet critical account see Jawaharlal Nehru, *Mahatma Gandhi* (Bombay, London: Asia Publishing House, 1966).

[26]Whereas Fanon associated decolonization with "rising gusts of wind," Gandhi identified *swaraj*, or self-rule with the unperceived growth of the banyan tree.

# Chapter I

[1]*Peau noire, masques blancs*, pp. 177-82. The larger issues involved in Hegel's dialectics of conflict are not discussed here as Fanon's concept of creative conflict specifically belongs to the lesser conflict in Hegel's master-slave relationships. The latter, however, forms part of Hegel's

larger discussion of the dialectics of conflict in general. See George W.F. Hegel *Phenomenology of Spirit* (1807), trans. A.V. Miller, text and forward by J.N. Findlay (Oxford University Press, 1977), pp. 111-19. The discussion of Hegel's concept is drawn from this section.

With the revival of Hegelian thought in Europe after World War II, French-educated intellectuals, including Jean-Paul Sartre and Albert Memmi, as well as Fanon, were influenced by the master-slave relationship. See Albert Memmi, *The Colonizer and the Colonized*, trans. H. Greenfield (New York: Orion Press, 1965), and Jean-Paul Sartre, *Anti-Semite and Jew*, trans. G.J. Becker (New York: Schocken Books, 1965).

[2] For other treatments of Hegel's influence on Fanon see Gendzier, *Frantz Fanon*, pp. 22-27, 32, 53; and Zahar, *L'Oeuvre de Frantz Fanon*, pp. 20-24.

[3] Hegel, *Phenomenology of Spirit*, p. 114.

[4] *Ibid.*

[5] George W.F. Hegel, *The Philosophy of Right* (Oxford: Clarendon Press, 1942).

[6] *Peau noire*, p. 179.

[7] Aimé Césaire, *Et les chiens se taisaient*, a tragedy in *Les Armes miraculeuses* (Paris: Gallimard, 1970), pp. 105-07. Fanon quoted part of this passage in *Peau noire*, pp. 162-3.

[8] *Les Damnés de la terre*, pp. 11, 13.

[9] These ideas are scattered throughout *Black Skin White Masks*, but are especially well treated in chapter six "The Negro and Psychopathology." see *Peau noire*, pp. 117-71. For another treatment of the same subject see chapter one, "The Negro and Language," *ibid.*, pp. 15-34, and *Toward the African Revolution*, pp. 19-21.

[10] *Ibid.*, pp. 172-82.

[11] *Ibid.*, p. 178.

[12] *Peau noire*, pp. 178-80, 181. Elsewhere Fanon illustrated this non-recognition in a number of ways. By the following dialogue—no doubt a composite which could have occurred anywhere in the colonial world between colonizer and colonized—he showed how the black man is not recognized and "kept in his place" through simple mechanisms of speech and style: "Oh I know the blacks; one ought to address them kindly, ask them about their country; it is important to know how to speak to them . . . ." "I am not exaggerating," Fanon continued, "a white man addressing a black man behaves exactly as an adult with an urchin, and he starts smirking, whispering, patronizing and cozening him. It is not just one white man that I have observed, but hundreds, and our observations were not restricted to any particular class . . . . I am in a position to claim an essential objectivity, I have studied this fact among doctors, policemen, employers." *Peau noire*, p. 26. Or again: "The doctors in the out-patients department" talk down to blacks. "Twenty European patients come into the room one after the other: 'Sit down Sir, . . . . What may I do for you?—What is your problem . . . .' Then a black or an Arab enters: 'Sit there fellow—What's bothering you?—Where does it hurt—that is when they do not say "You no feel good, no?' " *Peau noire*, p. 27.

[13] Fanon's Doctoral thesis was presented in 1951. His graduation date is sometime between 1951 and 1952. I am grateful to Fanon's widow, Mme. Marie-Josephe (Josie) Dublé Fanon and Dr. François Sanchez, Fanon's former friend and colleague, for showing me a copy of the thesis and for discussing some of its aspects with me. (Algiers, 16 and 18 August 1972).

[14] "Troubles mentaux et syndromes psychiatriques dans L'hérédo-dégénération-spino-cérébelleuse: Un Cas de maladie de Friedreich avec délire de passion," pp. 15-16.

[15] *Ibid.*, p. 16.

[16] Lacan had used the concept of reciprocal or mutual desire to explain how personalities

"mediated" with each other. See for example Jacques Lacan, "Le Stade du miroir comme formatuer de la fonction du "Je": Telle qu'elle nous est révélée dans l'experience psycho-analytique," in Jacques Lacan, *Ecrits* (Paris, 1970), pp. 89-97.

[17]"Troubles mentaux et syndromes psychiatriques," pp. 64-68. He also borrowed the concept of language from Lacan which he later used in the first chapter of *Peau noire.*

[18]Lucien Lévy-Brühl, *L'Ame primitive* (Paris, 1927), p. 318. Fanon discussed this idea in "Troubles mentaux et syndromes psychiatriques," pp. 66 and 69. As a matter of fact, he seemed especially influenced not only by *L'Ame primitive*, but also by Lévy-Brühl's *La Mythology primitive: Le Monde mythique des Australiens et Papous* (Paris, 1935). These ideas are scattered throughout *Les Damnès de la terre.*

[19]Gendzier, *Frantz Fanon*, pp. 19, 62-71.

[20]"Troubles mentaux et syndromes psychiatriques," pp. 64-68.

[21]*Peau noire*, chap.VI

[22]See chaps. V and VI of this book.

[23]Geismar, *Fanon*, pp. 51-52.

[24]"Troubles mentaux et syndromes psychiatriques," pp. 68-69.

[25]Geismar, Fanon, pp. 61-74, 128-39; Gendzier, *Frantz Fanon*, pp. 72-109.
    The Front de Libération Nationale was the Algerian political party responsible for leading the Algerians to war against the French, and for conducting the war (1954-1962). Its founding was proclaimed on 1 November 1954.

[26]Frantz Fanon and C. Geronimi, "Le TAT chez la femme musulmane. Sociologie de la perception et de l'imagination," *Congrès des médecins aliénistes et neurologues de France et des pays de langue Française*, LIV session, Bordeaux (30 août-4 septembre, 1956), pp. 364-86.

[27]Frantz Fanon and J. Azoulay, "La Socialthérapie dans un service d'hommes musulmans: difficultés méthodologiques," *L'Information psychiatrique*, 30 année, 4 série, no. 9, (Paris 1954), 349-61. For a further discussion of women see B. Marie Perinbam, "The Parrot and the Phoenix: Frantz Fanon's View of the West Indian and Algerian Woman," *Journal of Ethnic Studies*, 1, no. 2 (1973), 45-55.

[28]Frantz Fanon and François Sanchez, "Attitude du musulman maghrébian devant la folie," *Revue pratique de psychologie de la vie sociale et d'hygiène mentale*, no. 1 (1956), 24-27: Frantz Fanon, "Reflexions sur l'ethnopsychiatrie," *Conscience maghrébine*, no. 3 (1955); Frantz Fanon and R. Lacaton, "Conduites d'aveux en Afrique du Nord" *Congrès des médecins aliénistes et neurologues de France et des pays de langue française*, LIII session, Nice (5-11 septembre, 1955), 657-660.

[29]F. Fanon and C. Geronimi, "L'Hôpitalisation de jour en psychiatrie: valeurs et limites," *La Tunisie Médicale*, no. 10 (1959), 689-732.

[30]It should be pointed out that before going to Algeria in November 1953, Fanon had already produced articles on the relevance of culture to therapy. See for example, François Tosquelles and Frantz Fanon, "Sur quelques cas traités par le methode de Bini," *Congrès des médecins aliénistes et neurologues de France et des pays de langue française*, LI session, Pau, (20-26 juillet, 1953), 539-44. (In 1938, Cerlitte and Bini described a method of producing convulsions by electricity and began its use in the treatment of schizophrenia); François Tosquelles and Frantz Fanon, "Indications de la thérapeutique de Bini dans le cadre des thérapeutiques institutionnelles," *ibid.*, pp. 545-52; François Tosquelles and Frantz Fanon, "Note sur les techniques de cures de sommeil avec conditionnement et contrôle electro-encéphalographique, *ibid.*, 617-20.

[31] Algerians were also identified with stereotypes from the reptillean and insect world, suggesting slime and cunning. See for example, *Les Damnés de la terre*, pp. 41-42, while blacks were most often associated with biological stereotypes, such as "rape . . . penis . . . athletic [prowess], potency . . . savagery, and animal devil, and sin." *Peau noire*, pp. 106, 126-27, 130, 136-37, 148, 157, 165 *et passim*.

[32] Frantz Fanon, *Sociologie d'une révolution*, pp. 21-55.

[33] *Ibid.*, pp. 29-30.

[34] Mme. Fanon stresses that Fanon travelled throughout Algeria at war to collect data for the book which he was planning to write. The latter appeared as *L'An V de la révolution algérienne*. Interview with Mme. Josie Fanon (Algiers, 16 and 18 August, 1972).

[35] *Sociologie d'une révolution*, chaps. 6 and 2.

[36] Bertène Juminer, "Homage to Frantz Fanon," *Présence africaine*, XII, no. 40 (1962), 139.

[37] *Peau noire*. pp. 70, 108, 183-90.

[38] Interview with Messers Makhlouf Longo, Mohammed Menacer, and Abdelkader Charef, male nurses at the Blida Hospital, now named for Fanon as L'Hôpital Psychiatrique Frantz Fanon (Blida, 12 August, 1972).

[39] Interview with Mme. Dominique Desanti, Stanford University (Palo Alto, 4 April 1972). Mme. Desanti was a prominent member of the Parti Communist Français for about ten to fifteen years. She was also a friend of Sartre, was in Algeria, and knew Fanon and several members of the Front de Libération Nationale.

[40] Interview with Messers Makhlouf Longo, Mohammad Menacer, and Abdelkader Charif at L'Hôpital Psychiatrique Frantz Fanon (Blida, 12 August 1972).

[41] Geismar, *Fanon*, pp. 43-44, 51-53, 63-65, 67-70, 126-27 *et passim*. Gendzier reports that "it seems clear that Frantz was a highly sensitive child and a difficult man. Incidents of playmates attacking and being met with unexpectedly harsh rejoinders are frequent, as are stories that reflect his extreme self-consciousness and his defensiveness at an early age . . . . Both his brother Joby and his mentor Dr. Tosquelles . . . independently of one another, have spoken about the combination of defensiveness and aggresiveness which they recognized in Fanon's make-up." Gendzier. *Frantz Fanon*, pp. 11-12.

[42] *Les Damnés de la terre*, pp. 38–39.

[43] *Peau noire*, pp. 108, 183-87, 190.

# *Chapter II*

[1] Geismar, *Fanon*, p. 12; Gendzier, *Frantz Fanon*, p. 10. My discussion with Mme. Josie Fanon (Algiers, 16 and 18 August 1972), with Mlle Solange Ravenet, the music teacher of Fanon's sister (Grasse, 24 July 1973), and with M. Eucker Fanon, the uncle of Frantz (Fort-de-France, 4 January 1975) do not support this view. For a discussion of Martinican social structure, see Peter Geismar, *Fanon*, pp. 5-28; Pierre Bouvier, *Fanon*, (Paris: Editions Universitaires, 1971), pp. 13-18; Arvin Murch, *Black Frenchman: The Political Integration of the French Antilles* (Cambridge, Mass.: Schenkman Pubs. Co., 1971); David Lowenthal, "Race and Color in the West Indies," *Daedalus* (Spring, 1967), 580-621, and throughout this chapter, especially footnote 14.

[2] *Toward the African Revolution*, p. 26.

[3] Interview with Mlle. Solange Ravenet (Grasse, 24 July 1973).

[4]Of his siblings, Fanon seemed closest to his oldest brother, Joby, who worked for the French Ministry of Finance (Customs Division). Joby was followed by Felix, who was an engineer for the Department of Public Works in Fort-de-France, and by Willy, who worked with the Ministry of Education in Paris. His three sisters all married. Murielle lived and worked in France. Marie-Flore married M. Renard, a teacher at a local lycée, and at one time mayor of the town of Le Robert. Although not all lawyers and doctors, the Fanon children were successful achievers. Mme. Elènore Fanon, his mother, was most proud of Frantz. Interview with Mlle. Solange Ravenet, Marie-Flore's piano teacher (Grasse, 24 July 1973). See also Geismar, *Fanon*, pp. 8-9.

[5]For a description of Fort-de-France, see Geismar, *Fanon*, pp. 5-12.

[6]Interview with M. Eucker Fanon (Fort-de-France, 4 January 1975).

[7]*Peau noire*, pp. 37, 91, 108, 122, 156; *Toward the African Revolution*, p. 26.

[8]Emmanuel Hansen, *Frantz Fanon: Social and Political Thought* (Ohio State University Press, 1977), pp. 16-17.

[9]Geismar, *Fanon*, p. 30.

[10]Fanon also had not been aware of the racism in the Arab world. In 1952 he wrote: "Some ten years ago I was astonished to learn that the North Africans despised men of color. It was absolutely impossible for me to make any contact with the local population . . . . The Frenchman," he concluded, "does not like the Jew, who does not like the Arab, who does not like the Negro." *Peau noire*, p. 85.

[11]*Toward the African Revolution*, pp. 19, 26.

[12]Interview with male nurses at L'Hopital Psychiatrique Frantz Fanon (Blida-Joinville, 13 August 1972).

[13]I found this to be the case in Martinique where Fanon is read very little. And because many Martinicans had never heard of his father (who died in 1947), the assumption was that Fanon was not worth knowing. (Fort-de-France, 4 January 1975).

[14]The 1954 census indicates that the white creole population numbered approximately 1,674, or 0.7 per cent of the total population of 239,130. There were about one hundred and fifty white creole patronyms, some representing as few as one or two families. They tended to be endogamous, and formed an exclusive sub-group.

Of these one hundred and fifty patronyms, twenty-eight per cent of the white population, thirty-seven per cent arrived between 1713 and 1789, and made up twenty-two per cent of the white population. Families arriving in the nineteenth century, represented thirty-five per cent of the total white population. The majority of white Martinicans, therefore, arrived in the island before the nineteenth century, a phenomenon of which Fanon seemed aware.

He threw no light on their origins, but the majority came from Normandy down to the Val-de-Loire , from Gascogne, and from Provençe. In the second half of the eighteenth century, many seemed to have come from regions around Bordeaux and Marseille. Additionally, immigrants came from Britanny, with a lesser per cent from Ile-de-France and Paris. Fewer came from Poitou, Anjou, Saintonge, Ile-de-Ré, Touraine, Picardie, Lorraine and Champagne. Still others came from Ireland, Holland, Italy, Great Britain, Spain, and even Turkey. Poverty, land hunger, and the desire to seek a fortune are among some of the reasons why they left Europe. In the seventeenth century, many went as voluntary *engagés*; others were frequently forced or tricked into going.

According to population estimates, there may have been about seven hundred whites in Martinique in 1639. By 1664, there were 1,081 who formed 30.8 per cent of an approximate population total of 3,500. By 1672, there were about 5,000 showing an increase of 3,919 in eight years; and in 1692 when the total population was 19,613, the number had increased to 6,413 or an increase of 1,413 in twenty years. On the eve of the French Revolution, Martinican whites numbered roughly 10.7 per cent of a total population of approximately 100,000, which suggests that their relative numbers had diminished from about one third to about one tenth of the estimated total population in about two hundred years. According to the 1877 census which may have been incomplete, of the total population of 161,995, approximately 1,000 or 0.61 per cent were white. Thus in three hundred and fifteen years (1639-1954), the white population had decreased from 100 per cent to 0.7 per cent of the total population. See *Annuaire de la Martinique 1952-1956* (Paris, 1957), chap. III. According to Edith Beaudoux-Kovats and Jean Benoist (1972), the total number of white creoles was 2,399 including those who resided elsewhere but who were still based in the Antilles. Edith Beaudoux-Kovats and Jean Benoist (ed.), *L'Archivel inachevè: Culture et sociètè aux Antilles françaises* (Montréal, Les Presses de L'Université de Montréal, 1972), pp. 112-13. See also Jean Benoist, "Une civilisation antillaise," in Jean Benoist (ed.) *Les Sociétés antillaises* (Montréal: Centre de Recherches, Caraîbes, 19750, p. 18; Jean Benoist, "Les composantes raciales de la Martinique," *ibid.*, p. 17.

For a discussion of motives for migration see Gabriel Debien," Les Engagés pour les Antilles, (1634-1715)," *Revue d'histoire des colonies*, XXXVIII (1951), chap. VII. "Causes de départs: Salaires elèves? Promesses de terres? réclame?" pp. 158-70. See also Louis Philippe May, *Histoire economique de la Martinique* (Paris: Librarie des Sciences Politiques et Sociales, 1972), pp. 31-43; Jean Baptiste de Tertre, *Histoire genérale des Antilles habitées par les Français*, 4 vols. (Paris, 1667-1671), vol. 1, p. 108; Edith Kovats-Beaudoux [sic], "Une minorité dominante: Les blancs créoles de la Martinique," in Brian Weinstein, "The French West Indies: Dualism from 1848 to the Present," in Martin L. Kilson and Robert I. Rotberg (eds.), *The African Diaspora* (Cambridge: Harvard University Press, 1976), p. 240; August Armet, "Exquisses d'une sociologie politique de la Martinique: De l'assimilation au sentiment national," unpub. dissertation for Doctorat de Troisième Cycle (Université de Paris, 1970), p. 179. Cited in Brian Weinstein, "The French West Indies," p. 241.

Finally, a word on population estimates. They were for the most part unreliable. While different estimates are suggested, it seems certain that census figures for 1664, to which most authors refer, were incomplete. Elsewhere white populations either show discrepancies or seemingly wide and unaccountable fluctuations. See for example L. Peytraud, *l'Esclavage aux Antilles française avant 1789* (Paris: Hachette, 1897), pp. 5-6; Louis-Philippe May, *Histoire economique de la Martinique*, pp. 53-56.

[15]Gendzier, *Frantz Fanon,* pp. 10-11.

[16]*Peau noire*, pp. 39-40.

[17]*Ibid.*, p. 134, note. Fanon was of course referring to "associational whiteness," which means that if one is associated with "white" achievements, one is accordingly perceived as "white," regardless of skin color.

[18]Geismar, *Fanon*, pp. 43-44, 51-53, 63-65, 67-70, 126-57 *et passim*; Gendzier, *Frantz Fanon*, pp. 11-12. See also chap. 1.

[19]Interview with Mme. Josie Fanon (Algiers, 16 and 18 August 1972), and M. Eucker Fanon (Fort-de-France, 4 January 1975).

[20]See for example the well known dedication which he wrote in a copy of his thesis presented to brother Felix: " . . . I have a horror of weaknesses—I understand them, but I do not like them." Gendzier, *Frantz Fanon*, p. 12.

[21]Dominque Desanti reminds us that Fanon believed that he was going to be the visionary and ideologue of the Third World. Interview at Stanford University (Palo Alto, 4 April 1972).

[22]*Peau noire*, chaps. I, II, III. Capécia's two novels both dealt with this problem (*Je suis martiniquise* [1948] and *La Négresse blanche* [1950]). Maran's Jean Veneuse appeared in *Un homme pareil aux autres* (1947).

[23]The Compagnie des Iles d'Amérique, created by Cardinal Richelieu in 1635, was responsible for this act of possession. The Company itself was organized by Nicolas Fouquet, father of the powerful Superintendent of Finances who served in Marzarin's administration. It went out of business in 1645. As the potential of the sugar colonies grew, a number of joint-stock trading enterprises came into existence in the seventeenth and eighteenth centuries, for purposes of transporting slaves and exploiting the sugar resources. Most of them, including the Compagnie des Iles d'Amérique, and its predecessor the Compagnie de Saint Christophe (1626-1636) which settled Guadeloupe, were created by royal charter, and were granted monopoly rights. Frequently the companies' goals were unrealistic—given their limited capital resources, technical and managerial skills. Not surprisingly, many early enterprises failed within a few years. During the seventeenth and eighteenth centuries, several of these companies were created, incuding the Compagnie de Guinée (1685), which was awarded the Asiento trade in 1701. André Ducase, *Les Négiers ou le trafic des esclaves* (Paris, 1948), pp. 30-33.

[24]Sugar culture was introduced into Martinique about 1635 by the directors of the Compagnie des Iles d'Amérique, although industrial techniques and organization did not develop on a large scale until about 1654, when Dutch planter *émigrés* arrived from Brazil. Expelled by the Portuguese on religious grounds, several migrated west into the Antilles. About 1654, a band including slaves migrated to Martinique, where it is reported that one of the Dutch slaves communicated his technical knowledge to the Martinican settlers. Louis-Philippe May, *Histoire économique de la Martinique*, pp. 88-89; C. A. Banbuck, *Histoire politique, economique et social de la Martinique sous l'ancien régime, 1695-1789* (Paris: Librairie des Sciences Politiques et Sociales, 1972), pp. 224-25.

Martinique was valuable because of its high sugar yield in proportion to available arable land. It was a formidable competitor, especially for rival concerns in Guadeloupe. Although there were only fourteen sugar mills on the island in 1670, by 1675, Martinique was exporting 43,000 hundredweight of sugar to France, as compared with 48,000 hundredweight (1674) of muscovado and white sugar from Guadeloupe and her dependencies. By 1720, there were more than 325 sugar plantations, which exported 120,000 hundredweight of sugar, 80,000 hundredweight of it was white, as compared with 44,000 hundredweight from Guadeloupe. Seventeen hundred and fifty-three was the peak year for the century when Martinique exported 411,000 hundredweight. Sugar production did not again reach this level until seventy years later. In 1770, Guadeloupe exported 158,000 hundredweight of sugar, 85.6 per cent of which was white sugar. Martinique passed her productive peak years between approximately 1742 and 1767, although this may not have been apparent to observers. John J. McCusker, "The Rum Trade and the Balance of Payments of the Thirteen Continental Colonies, 1650-1775," Unpub. Dissertation (University of Pittsburgh, 1970), 2 vols., Vol. II, pp. 325, 327-30.

[25]Although first promulagted in March 1685, subsequent legislation was added in the form of royal *ordonnances, déclarations* and *édits* on at least twelve separate occasions between 1713 and 1762. The complete 12 volume Code was finally published in 1770 under the title of *Le Code noir ou receuil des règlements rendus jusqu'à present*. For an English summary of the code, see William Renwick Riddel, "Le Code Noir," *The Journal of Negro History*, X, no. 3 (July, 1925), pp. 296-314. The original text is reproduced in L. Petraud, *L'Esclavage aux Antilles françaises*, pp. 158-66. See also F. A. Isambert *et al., Receuil général des anciens lois françaises*, 29 vols. (Paris, 1821-1833), XIX, pp. 494-504.

[26]Quoted in Pierre Paraf, *Le Racism dans le monde*, 4 ed. (Paris, 1972), p. 158-59.

[27]Quoted in C. A. Banbuck, *Histoire politique de la Martinique*, p. 309. See also Antoine

Gisler, *L'Esclavage aux antilles française (XII-XIX Siècle): Contribution au problème de l'esclavage* (Fribourg: Editions Universitaires Fribourg Suisse, 1964), pp. 99, 100. For an interesting discussion of the status of black freemen in the French Antilles see Léo Elizabeth, "The French Antilles," in David W. Cohen and Jack P. Greene (eds.), *Neither Slave Nor Free* (John Hopkins University Press, 1972), pp. 134-71.

[28]Gabriel Debien, *Destinées d'esclaves à la Martinique (1746-1778): Notes d'histoire coloniale* no. 57, p. 26. *Extrait du bulletin de l'institut français d'Afrique Noire*, XXII (Jan.-April, 1960).

[29]In the late 1950's the average sugar worker in Martinique was earning 104 francs (metropolitan) for a 46-hour week. His French counterpart in the beet root industry was earning on an average 122 francs for approximately the same amount of work. In 1955, there were 3,000 permanent workers in the sugar industry; 2,500 salaried permanent agricultural workers; 2,100 seasonal workers. There also were about 5,000 small independent cane farmers who did most of their own work. *Assemblée de l'Union Français proposition no. 201 (1956) de la Commission des Affaires economique*. Cited in Monique Lagon, "Le Sucre des Antilles, de la Réunion," *Economie et Politique*, 63 (Oct.), 59. In 1954, the total population was 239,130.

[30]*Peau noire*, pp. 53, 165-66.

[31]Léo Elizabeth, "The French Antilles," pp. 134-71. See especially, p. 166.

[32]*Peau noire*, pp. 183-84.

[33]B. Marie Perinbam, "Fanon and the Revolutionary Peasantry: The Algerian Case," *Journal of Modern African Studies*, 11. 3 (1973), 427-45.

# Chapter III

[1]This was not, however, his first departure from Martinique. In 1943, he went to Dominica as a volunteer in the Caribbean Free French Movement. He had just completed the first part of the baccalaurete degree, and completed his lycée education after his return from Europe in 1946.

[2]By the end of the 1950's India, Ceylon, Burma, and Malaysia were independent from the British, and Indonesia from the Dutch. With the exception of Algeria, the Maghribian protectorates were also independent by the end of the 1950's. The swift flow of events between 1957 and 1965 also brought independence to most of sub-Saharan Africa, and to the larger Caribbean islands. By the mid-1960's, there were few dependencies on the colonial periphery as the age of empire officially drew to a close.

[3]The French Union came into existence in 1946 together with the Fourth Republic. It was intended to replace the French Empire, but within less than a decade it began to disintegrate. In 1954, Cambodia, Laos, North and South Vietnam left the Union. As a result of nationalist pressures, the French government recognized the independence of the North African protectorates of Morocco and Tunisia in 1956. By 1958, Guinea voted to leave the Union, followed in 1960 by the majority of the French sub-Saharan states. In 1962, Algeria also left the Union. Today, only the *départements* of Martinique, Guadeloupe, Réunion and Guyane, together with some small scattered islands and territories are reminders of the French Union.

[4]Elsewhere he talked about growing up with the notion that the "Gauls are our ancestors." *Peau noire*, pp. 122, 155, 166.

[5]*Ibid.*, pp. 22, 85, 95-6, 122.

[6]During the Algerian war, Salan was Chief of the Organization Armée Secrète, a right-wing terrorist organization created by Algerian settlers whose activities apparently were under the

covert leadership of French army officers, and former members of the Bureau of Psychological Warfare. Although deeply factionalized, one of the Organization's goals was an independent Algeria under white rule. During the Algerian war of liberation, the Organization and its predecessor, Le Main Rouge, claimed "to its credit two attempts at murdering the German arms dealer Otto Schlueter (who sold American weapons to the Front de Libération National: FLN); a more successful sabotage effort against a German ship carrying arms to North Africa; the November 1958 assassination of Ait Ahcene, the FLN representative in Germany; and more than ten other attacks on those cooperating with the Moslem inhabitants." Geismar reports that le Main Rouge made at least one attempt on Fanon's life in Rome, probably some time in 1959. Geismar, *Fanon*, p. 143.

[7] Fanon's identification with Algeria and its people at war is scattered throughout his later writings. See for example, *Toward the African Revolution*, p. 97.

[8] Simone de Beauvoir, "Fanon chez Sartre," from Simone de Beauvoir, *La Force des choses*, excerpted in *Jeune Afrique*, no. 162 (16-22 Dec., 1963), 26-27.

[9] Interview with male nurses at L'Hôpital Psychiatrique Frantz Fanon (Blida, 13 August, 1972).

[10] Geismar, *Fanon*, p. 43. Joby his brother also worked in the campaign, and reportedly drew Fanon's attention to the fact that successful political campaigns must involve all of the people, including the masses. Hansen, *Frantz Fanon*, p. 27.

[11] *Peau noire* was not Fanon's first attempt at writing. In his youth he wanted to be a dramatist, and between 1949 and 1950, he wrote three unpublished plays: "Les Mains paralleles," "L'Oeil se noie," and "La Conspiration," ("Parallel Hands," "The Drowning Eye," and "The Conspiracy"). Mme Josie Fanon permitted me to see a part of the first play. Apparently all three addressed themselves to issues which he later raised in *Peau noire*: e.g. the question of identity, existentialist themes, political activism, and racism. In 1972, I learned that Claude Lanzmann of *Les Temps modernes* also had a copy of the plays. Fanon apparently did not want them to be published. Interview with Mme Josie Fanon (Algiers, 16 August, 1972).

[12] For a discussion of "open" and "closed" societies of the sort about which Fanon spoke, see R. Dahrendorf, *Class and Class Conflict in Industrial Society* (Stanford: Stanford University Press, 1959); see also Burton B. Silver, "Social Mobility and Intergroup Antagonism: A Similation," *Journal of Conflict Resolution*, XVII, no. 4 (Dec. 1973), 605-23 for another interpretation of the "open" and "closed" societies.

[13] Other analyses of similar models which have been applied to the Third World include Lloyd Braithwaite, "Social Stratification and Cultural Pluralism," pp. 816-31; reprinted in Horowitz (ed.), *People and Culture*, pp. 95-116; Burton Benedict, "Stratification in Plural Societies," *American Anthropologist*, 64, no. 6 (1962), 1235-45. See also *Toward the African Revolution*, p.18-19, 26, and *Peau noire*, chapter two, especially p. 40.

[14] The above discussion of the black Martinican peasant masses and the lighter-skinned bourgeoisie and whites forms part of his woefully inadequate discussion of colonial class structures. Criticizing Fanon's class analysis in general, Caute regretted these shortcomings. Commenting on his confused thinking, Caute added that while Fanon defined social classes according to Marxist criteria (i.e. relationship to the means of production), he assessed political behavior according to other criteria, such as the level of livelihood, and the extent of integration into the colonial system. This is methodologically a departure from Marxism, Caute observed, and reveals instead the influence of Sartre's *Critique of Dialectical Reason* (1960), especially Fanon's emphasis on "need" and "scarcity" as the "historically and economically primary causes of social violence." Caute, *Frantz Fanon*, pp. 81-82.

[15] Much of Fanon's data for the model of the conflict plural society is found in *Sociologie d'une révolution*.

[16]See for example, "L'Algeria se devoile," "La Voix de l'Algérie," in *Sociologie d'une révolution*, pp. 21-55, 57-88, and "The 'North African Syndrome', " *Toward the African Revolution*, pp. 3-16.

[17]"Letter to the Resident Minister (1956)," *Toward the African Revolution*, pp. 52-54.

[18]de Beauvoir, "La Force des choses," p. 26.

[19]*Sociologie d'une révolution*, p. 22, see also note 1, p. 24.

[20]*Toward the African Revolution*, pp. 3-16; *Sociologie d'une révolution*, pp. 125-27.

[21]Frantz Fanon and C. Geronimi, "Le TAT Chez les femmes musulmanes: sociologie de la perception et de l'imagination," pp. 364-68.

[22]See for example, Michel Launay, *Pays algériens: La Terrre, la vigne et les hommes* (Paris, 1963), pp. 132-40, 145-6, 153-60; *L'Echo d'Alger* (Algiers, 16 June, 1936); *Les Damnès de la terre*, pp. 43-44. See also Chapter IV.

[23]*Recueil des délibérations du congrès colonial national, Paris, 1889-90* (Paris, 1890), pp. 84-85.

[24]Arthur Girault, *Principles de colonisation et de législation coloniale*, Third ed. (Paris, 1907), p. 91.

[25]For a discussion of the rapidly changing political processes between the 1930's and the 1950's see Gendzier, *Frantz Fanon*, pp. 121-39; William B. Quandt, *Revolution and Political Leadership: Algeria, 1954-1968* (Cambridge, Mass: Harvard University Press, 1969), chaps. 3-7, David and Marina Ottaway, *Algeria: The Politics of a Socialist Revolution* (University of California Press: Los Angeles, 1970), chaps 1-3; Donald C. Gordon, *North Africa's French Legacy* (Camridge, Mass: Harvard University Press, 1962); *The Passing of French Algeria* (London: Oxford University Press, 1966).

[26]*Toward the African Revolution*, p. 15.

[27]*Les damnès de la terre*, pp. 72-73, 76-78, 79. William Quandt's study of the Algerian revolutionary leadership tends to support this thesis. Quandt, *Revolution and Political Leadership*, see especially chapters III-VII. for a general discussion of these and related topics see Philip Worchel, Philip G. Hester, Philip S. Kopala, "Collective Protest and Legitimacy of Authority," *The Journal of Conflict Resolution*, XVIII, no 1 (March, 1974), 40; R. Flacks, "Protest or Conform: Social Psychological Perspectives on Legitimacy," *Journal of Applied Behavioral Science*, V (1969), 132.

[28]"Rôle de la lute armée": "De l'insurrection du 1 novembre . . . à la Révolution démocratique," *el-Moudjahid,*, nos. 53-54 (1/11/59), in *La Révolution algérienne par les textes: Documents presentès par André Mandouze* (Paris: François Maspero, 1961), p. 33.

[29]For the French justification of the use of violence see Jules Harmand, *Domination et colonisation* (Paris, 1910), pp. 339-324-34, 350. For Fanon's quote see *Les Damnès de la terre*, p. 83; and for a discussion of the dissidents' link with the peasantry, see Perinbam, "Fanon and the Revolutionary Peasantry," 442-44.

[30]See "Introduction: The Meaning of Violence," footnotes 1,3 *et passim*.

[31]J. S. Furnivall, *Colonial Policy and Practice: A Comparative Study of Burma and Netherlands India* (London: Cambridge University Press, 1948), pp. 303-13; *Netherlands India: A Study of Plural Economy* (Cambridge University Press, 1939). Furnivall also discussed his model in shorter studies. See for example J. S. Furnivall, "The Political Economy of the Tropical Far East," *Journal of the Royal Central Asiatic Society*, 29 (1942), 95-210; and Furnivall, "Some Problems of Tropical Economy," in Rita Hinden (ed.), *Fabian Colonial Essays* (London: Allen and Unwin, 1945), pp. 161-84.

³²Furnivall, *Colonial Policy*, pp. 304-08, 310, 311; "Some Problems of Tropical Economy," p. 167-68.

³³See M.G. Smith, "Social and Cultural Pluralism," in Vera Rubin (ed.), *Annals of the New York Academy of Sciences*, 83, art. 5 (1960); M.G. Smith, "A Framework for Caribbean Studies," *Caribbean Affairs Series*, (Extra-Mural Department, University College of the West Indies, 1955). Both articles have been reprinted in M.G. Smith, *Plural Society* pp. 18-91. Two of Smith's other studies which are germane to this topic are M.G. Smith, *Stratification in Grenada* (Berkeley: University of California Press, 1965); and M.G. Smith, *West Indian Family Structure* (Seattle: University of Washington Press, 1962).

³⁴See for example, Wendell Bell and Walter E. Freeman (eds.), *Ethnicity and Nation-Building: Comparative, International and Historical Perspectives* (London: Sage Publications, 1974).

# Chapter IV

¹Fanon died at the Bethesda National Institute of Health on 6 December 1961, where he had been since about mid-October. For an account of his death and alleged associations with the C.I.A. see Geismar, *Fanon*, pp. 184-86; and Joseph Alsop's column in the *International Herald Tribune* (22-23 Feb., 1969).

²Interview with Mme. Josie Fanon (Algiers, 16 and 18 August, 1972). Mme, Fanon's point of view is supported by Hansen, *Frantz Fanon*, pp. 37-43, and Pierre Bouvier, *Fanon*, (Paris: Editions Universitaires, 1971), p. 49.

³Zahar, *L'Oeuvre de Frantz Fanon*, p. 7; Geismar, *Fanon*, pp. 72-73; Gendzier, *Frantz Fanon*, p. 59; de Beavoir, "Fanon chez Sartre," p. 26.

⁴For a good discussion of Tosquelles' influence on Fanon's medical training, see Gendzier, *Frantz Fanon*, pp. 63-71, and p. 276, note 5. Gendzier remarks that : "Tosquelles thought in terms of a unitary vision, a community of medicine, in which the results of each would be shared by all, to the common benefit of the man of science as well as the patient." Finally, she says, "therapy was understood by Tosquelles, and later by Fanon, to operate within an institutional framework . . . . It coincided with their view on the role of medicine in the community, on the responsibility of the doctor towards the entire community, and in a more general way, it reflected their reluctance to consider the individual in isolated treatment." Summary of the proceedings of the *Congrès des médecins aliénistes et neurolgistes de France et des pays de langue française*, 51st session, Pau, July 20-26, 1953. At this session Tosquelles and Fanon presented their philosophy of psychiatry in a joint paper entitled "Indications de le thérapeutique de Bini dans les cadres de thérapeutiques institutionnelles," pp. 545-552; and "Discussion de rapport de psychiatric," pp. 101-03. The kernel of Fanon's theory of alienation, as well as his insights into environmental roles are evident in this early training. For an assessment of Fanon's contribution to psychiatry, see Paul Adams, "The Social Psychiatry of Frantz Fanon," *American Journal of Psychiatry*, 127 (Dec. 1970), 109-14.

⁵The date of Fanon's marriage is uncertain. While Geismar and Zahar suggest 1952, Caute and Gendzier indicate 1953. Hansen gives 1953, and Philip Lucas suggests 1950. My own work in Algeria (August, 1972) produced the same range of dates. Geismar, *Fanon*, p. 52; Zahar, *L'Oeuvre de Frantz Fanon*, p. 7; Caute, *Frantz Fanon*, p. 99; Gendzier, *Frantz Fanon*, p. 272; Hansen, *Frantz Fanon*, p. 55; Philippe Lucas, *Sociologie de Frantz Fanon* (Algiers: Société Nationale d'Edition et de Diffusion, 1971), p. 195.

⁶Fanon had an illegitmate daughter by a woman in Lyon. After his death, she accompanied

Joby, his brother on a visit to Martinique where she met their mother. At the time, she was a student in Paris. Geismar, *Fanon*, pp. 46-47.

[7] Although Algerians eschewed the personality cult, after the war they renamed many street and place names after war heroes. In Algiers, a Boulevard Frantz Fanon and a high school are named for Fanon. The hospital in the town of Blida is named "L'Hôpital Psychiatrique Frantz Fanon."

[8] The Front de Libération Nationale (F.L.N.) was the political organization responsible for conducting the war, which led Algerians to liberation. The Front was proclaimed on 1 November 1954 (the day the war broke out), and its initial membership consisted of dissidents from Massali al-Hajj's Mouvement pour le Triomphe des Libertés Democratiques (M.T.D.L.D.). For a discussion of the period just prior to the outbreak of hostilities, see David and Marina Ottaway, *Algeria: The Politics of a Socialist Revolution* (Berkeley and Los Angeles: University of California Press, 1970), pp. 9-26; Alf Andrew Heggoy, *Insurgency and Counterinsurgency in Algeria* (Bloomington: Indiana University Press, 1972), pp. 2-49; Quandt, *Revolution and Political Leadership*, chaps. 1 to 7.

[9] The Berberphone populations (about twenty per cent of the total North African population) are found mainly in Algeria, in the Kabylia and Aurès mountains of the eastern Atlas ranges, in the Mzab, and in the Hoggar mountains. They are also found in western Libya, north-western Tunisia, and in Morocco. The classical study of Berber history is Ibn Khaldun's *Histoire des Berbères*, trans. Baron de Slane, 3 vols. (Paris, 1925). Trans. David Seddon (London: Frank Cass, 1973); Georges Marçais, *La Berbérie musulmane et L'Orient au moyen age* (Paris, 1946); Pierre Bourdieu, *The Algerians*, trans. Alan C. M. Ross (Boston: Beacon Press, 1961), chapters, I, II, III.

[10] The Arab expansion into Europe and Asia is one of the more significant historical occurances. In approximately fifty years, they had extended their influence from the China Sea to the Atlantic Ocean. Between 637-644, they overthrew the Persian Empire, and conquered Syria and Egypt in 634-636, and 640-642 respectively. By 711, they were in Spain. For further reading on the the subject see Abdallah Laroui, *the History of the Maghrib: An Interpretative Essay*, trans. Ralph Manheim (Princeton University Press, 1977) pp. 79-242. Originally published as *L'Histoire du Maghreb: Un Essai de synthèse* (François Maspero: Paris, 1970); Ch-André Julien, *Histoire de l'Afrique du Nord: Tunisie, Algérie, Maroc de la conquête arabe à 1830* (Paris, 1961).

[11] For further reading see Ch-André Julien, *Histoire de L'Afrique du Nord*, pp. 250-309; *Histoire de l'Algérie contemporaine: La Conquète de les débuts de la colonisation* (1827-1871), (Paris, 1964), pp. 1-20; M. Abun-Nasr, *A History of the Maghrib* (Cambridge University Press, 1971), pp. 166-177. See also Marcel Colombe, "L'Algérie Turque," in Jean Alazard *et al, Initiation à l'Algérie* (Paris, 1957), pp. 99-123. Ch-André Ageron, *Histoire de l'Algérie contemporaine* (Paris, 1970), pp. 6-7; Douglas Johnson, "Algeria: Some Problems of Modern History," *Journal of African History*, V. 2 (1964), 225, 228, 229; Raphael Danzinger, *Abd al-Qadir and the Algerians: Resistance to the French and Internal Consolidation* (Holmes and Meier Publishers: New York, London, 1977), p. 3.

[12] *Les Damnés de la terre*, pp. 6, 9.

[13] Some French seemed appalled by these losses. See for example the statement by the deputy, Hippolyte Passy: "Never before in history was there a colonization that required the support of 40,000 bayonets." René Vâlet, *L'Afrique du Nord: Devant le parlement au XIX ème siècle (1828-1838, 1880-1881)* (Algiers, 1924), p. 135. Quoted in Gordon, *The Passing of French Algeria*, p. 14, note 22. In 1846 alone, it took about 108,000 troops, about one-third of the French army, to conquer about 50,000 fighting Algerians. The 1871 rising in Oran occupied 60,000 French troops for a year; and the revolt of 1879 harassed nine French battalions and

eight squadrons. Julien, *Histoire de l'Algérie contemporaine*, p. 178; Jamal M. Ahmed, "The Islamic Factor in the Awakening of Algeria," in C. Allen and R. W. Johnson (eds.), *African Perspectives* (Cambridge University Press, 1970), p. 117.

[14]*Les Damnés de la terre*, p. 49. Jamal M. Ahmed expressed a similar idea in a different way when he wrote: "The war of Algerian Liberation started on . . . 21 November 1832 . . . [ when] abd-al-Qadir . . . entered Mascara . . . ; the first of November 1954 which is the more modern date is only the contemporary version of that armed uprising." Jamal M. Ahmed, "The Islamic Factor in the Awakening of Algeria," p. 115. For other accounts of the continuing conflict see Mostefa Lacherof," Constantes politiques et militaires dans les guerres colonies d'Algérie (1830-1960)," *Les Temps Modernes* (Dec. 1960-Jan. 1961), 727-800; "Nationalism Algérien," *Les Temps Modernes* (Sept.-Oct. 1956), 214-55; *Toward the African Revolution*, p. 81.

[15]For a study of French colonial land policies see John Ruedy, *Land Policy in Colonial Algeria: The Origins of Rural Public Domain* (University of California Press: Berkeley: 1967). See also Gerard Chaliand, *L'Algérie, est-elle socialiste?* (Paris, 1966), p. 83; Pierre Nora, *Les Français d'Algérie* (Paris, 1951), pp. 232-233. For additional statistical data see Ch-Robert Ageron, *Histoire de l'Algérie contemporaine*, pp. 78-83.

[16]In 1964, only about 450,000 peasants possessed one to ten hectares of land. Gerard Chaliand, *L'Algérie est-elle socialiste?* p. 83. A Hectare equals 2.471 acres.

[17]*Les Damnés de la terre*, p. 66, 68, 76, 79, 80-81.

[18]*Les Damnés de la terre* pp. 6-7, 8-9, 17; *Sociologie d'une révolution*, p. 39-52, 59.

[19]See Perinbam, "Fanon and the Revolutionary Peasantry," 435-36 for a discussion of the role of the landless peasantry.

[20]*Les Damnés de la terre*, pp. 5-62.

[21]In 1957, about 7 million people were in the mixed communes, and 3,800,000 were in self-governing communes, of a total population of just over ten million. *Petite encyclopedie, africaine et malgache: Afrique du Nord, Algérie Maroc-Tunisie*, Fourth ed. (Paris: Larousse, 1964), p. 74.

[22]See J. Desparmet, "Les Réactions nationalitaires en Algérie," chapter II "La Vieille poésie nationale," *Bulletin de la Société de Géographie d'Alger et de L'Afrique du Nord* (1933), 438-56, especially 438. See also *ibid*, 35-54, 173-84.

[23]Danziger, *Abd Al-Qadir and the Algerians*, pp. 223-37.
[24]*Les Damnés de la terre*, p. 32, 47-49, 68, 141. See also chapter 1.

[25]Many Algerians resisted the adoption of French citizenship on the grounds that the *senatus consulate* (1865) was discriminatory because it denied Algerian Muslims French citizenship unless they renounced their status under Islamic law. This seemed particularly true when the Crémieux *décret* of 1870 automatically naturalized the indigenous Jewish population without reference to Jewish law. The discriminatory clauses were later removed.

[26]Perinbam, "Fanon and the Revolutionary Peasantry," 429-32.

[27]Gendzier, *Frantz Fanon*, pp. 95-6; *Toward an African Revolution*, p. 12; *Les Damnés de la terre*, pp. 170-72.

[28]de Beauvoir, "Fanon chez Sartre," p. 26.

[29]Léon Blum, *Mémoire*, quoted in *La Révolution algérienne par les textes: Documents presentés par André Mandouze*, p. 48.

[30]"Principe et fin de la Révolution algérienne: De la résistance pacifique," Extrait du discours du Délégué algérienne à Conférence de Solidarité des peuples afro-asiatiques, Cairo, (Dec. 1957), *Ibid*, pp. 29-30.

# Chapter V

[1]*Les Damnés de la terre*, pp. 53-62.

[2]This chapter and the following develop the idea expressed in this paragraph.

[3]Perinbam, "Fanon and the Revolutionary Peasantry," 432-36; B. Marie Perinbam, "Violence, Morality and History in the Colonial Syndrome: Frantz Fanon's Perspectives." *Journal of Southern African Affairs: An Interdisciplinary Research Quarterly*, 111, no. 1 (Jan. 1978), 10-29; B. Marie Perinbam, "Frantz Fanon's View of the West Indian and Algerian Woman," 45-55.

[4]Like his marriage date, the date of Fanon's departure from Algeria is unclear. According to his widow, Mme. Josie Fanon, the family left Blida in 1956. See David C. Gordon, *The Passing of French Algeria*, p. 122, note 34. The December 1961 issue of *El-Moudjahid*, however, records the departure date as 28 January 1957. See "Frantz Fanon, notre frère," *El-Moudjahid*, 111, no. 88 (21, December 1961), p. 647.

[5]Zahar, *L'Oeuvre de Frantz Fanon*, p. 86.

[6]*Toward the African Revolution*, pp. 52-3.

[7]*Peau noire*, pp. 37-91, 108, 122, 156; *Toward the African Revolution*, p. 26. For a fuller discussion of Fanon's views on racism and culture see *Les Damnés de la terre*, pp. 141-75.

Fanon's presentation on "Racism and Culture" was later published in *Présence Africaine* (June-November, 1956), and has since appeared in *Toward the African Revolution*, pp. 31-44. During his discussion, Fanon elaborated on two major themes. First, he criticized French assimilationist policies for denying colonized peoples access to indigenous cultures from which they derived their identity. To this extent, his thesis was compatible with those of the older generation of poets and analysts of negritude who were present at the Congress, such as Léopold Senghor, Aimé Césaire, Alioune Diop, the editor of *Présence Africaine*, and Jacques Alexis, the Haitian writer.

Fanon's second thesis, however, hinted at the differences which were later to develop between his thought and that of his friends. Elaborating on the problem of constantly being evaluated by alien assimilationist norms, which assumed a curve extending from "inferior/primitive" to "superior/civilized," he condemned its use as a "logical" justification for European expansion into non-Western societies. Finally, he criticized racists and racism, including that of the United States. Perceiving a correlation between racism and socio-economic conflicts inherent in capitalism, he concluded that because capitalism had produced material achievements for which the poor and oppressed develop consumer tastes, ironically oppressed peoples came to identify with their oppressors.

Fanon's politicization of racism, as well as his inclusion of black Americans in the category of the "colonized" was his contribution which, at the time, marked a separation from the earlier poets and analysts of negritude. Americans present at the Congress included Richard Wright, and James Baldwin who wrote of the general atmosphere of the Congress in *Nobody Knows My Name*, pp. 13-55. For a full account of the Congress proceedings see *Présence Africaine* (June-November 1956), the entire issue.

[8]Caute's observations on the situation are worth quoting: "Senghor, who told the congress that the British and American Negroes were pragmatists, whereas the French were Cartesian, concluded, 'That's why, quite often, you don't follow us, as we don't follow you' . . . . James Baldwin's account of the congress in terms of his own reactions to the rhetoric of Senghor and Césaire, and in terms of his description of the short shrift given the Bible-clutching black 'Anglo-Saxons' by the black French rationalists, indicates that Senghor's allusion to mutual non-comprehension was not wide of the mark." Caute, *Frantz Fanon*, p. 26.

[9]*Toward the African Revolution*, pp. 153-7.

[10]*Les Damnés de la terre*, pp. 141-65.

[11]*Ibid.*, p. 154-5.

[12]See Introduction, note 5.

[13]Gendzier, *Frantz Fanon*, p. 99.

[14]*El-Moudjahid*, was first published in June 1956. In the fall of 1957, the press was transferred to Tunisia, and later to Morocco. A total of eight issues of the journal were published, of which the fifth and seventh are missing. It is said that complete copies of the journal are in private hands in Algeria. Most of the articles written, but unsigned, by Fanon have been identified by Mme. Fanon, and later published in *Toward the African Revolution*. In 1962, a special three volume edition of *El-Moudjahid* was published in Yugoslavia, a copy of which is in the collections of the Hoover Institution on War Revolution and Peace, Stanford University, Palo Alto.

Fanon's articles in *Résistance Algérienne* have not been identified.

[15]For a discussion of Fanon's contribution to the revolutionary literatures, see Gendzier, *Frantz Fanon*, pp. 140-50.

Both Geismar and Gendzier attribute Fanon's involvement in the F.L.N., especially during the Tunisian period, to Pierre Chaulet, a second-generation Algerian of European origin. Having completed his medical training at Algiers, Chaulet met Fanon at Blida, where the two became fast friends, even working together in the nationalist health centers in Tunisia. Geismar, *Fanon*, pp. 93-4; Gendzier, *Frantz Fanon*, p. 91.

[16]For Peter Worlsey's account of his meeting with Fanon at the Congress, see "Revolutionary Theories," *Monthly Review*, 21, no. 1 (May, 1969), 30-1; and Peter Worsley, "Frantz Fanon and the 'Lumpenproletariat'," Ralph Milliband and John Saville (eds.), *The Socialist Register*, 1972 (London: The Merlin Press, 1972), p. 193.

[17]Geismar, *Fanon*, pp. 162-69.

[18]Apropos of Fanon's last request to be sent to Cuba, Hansen relates this to a "withdrawal syndrome." "This tendency to withdraw from an intolerable situation," he observed, "seems to have characterized Fanon all his life. When Martinique fell to the Vichy forces, he "withdrew" from the island by enlisting in the French army; while in North Africa, he "withdrew" by volunteering for service in Europe; in Paris, he "withdrew" to Lyon; from Lyon he "withdrew" to Algeria; in Accra, he wanted to "withdraw by asking for a diplomatic post to Cuba . . . . For a man committed to praxis, [this withdrawal] is rather difficult to explain." Hansen, *Frantz Fanon*, p. 55, note 38.

It is debatable whether "withdrawal syndrome" is the appropriate term to describe his behavior. The reverse could also be true: that as the man commited to praxis, he wanted to be in a situation where his contribution would count for something.

[19]Following the "official position," Gendzier denies that Fanon was a close friend of Abane Ramdan, although she reverses herself later in her text. My sources in Algeria, including Mme. Fanon, confirm that Fanon and Ramdan were the closest of friends, and that they shared similar ideological perspectives. This therefore adds credence to de Beauvoir's quotation of Fanon that: "I have two deaths on my conscience which I will not forgive myself for: that of Abane and that of Lumumba." Why Fanon should have felt guilty about these deaths is not clear. Gendzier, *Frantz Fanon*, pp. 197, 285, note 6; interview with Mme, Josie Fanon (Algiers, 16 and 18 August, 1972); de Beauvoir "Fanon chez Sartre," p. 26.

[20]Caute, *Frantz Fanon*, p. 75.

[21]Hannah Arendt, *On Violence* (New York: Harcourt Brace and World Inc., 1969), p. 75.

[22]Gendzier, *Frantz Fanon*, p. 198.

[23]Elie Kedourie, *Nationalism in Asia and Africa* (New York: World Publishing, 1970), p. 139; Lewis Coser, "The Myth of the Peasant Revolt," *Dissent*, XIII, no. 3 (May-June, 1966), 298-303.

[24]"Rôle de L.A.L.N." *La Révolution algérienne par les textes: Documents du F.L.N.*, pp. 31-34.

[25]J. Desparmet, "Les Réactions nationalitaires en Algérie," chapter IV, "Elegies et satires politiques de 1830 à 1914," *Bulletin de la Société de Géographie d'Alger et de l'Afrique du Nord*, 34, no 133-136 (1933), 38; chapter 11, "La Vielle poésie nationale" (1933), 450-51. See also J. Desparmet, "Les Réactions nationalitaires en Algérie," chapter 1, "Le Vieux génie maure," *Bulletin de la Société de Géographie d'Alger et de l'Afrique du Nord* (1933), 173-84.

[26]*Les Damnés de la terre*, pp. 32, 67-8, 147, 169.

[27]Perinbam, "Fanon and the Revolutionary Peasantry," 427-32. See also Gil Carl Alroy, *The Involvement of Peasants in Internal Wars* (Princeton, 1966), Research Monograph, no. 24, p. 2; Martin Staniland, "Frantz Fanon and the African Political Class;" *Memo*, no. 12, *Institute of Development Studies* (Brighton, July 1968), pp.10, 14-15; 18; F. Mulumbu-Mvuluya, "Introduction a l'étude du rôle des paysans dans les changements politiques," *Cahiers économiques et sociaux* (Kinshasa), VIII, 3 (September, 1970), 439-42. For other discussions of the non-revolutionary peasantry, see Romano Ledda, "Les Classes sociales et la lutte politique," *Revue internationale du socialisme*, Rome (22 August, 1967), 594-615; and I Potekhin, "Land Relations in African Countries," *Journal of Modern African Studies*, Cambridge, 1, no. 1 (April, 1963), 39-59.

[28]Interview work in Algeria (August, 1972).

[29]"L'Assemblée du peuple," *El-Moudjahid*, no. 9 (20/8/57), in *La Révolution algérienne par les textes*, pp. 102-04, See also pp. 109-110, 115.

[30]*Les Damnés de la terre*, pp. 5, 6, 25, 45, 51-53.

[31] Sydney Hook, "The Ideology of Violence," *Encounter* (April, 1970), 34-35.

[32]Zahar, *L'Oeuvre de Frantz Fanon*, pp. 97-98; Nguyen Nghe, "Frantz Fanon," *La Pensée* (Paris, 1963), 23-36. See especially pp. 27-28.

[33]*Les Damnés de la terre*, pp. 45, 52, 233.

[34]*Sociologie d'une révolution*, pp. 57-88.

[35]*Ibid.*, pp. 113-41.

[36]*Ibid.*, pp. 21-55.

[37]"Les Femmes et la révolution," *La Révolution algérienne par les textes*, pp. 105-07. See also Perinbam, "Frantz Fanon's View of the West Indian and Algerian Woman," 45-55.

[38]Perinbam, "Fanon and the Revolutionary Peasantry," 442-44.

[39]Significantly, group-work therapy was successful only in those European wards where the therapy was compatible with the culture. Muslim patients responded less to European therapy, a phenomenon which was not lost on Fanon. Gendzier, *Frantz Fanon*, pp. 77-85.

[40]*Les Damnés de la terre*, pp. 82, 215-25.

[41]Bernard J. Siegal, "Defensive Cultural Adaptation," in Hugh D. Graham and Ted R. Gurr (eds.), *Violence in America: Historical and Comparative Perspectives* (Beverly Hills: Sage Publication, 1979), pp. 455-71; Ralph H. Turner, "Integrative Beliefs in Group Crisis," *The Journal of Conflict Resolution*, XVI, no. 1 (March, 1972), 25-40.

[42]Emile Durkheim, *Suicide: A Study in Sociology*, trans. J.A. Spaulding and George Simpson, ed. (Glencoe, Ill.: The Free Press, 1951).

[43]Interview with male Muslim nurses at Blida, who had worked with Fanon (12 August, 1972).

[44]*Les Damnés de la terre*, p. 216.

[45]*Ibid.*, pp. 229-33.

[46]Perinbam, "Violence, Morality and History in the Colonial Syndrome," 10-12.

[47]For an interesting study of the epic political theorist who derives his inspiration from the moral order see Sheldon S. Wolin, "Political Theory as a Vocation," 1078-82.

[48]*Les Damnés de la terre*, p. 44.

[49]*Ibid.*, pp. 44, 48, 75-6.

# Chapter VI

[1]See Zahar, *L'Oeuvre de Frantz Fanon*; Caute, *Frantz Fanon*, chapters III and VI; Hansen, *Frantz Fanon*, chapters III, IV, V.

[2]*Les Damnés de la terre*, p. 9.

[3]For a discussion of Fanon's view of man in a "state of nature," prior to the introduction of the evils of colonialism, see Hansen, *Frantz Fanon*, pp. 59-69.

[4]Evidence of these borrowings are in Fanon's later works which he either wrote in Algeria, or completed after his departure in 1957.

[5]Caute, *Frantz Fanon*, p. 33; *Les Damnés de la terre*, pp. 232–3.

[6]Jean-Paul Sartre, "Orphée noir," preface to *Anthologie de la nouvelle poésie nègre malgache* (Paris: Presses Universitaires de France, 1948), pp, XL et seq.; *Peau noire*, pp. 109-114.

[7]*Les Damnés de la terre*, pp. 27-8.

[8]The idea of setting the non-revolutionary image of the peasantry upside down did not originate with Fanon. Both the Fifth (1924) and the Sixth (1928) International recognized this as a necessity "in backward countries and in certain colonies." Emile Burns (compiler), *A Handbook of Marxism* (New York, 1935), pp. 139-40. Despite the recommendation, however, Fanon was ambivalent about rural traditional leaders. He knew that, in some instances, they owed their position to the colonial power, and that in forming a screen between the young westernized nationalists and the bulk of the people, "they were also protecting their interests," preventing "modern ideas from dislocating the indigenous society which would call into question the unchanging nature of feudalism . . . [and which would] even take the bread out of their mouths." *Les Damnés de la terre*, p. 85.

[9]Hannah Arendt, "Reflections on Violence," *New York Review of Books*, (Feb. 27), p. 29.

[10]Interviews with Mme. Dominique Desanti, Palo Alto (4 April, 1972); and with Mme Josie Fanon, Algiers (16 and 18 August, 1972). Both Caute and Hansen agree with these conclusions, See Caute *Frantz Fanon*, pp. 93-4; Hansen, *Frantz Fanon*, p. 122.

[11]Hansen, *Frantz Fanon*, pp. 60-62.

[12]Nguyen Nghe, "Frantz Fanon et les problèmes de l'independence," *La Pensée* (Feb., 1963), p. 30, Hansen, *Frantz Fanon*, p. 142; Caute, *Frantz Fanon*, pp. 80-81.

[13]Fanon, of course, has been criticized for denying the urban worker a role in the "historic mission." See for example, Michel Pablo, "Les damnés de la terre," *Quatrième Internationale*, 15 (1962), 62. Fanon may, however, have been influenced by the position of the French Communist Party *vis à vis* Algeria. For example, in 1949, the Communist Party, under the

leadership of Maurice Thorez, showed its opposition to the Indo-China war against Ho Chi Minh and the Vietcong by refusing to load arms destined for Indo-China. Ho Chi Minh apparently expressed appreciation. Four years earlier, however, when the May riots broke in Constantine, (a *département* of Algeria), the Communist Party called for punishment of the ring-leaders, and opposed any suggestion for Algerian independence at any time, neither then nor in the future. And in March 1956, the assembled deputies at the Communist Party meetings voted in favor of special powers that gave the French government wide freedoms in Algeria. Aimé Césaire, Fanon's former tutor and friend, left the Party in disgust. As Caute points out, the Indo-China war was sufficiently remote from French Communist Party members to make an ideological decision possible. Algeria was, however, another matter. Many Party members knew Algeria well. Many more had relatives there. Party decisions affecting Algeria were therefore much more influenced by personal issues, rather than ideological considerations, as had been the case in Indo-China. Caute, *Frantz Fanon*, pp. 48-49.

[14]*Les Damnés de la terre*, pp. 9, 19-20.

[15]Caute, *Frantz Fanon*, p. 81.

[16]*Les Damnés de la terre*, p. 22.

[17]*Peau noire*, p. 165.

[18]*Les Damnés de la terre*, p. 21.

[19]Hansen, Frantz Fanon, p. 126; Richard Ralston, "Fanon and His Critics: The New Battle of Algiers," *Cultures et développement: revue internaitonal des sciences du développement*, Louvain, VIII, no. 3 (1979) 474-5.

[20]*Les Damnés de la terre*, p. 36.

[21]C. G. Jung, *Four Archetypes*, trans. R. F. C. Hull. Extracted from *The Archetypes and the Collective Unconscious*, vol. 9, part 1, *Collected Works* (Princeton University Press, 1969), p. 35.

[22]*Les Damnés de la terre*, pp. 21-22.

[23]*Ibid.*, pp. 31-32, 44. It is clear that Fanon was familiar with the political "bandit" phenomenon. "Between 1941 and 1949 [the year that he returned from France to Martinique] in the southern part of the island—where Fanon began his political apprenticeship—a field hand by the name of René Beauregard—or Mister René as he came to be known—took it upon himself to break the *Béké's* hold on the lives of the people of Rue Cases-Nègres. For eight years, sheltered and fed by the people of the region in spite of a price . . . on his head, Beauregard's exploits dominated the consciousness of the whole colony. He challenged . . . the established structure of the colonial order with uncanny coups of . . . surprise attacks against his enemies. The colonial regime vainly made attempts to discredit him in the eyes of the population . . . . Finally trapped and wounded, in the early hours of October 1, 1949, Beauregard cheated the colonial guillotine with a well-placed discharge of his gun to his rebel's heart." Christian Filostrat, correspondence, 28 June 1981. From preface (p. xi) by Christian Filostrat to *Black Shack Alley*, translation of Joseph Zobel's *La Rue Cases-Nègres* by Keith Q. Warner, (Washington, D.C.: Three Continents Press, 1980).

[24]Siegal, "Defensive Cultural Adaptation," pp. 455-71; Turner, "Integrative Beliefs in Group Crisis," pp. 25-40.

[25]*Les Damnés de la terre*, pp. 39-42.

[26]Perinbam, "Fanon and the Revolutionary Peasantry," 437-45; Perinbam, "Frantz Fanon's view of the West Indian and Algerian Woman." pp. 45-55.

[27]Siegal, "Defensive Cultural Adaptations," pp. 455-71; Turner "Integrative Beliefs in Group Crisis," pp. 25-40.

[28]For Discussions of millenarianism as an ancient phenomenon, see Norman R. C. Cohn, *The Pursuit of the Millenium* (Fairlawn, N. J.: Essential Books, 1957), which is a study of European medieval millenarian movements; Peter Worsely, *The Trumpet Shall Sound* (London, 1957), which is a study of the Pacific "cargo" cults. For an illuminating discussion of the progressive politicizing and modernization of millenarian movements, see E. J. Hobsbawm, *Primitive Rebels: Studies in Archaic Forms of Social Movements in the Nineteenth and Twentieth Centuries* (New York: The Norton Press, 1956). For a different approach see Perinbam, "Fanon and the Revolutionary Peasantry," pp. 427-445.

[29]Eric R. Wolf, *Peasant Wars of the Twentieth Century* (New York, Evanston and London: Harper and Row, 1969) pp. xii, 292-93, 289.

[30]Hobsbawm, *Primitive Rebels*, pp. 5, 57-107.

[31]"The colonial world," Fanon remarked "is a Manichean world . . . [and] the settler paints the native as the quintessance of evil." *Les Damnès de la terre,* p. 10.

[32]*Ibid.,* pp. 7-8, 18.

[33]The two terms together suggest that the struggle against *dar-al-harb* continues until conquest or submission is realized.

[34]Letter to *El Moudjahid*, 19 June, 1956 from Hamide Zabana. *El Moudjahid*, no. 1, s.d. (June, 1956), in Patrick Kessel and Giovanni Pirelli, *Le Peuple algèrien et la guerre: Lettres et temoignages d'algèriens, 1954-1962* (Paris: François Maspero, 1962), pp. 46-47.

[35]Allen and Johnson (eds.), *African Perspectives: History, Politics and Economics of Africa* (Cambridge University Press, 1970), pp. 113-41 See especially pp. 121-22.

[36]Quoted in C. S. Maier and D. S. White (eds.) *The Thirteenth of May: The Advent of de Gaulle's Republic* (New York: Oxford University Press, 1968), p. 98. Quoted by Gendzier, *Frantz Fanon*, pp. 130-31.

[37]Mohammad El-Mili, "The Algerian roots of Fanon's thought," *al-Thaqafa* (November, 1971), 22-45. I am grateful to Dr. Karl Stowasser of the University of Maryland for his translation of the article.

[38]*International Herald Tribune* (22-23 Februrary, 1969).

[39]Geismar, *Fanon*, pp. 182-87.

[40]Interview with Fanon's close friend, Algiers (25 and 26 June, 1971); and with Mme. Josie Fanon, Algiers (16 and 18 July, 1972).

[41]*International Herald Tribune* (22-23 February, 1969).

[42]Geismar, *Fanon*, pp. 186-87.

[43]*El Moudjahid*, no. 88 Dec. 21 (1961).

[44]Aristide Zolberg and Vera Zolberg, "The Americanization of Frantz Fanon," *Public Interest*, no. 9 (1969), 49-63.

# *Conclusion*

[1]Perinbam, "Violence, Morality and History," pp. 21-22.

[2]One such study which attempts this is E. Victor Wolfenstein, *The Revolutionary Personality: Lenin, Trotsky, Gandhi*, (New Jersey: Princeton University Press, 1967). See also James C. Davies (ed.), *When Men Revolt and Why: A Reader in Political Violence and Revolution* (New York: The Free Press, 1971); Edgar Snow, *Red Star Over China* (1938), rev.

ed. (New York: Grove Press, 1968); Ted R. Gurr, *Why Men Revolt* (Princeton University Press, 1970).

³See Wolfenstein, *The Revolutionary Personality*, pp. 26-47, 73-124, 138-191, 275-318; and Erik Erikson, *Gandhi's Truth and the Origins of Militant Non-Violence.*

⁴See for example, Mohammad El Mili, *al-Thaqafa* (March 1971), 10-25; (May, 1971), 40-54; (Nov. 1971), 22-45. For a discussion of the "official" Algerian view of Fanon's role in the revolution, see Gendzier, *Frantz Fanon*, pp. 231-60.

⁵Geismar, *Fanon*, p. 3.

⁶Quoted from *Le Monde* by François Maspero, Fanon's publisher of *Les Damnès de la terre*, in "Homage to Frantz Fanon," p. 150.

⁷James H. Billington, *Fire in the Minds of Men* (New York: Basic Books, 1980).

⁸James C. Davies, "The J-Curve of Rising and Declining Satisfactions as a Cause of Revolution and Rebellion," in Hugh D. Graham and Ted R. Gurr (eds.), *Violence in America*, pp. 411-37. See also James C. Davies, "Towards a Theory of Revolution," *American Sociological Review*, vol. 27 (Feb, 1962), 1-19.

⁹For an early expression of this idea, see Abraham H. Maslow, *The Journals of A.H. Maslow*, 2 vols. (Monterey, Ca.: Brooks/Cole Publishing Company, 1979), vol 11, p. 952, 963, 964.

¹⁰Aristotle, *Politics*, trans. H. Rackman (London and Harvard: Harvard University Press, 1932). Quoted in Davies, *When Men Revolt and Why*, pp. 86-7.

¹¹Henry Bienen, *Violence and Social Change: A Review of Current Literature* (Chicago and London: University of Chicago Press, 1968), p. 7-10.

¹²Harry Eckstein (ed.), *Internal War* (New York: Macmillan Co. 1964), pp. 3-6.

¹³Bienen, *Violence and Social Change*, pp. 7-10.

¹⁴For some examples of this type of literature, see Jack Woddis, *Africa: Roots of Revolt*, (New York: The Citadel Press, 1962); *New Theories of Revolution: A Commentary on the Views of Frantz Fanon, Règis Debray, and Herbert Marcuse*, and H. R. Cowie, *Revolutions in the Modern World* (Sydney, Australia: Thomas Nelson, 1979), pp. 188-225; John Dunn, *Modern Revolutions: An Introduction to the Analysis of Political Phenomenon* (Cambridge University Press, 1972); Lilyan Kesteloot, *Intellectual Origins of the African Revolution*, trans. from the French by Alexandre Mboukou (Rockville Md: New Perspectives, 1973); Lewis Coser, "Fanon and Debray: Theorists of the Third World," in Irving Howe (eds.), *Beyond the New Left*, pp. 120-34; Michael Freeman, "Review Article: Theories of Revolution," *British Journal of Political Science*, 2 (1972), 339-59; Museveni, Yoweri, T. "Fanon's Theory of Violence: Its Verification in Liberated Mozambique," in Nathan Shamuyarira (ed.), *Essays on the Liberation of Southern Africa* pp. 1-24; Robert Blackey, "Fanon and Cabral: A Contrast in Theories of Revolution for Africa," pp. 191-209.

For studies of the struggle see Norman Miller and Roderick Aya (eds.) *National Liberation: Revolution in the Third World* New York: Free Press, 1971); John Marcum, *The Angolan Revolution*, vol. 1 (1950-1962) (Cambridge, Mass. M.I.T. Press, 1969); Alan Isaacman, *Mozambique: The Africanization of a European Institution* (Madison University of Wisconsin Press, 1972); Leo Huberman and Paul M. Sweezy (eds.), *Règis Debray and the Latin American Revolution* (New York: Monthly Review Press, 1968); James H. Mittleman, "Mozambique: The Political Economy of Underdevelopment," *Journal of Southern African Studies*, vol. 111, no. 1 (Jan., 1978), 35-54; René Lefore, *Ethiopie, la révolution hèrètique* (Paris: Maspero, 1981).

¹⁵Although I have used these four revolutions to illustrate a point, it is important to indicate

that they differ in range, scope and objectives. Whereas on the one hand in France the revolution was effected by a combination of the *bourgeoisie* and segments of the peasantry, in England it was mainly the work of the capitalist landlords and the *bourgeoisie*. On the other hand, where landlords and state bureaucrats resisted the revolutionary process, and where the *bourgeoisie* was too small and weak—as was the case in Russia and China, and for that matter Algeria—peasant revolutionaries were organized by ideologues in the role of mass mobilizers. Barrington Moore, *Social Origins of Dictatorship and Democracry: Lord and Peasant in the Making of the Modern World* (Boston, 1966).

[16] Crane Brinton, *The Anatomy of Revolution* (New York: Vintage Books, 1952), chapters 8, 9.

[17] Arendt, *On Violence*. See especially, pp. 59-87.

[18] At the request of Mme. Fanon, Sartre's preface did not appear in subsequent French printings. For the English version see Frantz Fanon, *The Wretched of the Earth*, pp. 1-31.

[19] Melvin J. Lasky, "The Birth of a Metaphor: On the Origins of Utopia and Revolution," part II, *Encounter*, vol. 34, no. 3 (March, 1970), 42.

[20] *Ibid.*, pp. 41-42.

[21] Melvin J. Lasky, "The Birth of a Metaphor: On the Origins of Utopia and Revolution," part I, *Encounter*, vol 34, no., 2 (Feb., 1970), 39-40.

[22] *Ibid.*, p. 38.

[23] *Ibid.*, pp. 37, 45.

[24] Lasky, "The Birth of a Metaphor," part II, p. 34.

[25] *Les Damnès de la terre*, pp. 6, 14, 21, 29, 33, 37, 41, 78, 82, 88, 107.

[26] *Ibid.*, pp. 230-33. The emphasis is mine.

# Glossary of Select Terms

A.L.N.         Armée de Libération Nationale. The Algerian nationalist army, the military arm of the F.L.N.

C.C.E.         Comité de Coordination et d'Exécution. The Executive body of the F.L.N. between 1956-1958.

C.G.T.         Confédération Générale du Travail. A French Communist dominated labor union.

C.N.R.A.         Conseil National de la Révolution Algérienne. Legislative body of the F.L.N. from 1956 to 1962.

C.R.U.A.         Comité Révolutionaire d'Unité et d'Action. A revolutionary organization founded in April 1954. Replaced by the F.L.N. in November 1954.

F.L.N.         Front de Libération Nationale (November 1954). The Algerian nationalist organization which became the country's official party after independence.

F.N.L.A.         Frente Nacional para Libertacão de Angola. An Angolan nationalist movement led by Holden Roberto.

G.P.R.A.         Gouvernement Provisoire de la République Algérienne. The provisional wartime government of the Algerian nationalists.

M.P.L.A.         Movimento Populare para Libertação de Angola. An Angolan nationalist movement led by Agosthino Neto.

M.T.L.D.         Mouvement pour le Triomphe des Libertés Démocratiques. A nationalist movement led by Massali al-Hajj before the war of liberation. Formed in 1946.

O.A.S.         Organisation de l'Armée Secrète. The French terrorist organization formed in 1961.

O.A.U.              Organization of African Unity. An organization of African states based in Addis Ababa.

P.P.A.              Parti du Peuple Algérien (1937). An Algerian nationalist party led by Massali al-Hajj, replaced by the M.T.L.D. (1946).

U.D.M.A.            Union Démocratique du Manifeste Algérien. An Algerian nationalist party founded by Ferhat Abbas in 1946.

U.G.E.M.A.          Union Générale des Etudiants Musulmans Algériens. The wartime nationalist student organization.

U.G.T.A.            Union Générale des Travailleurs Algériens. The Algerian labor federation. Founded 1956.

U.N.F.A.            Union Nationale des Femmes Algériennes. The Algerian women's organization.

U.P.A.              Union Populaire Algérienne. An Algerian nationalist party formed by Ferhat Abbas in 1938.

*Appendix I*

# Main Events in Fanon's Life

| | |
|---|---|
| 20 July 1925: | Frantz Fanon born in Fort-de-France, Martinique. |
| 1939-1943: | Attended the all-black Lycée Schoelcher Fort-de-France, where he came under the influence of Aimé Césaire, then a teacher of literature. |
| 1943: | Went to Dominica as a volunteer in the Caribbean Free French Movement. |
| 1944: | Served with the Free French armies in Guercif in Morocco, and Bougie in Algeria. Served also in the valley of Doebs, where he was wounded at Besançon on the Swiss Frontier. Received a bravery citation from Colonel Raoul Salan. |
| 1946: | Completed his baccalaureate degree and lycée education after his return from Europe. |
| 1946: | Fanon and his elder brother, Joby, worked with Aimé Césaire's election campaign in Martinique. |
| 1947: | Death of Fanon's father. |
| 1947: | Fanon returned to France and enrolled in the dental faculty in Paris. Within the year, he moved to Lyon where he began training as a medical student. |
| 1950/51/52 or 53: | Married Marie-Josephe Dublé from Lyon. |
| 1952: | Graduated from the Faculty of Medicine and Pharmacy at Lyon. |
| 1952: | Returned to Martinique, where he practiced medicine in Vauclin, his mother's ancestral home in the southern part of the island. |
| Summer 1952: | Returned to France, and entered the hospital at Saint Alban-de-Lozere, near Mende in central France, where he began work as a resident under the direction of the distinguished social psychiatrist François Tosquelles. |
| 1952: | *Black Skin White Masks* published. |
| July 1953: | Passed the examinations in pathology, neurology, forensic medicine, and other areas, including an oral examination. This entitled him to the |

|  | rank of *Chef de service*, and director of one of France's psychiatric hospitals. |
|---|---|
| 1953: | Went to work at Pontorson, in Normandy. |
| November 1953: | Took up the position as *Chef de service* at the psychiatric hospital in Blida-Joinville, outside the capital city of Algiers. |
| 1 November, 1954: | Algerian war of liberation from France broke out. |
| September, 1956: | Addressed the First Congress of Black Writers and Artists in Paris. |
| January 1957: | Expelled from Algeria by the French authorities. Travelled first to France, and later settled in Tunis. In Tunisia, he worked at the government Psychiatric Hospital at Monouba (Tunis), and at the Centre (Neuropsychiatrique) de Jour (a day care center), with the Front de Libération Nationale: F.L.N.; and with the Armée de Libération Nationale: A.N.L. Later he was involved in the work of the seven F.L.N. health Centers in Tunis, and also taught at the University of Tunis. |
| December, 1958: | Attended the All-Africa Peoples' Conference in Accra (Ghana). |
| March 1959: | Addressed the Second Congress of Black Writers and Artists in Rome. |
| 1959: | His second book, *A Dying Colonialism*, published. |
| 1959: | Assassination attempt on Fanon's life in a Rome hospital by Le Main Rouge, a right wing terrorist organization. |
| 1959: | Working for the Gouvernement Provisoire de la République Algérienne: G.P.R.A., Fanon travelled to Cairo. As the G.P.R.A. representative, he also attended the Positive Action Conference for Peace and Security in Africa, and the Afro-Asia Solidarity Conference in Conakry (Guinea) in April 1959 and Addis Ababa (Ethiopia) respectively. |
| Summer 1959: | Attended the Third Conference of Independent African States. |
| 1960: | Participated in the Second All-African Peoples' Congress in Accra. |

| March 1960: | Assigned to post of permanent representative for the G.P.R.A. in Accra. |
| 1960: | Undertook a revolutionary journey through the Sahara from Mali to Algeria in an unsuccessful attempt to open a southern front. |
| 1960: | Visited the Soviet Union where he was treated with Myleran for granulocytic leukemia. |
| September 1961: | Arrived in Washington D.C. where he was later admitted to the National Institute of Health in Bethesda, Maryland. Read the page proofs for *The Wretched of the Earth*. |
| 6 December 1961: | Death of Frantz Fanon. |

## *Appendix II*

# Main Events During the Algerian Revolution

1954:  1 November.  Beginning of Algerian Revolution in the Aurès mountains.

1955:  April.  Bandung Conference.

1956:  24 February.  Creation of the Union Générale des Travailleurs Algériens: U.G.T.A.

July.  National Strike in Algeria.

20 August.  End of the Soummam Conference. Goals of the Algerian Revolution outlined.

1 November.  One day strike in commemoration of the second anniversary of the Algerian Revolution.

December.  Beginning of the Battle of Algiers.

1957:  9 January.  Creation of the Croissant Rouge Algérien.

28 January to 4 February.  National strike in Algeria.

Fall.  End of the Battle of Algiers.

December.  Conférence de Solidarité des peuples afro-asiatiques in Cairo.

1958:  15 April.  Pan-African Conference (independent states) in Accra.

27-30 April.  Third Maghribian Conference at Tangier for the unification of the Arab states of the Maghrib.

13 May.  European *coup de force* at Algiers.

19 September.  Constitution of the Gouvernement Provisoire de la République Algérienne: G.P.R.A.

1 November.           The Ouvrier Algérien, an organ of the U.G.T.A.
                      moved to Tunis.

5-12 Decem-           African Peoples Conference (non-independent
ber.                  states) in Accra.

1959:   January.      Congress of the Union Générale des Tra-
                      vailleurs d'Afrique Noire: U.G.T.A.N. in Cona-
                      kry.

29-31 May.            Meeting of the Comité directeur for the Confer-
                      ence of African Peoples at Tunis.

4-8 August.           Meeting of the Independent African States at
                      Monrovia. The Algerian flag flew at this
                      conference.

16 September.         General de Gaulle proposed Algerian self-
                      determination.

6-9 October.          Meeting of the Comité directeur of the Confer-
                      ence of African Peoples at Accra.

16 December           Meeting of the Comité National de la Révolu-
1959—18 Jan-          tion Algérienne: C.N.R.A. in Tripoli.
uary 1960.

1960:   28-31 January.  Second Conference of the African Peoples at
                      Tunis.

7-10 April.           Conférence pour la Paix et la Sécurité in Africa
                      at Accra.

12-15 April.          Conférence Afro-asiatique at Conakry.

27-29 June.           First round of talks between the F.L.N. and the
                      French government at Melun, Switzerland.

June.                 Third Pan-African Conference at Addis-Ababa.

6 October.

                      The Peoples Republic of China agreed to lend
                      assistance to the G.P.R.A.

7 October.        *De facto* recognition of the G.P.R.A. by the Soviet Union.

1961:   25-31 March.      Third Conference of the African Peoples at Cairo. Military *putch* at Algiers.

20 May.           Openings of negotiations between French representatives and those of the G.P.R.A. at Evian, Switzerland.

1962:   19 March.         Cease-fire and Peace Agreements concluded at Evian. The agreements were never actually signed by either party because the French refused formal recognition to the F.L.N. They handed over the country officially to a mixed French-Algerian "provisional executive."

# Bibliography

## Works by Frantz Fanon

*Les Mains paralleles. L'oeil se noie. La conspiration*, three unpublished pieces for the theatre, written in the period 1949-1950.

*Troubles méntaux et syndromes psychiatriques dans l'hérédodégénération-spino-cérébelleuse. Un cas de maladie de Friedreich avec délire de possesion*, Thesis, Lyon, 1951-52.

"Le syndrome nord-africain" in: *Esprit*, Paris, February 1952, reproduced in *Pour la révolution africaine*. Ecrits politiques. Petite collection Maspero, Paris, 1969, pp. 9-21.

*Peau noire, masques blancs*. Paris: Editions du Seuil, 1952.

"Sur quelques cas traités par la méthode de Bini" (in collaboration with Dr. F. Tosquelle, Saint-Alban), in: *Congrès des médecins aliénistes et neurologues de France et des pays de langue française, LIe session, Pau, 20-26 July, 1953*.

"A propos d'un cas de syndrome de Cotard avec balancement psycho-somatique" (in collaboration with Dr. Despinoy), in: *Les Annales médico-psychologiques*, volume 2, June, 1953, LIe session, Pau, 1953.

"Indications de thérapeutique de Bini dans le cadre des thérapeutiques institutionnelles: (in collaboration with Dr. F. Tosquelle), in: *Congrès*... 20-26 July 1953.

"Sur un essai de réadaptation chez une malade avec épilepsie morphéique et troubles de caractère graves" (in collaboration with Dr. Tosquelle), in: *Congrès* . . . , 20-26 July, 1953.

"Notes sur les techniques de cures de sommeil avec conditionnement et contrôle électro-encéphalographique" (in collaboration with Dr. Despinoy et W. Zenner), in: *Congrès* . . . , 20-26 July, 1953).

"La socialthérapie dans un service d'hommes musulmans. Difficultés méthodologiques", by doctors Fr. Fanon et J. Azoulay, Hôpital psychiatrique de Blida-Joinville, in: *L'Information psychiatrique*, 30e année, 4 série, no. 9, Paris, 1954.

*Introduction aux troubles de la sexualité chez les Nord-Africains* (in collaboration with doctors J. Azoulay and F. Sanchez), unpublished manuscript, 1954-55.

"Aspects actuels de l'assistance mentale en Algérie" (in collaboration with doctors J. Dequeker, R. Lacaton, M. Minucci, F. Ramée), Hôpital psychiatrique de Blida-Joinville, in: *L'Information psychiatrique*, 31e année, 4 série, no. 1, Paris, 1955.

"Antillais et Africains", in: *Esprit*, Paris, 1955

"Réflexions sur l'ethnopsychiatrie:, in : *Conscience maghrebine*, no. 3, 1955.

"Conduites d'aveux en Afrique du Nord" (in collaboration with Dr. R. Lacaton), in: *Congrès* . . ., LIIIe session, Nice, 5-11 September 1955.

*Conférence sur les catégories de l'humanisme moderne,* unpublished text of a lecture presented at Blida, 1955.

"Attitude du musulman maghrébin devant la folie" (in collaboration with Dr. F. Sanchez), in: *Revue pratique de psychologie de la vie sociale et d'hygiène mentale*, année 1956, no. 1.

"Lettre à un Français", 1956, in: *Pour la Révolution africaine*, pp. 46-49.

"Lettre au Ministre-Résident", 1956, in: *Pour la Révolution africaine*, pp. 50-53.

"Le T.A.T. chez les femmes musulmanes. Sociologie de la perception et de l'imagination" (in collaboration with Dr. C. Geronimi), in: *Congrès* . . ., LIV session, Bordeaux, 30 August—4 September 1956.

*Racisme et Culture*, text of a lecture presented to the First Congress of Black Writers and Artists. Paris, September, 1956.

"Conférence de presse". Report from the F.L.N. delegation at Tunis, in: *Le Monde*, Paris 5 June 1957.

"Déceptions et illusions du colonialisme français", in: *El Moudjahid*, no. 10, September 1957.

"L'Algérie face aux tortionnaires français", in: *El Moudjahid*, no. 10, September 1957.

"A Propos d'un plaidoyer", in: *El Moudjahid*, no. 12, November 1957.

"Les intellectuels et les démocrates français devant la révolution algérienne", in: *El Moudjahid*, 1, 15 & 30 December 1957.

"Aux Antilles, naissance d'une nation?", in: *El Moudjahid*, no. 16, January 1958.

"A propos d'un cas de spasme de torsion" (in collaboration with Dr. L. Levy), in: *La Tunisie médicale*, XXXVIe année, no. 9, Tunis, 1958.

"Le sang maghrébin ne coulera pas en vain", in: *El Moudjahid*, no. 18, February 1958.

"La farce qui change de camp", in: *El Moudjahid*, no. 21, April 1958.

"Décolonisation et indépendence", in: *El Moudjahid*, no. 22, April 1958.

"Une crise continuée", in: *El Moudjahid*, no. 23, May 1958.

"Lettre à la jeunesse africaine", in: *El Moudjahid*, no. 24, May 1958.

"Verítiés premières à propos du problème colonial", in: *El Moudjahid*, no. 27, July 1958.

"La leçon de Cotonou", in: *El Moudjahid*, no. 28, August 1958.

"Appel aux Africains", in: *El Moudjahid*, no. 28, August 1958.

"Lendemains d'un plébliscite en Afrique", in: *El Moudjahid*, no. 30, October 1958.

"La guerre d'Algérie et la libération des hommes", in: *El Moudjahid*, no. 31, November 1958.

"L'Algérie et Accra", in: *El Moudjahid*, no. 34, December 1958.

"Accra: L'Afrique affirme son unité et définit sa stratégie", in: *El Moudjahid*, no. 34, December 1958.

"Les tentatives déseperées de M. Debré", in: *El Moudjahid*, no. 37, February 1959.

"Fureur raciste en France", in: *El Moudjahid*, no. 42, May 1959.

"Premiers essais de méprobamate injectable dans les états hypocondriaques" (in collaboration with Dr. L. Levy), in: *La Tunisie médicale*, XXXVII année, Tunis, 1959.

"L'hospitalisation de jour en psychiatrie, valeurs et limites", I. Introduction générale, II. Considérations doctrinales (in collaboration with Dr. C. Geromini), in: *La Tunisie médicale*, XXXVII année, no. 10, Tunis 1959.

*L'An V de la révolution algérienne*. Paris, 1959, Maspero (new edition published as *Sociologie d'une révolution*. François Maspero, Paris, 1966).

"Le sang coule aux Antilles sous domination française", in: *El Moudjahid*, no. 58, January 1960.

"Unité et solidarité effective sous les conditions de la libération africaine", in: *El Moudjahid*, no. 58, January 1960.

"Cette Afrique à venir" 1950, in: *Pour la révolution africaine*, pp. 176-199.

Intervention à la "Conférence pour la paix et la sécurité en Afrique", Accra, 7-10 April 1960, extracts in *El Moudjahid*, no. 63, 25-4 1960, second edition of *L'An V de la révolution algérienne*.

Intervention, en qualité de représentant de l'Algérie à la Conférence afro-asiatique de Conakry, 12-15 April 1960, extracts in: *El Moudjahid*, no. 63, 25-4-1960.

"The Stages of Imperialism", in: *Provisional Government of the Algerian Republic, Mission in Ghana*, vol. 1, no. 6, December 1960.

"La mort de Lumumba: Pouvons-nous faire autrement?" in: *Afrique-Action*, no. 19, February 1961.

*Les Damnés de la terre*, Cahiers Libres, Paris: F. Maspero, 1961.

*Pour la révolution africaine*, Paris: F. Maspero, 1964.

# Bibliography

## Books

Abbas, Ferhat. *Le Jeune Algérien*. Paris: Jeune Parque, 1931.

_____. *La Nuite Coloniale*. Paris: Julliard, 1962.

Abun-Nasr, M. *A History of the Maghrib*. Cambridge University Press, 1971.

Ait Ahmed, Hocine. *La Guerre et l'après-guerre*. Paris: Editions de Minuit, 1964.

Agel, Jerome. *The Radical Therapist*. New York: Ballantine Books, 1971.

Ageron, Ch-André. *Histoire de l'Algérie contemporaine*. Paris, 1970.

Alleg, Henri. *La Question*. Paris: Editions de Minuit, 1958.

Alroy, Gil Carl. *The Involvement of Peasants in Internal Wars*. Princeton, N.J.: Center of International Studies, Princeton University, 1966.

*Annuaire de la Martinique 1952-1956*. Paris, 1957.

Arendt, Hannah. *On Revolution*. New York: Viking Press, 1965.

_____. *On Violence*. New York: Harcourt Brace and World, 1969.

Aron, Raymond, *La Tragedie algérienne*. Paris: Plon, 1957.

_____. *Main Currents in Sociological Thought*. New York: Basic Books, 1965.

Banbuck, C.A. *Histoire politique, économique et sociale de la Martinique sous l'ancien régime, 1695-1789*. Paris: Librairie des Sciences Politiques Sociales, 1972.

Barbour, Nevile, ed. *A Survey of North West Africa*. London: Oxford University Press, 1962.

Barnett, Donald, and Karari Njama. *Mau Mau from Within*. London: MacGibbon and Kee, 1966.

Beauvoir, S. de. *La Force des choses*. Paris: Gallimard, 1964. Trans. by Richard Howard as *Force of Circumstances*. New York: Putnam, 1964.

Bedjaoui, Mohammed. *La Révolution algérienne et le droit*. Brussels: Association Internationale des Juristes Démocrats, 1961.

Behr, Edward. *The Algerian Problem*. London: Hodder and Stoughton, 1961.

Bell, Wendell and Walter E. Freeman, eds. *Ethnicity and Nation-Building: Comparative, International and Historical Perspectives*. London: Sage Publications, 1974.

Bennabi, Malek. *Perspectives algériennes*. Algiers: Editions En-Nahda, 1964.

_____. *Mémoires d'un témoin du siècle*. Algiers: Editions Nationales Algériennes, 1965.

Berque, Jacques *Le Maghreb entre deux guerres*. Paris: Editions du Seuil, 1962.

Betts, Raymond F. *Assimilation and Association in French Colonial Theory*. New York: Columbia University Press, 1961.

Bienen, Henry. *Violence and Social Change: A Review of Current Literature*. Chicago and London: University of Chicago Press, 1968.

Billington, James H. *Fire in the Minds of Men*. New York: Basic Books, 1980.

Boudiaf, Mohamed. *Ou va l'Algérie?* Paris: Librairie de l'Etoile, 1964.

Bourdieu, Pierre. *The Algerians*. Boston: Beacon Press, 1962. Originally published as *Sociologie de l'Algérie*. Paris: Presses Universitaires de France, 1958.

Bourges, Hervé. *L'Algérie à l'épreuve du pouvoir*. Paris: Editions Grasset, 1967.

Bouvier, Pierre. *Fanon*. Paris: Editions Universitaires, 1971.

Brace, Richard and Joan Brace. *Algerian Voices*. Princeton, N.J.: Van Nostrand, 1965.

Brinton, Crane. *The Anatomy of Revolution*. New York: Vintage Books, 1952.

Buijtenhuigs, Robert. *Le Mouvement "Mau Mau": une révolte paysanne et anti-coloniale en Afrique Noire*. The Hague: Mouton, 1971.

Burns, Emile (compiler). *A Handbook of Marxism*. New York: 1935.

Cabral, Amilcar. *Revolution in Guinea*. New York: Monthly Review Press, 1969.

_____. *National Liberation and Culture*. Syracuse, New York: Program of Eastern African Studies, Syracuse University, *Occasional Paper*. No. 57, 1970.

_____. *L.S.M. Guinea-Bisseau: Toward the Final Victory— Selected Speeches and Documents from P.A.I.G.C.* Richmond, B.C. Canada: L.S.M. Information Center, 1974.

Calvert, Peter. *Revolution*. London: Pall Mall, 1970.

Caute, David. *Fanon*. New York: The Viking Press, 1970.

Césaire, Aimé. "Et les chiens se taisaient." A tragedy in *Les Armes miraculeuses*. Paris: Gallimard, 1970.

_____. *Discourse on Colonialism.* New York: Monthly Review Press, 1972.

Chaliand, Gérard. *L'Algérie est-elle socialiste?* Paris: Maspero, 1964.

Cohn, Norman R.C. *The Pursuit of the Millenium.* Fairlawn, N.J.: Essential Books, 1957.

Cowie, H.R. *Revolutions in the Modern World.* Sydney, Australia: Thomas Nelson, 1979.

Crawford, Fred R. ed. *Violence and Dissent in Urban America.* Atlanta: S.N.P.A. Foundation Seminar Books, n.d. (probably 1971-1972).

Crowder, Michael. *Senegal: A Study in French Assimilation Policy.* London: Oxford University Press, 1962.

Dahrendorf, R. *Class and Class Conflict in Industrial Society.* Stanford: Stanford University Press, 1959.

Danzinger, Raphael. *Abd al-Qadir and the Algerians: Resistance to the French and Internal Consolidation.* New York: Holmes and Meier Publishers, 1977.

D'Arcy, François, Annie Krieger, and Alain Marill. *Essais sur l'économie de l'Algérie nouvelle.* Paris: Presses Universitaires de France, 1965.

Davidson, Basil. *The Liberation of Guinée.* Harmondsworth, Middlesex: Penguin Books, 1969.

Davies, James C. *When Men Revolt and Why: A Reader in Political Violence and Revolution.* New York: The Free Press, 1971.

Debien, Gabriel. *Destinées d'esclaves à la Martinique (1746-1778): Notes d'histoire coloniale, no. 57. Extrait du Bulletin de l'Institut Français d'Afrique Noire,* 22. Jan. - April, 1960.

Debray, Régis. *Revolution in the Revolution?* New York: Grove Press, 1967.

DeKadt, Emanuel. *Patterns of Foreign Influence in the Caribbean.* London: Oxford University Press, 1972.

Ducasse, André. *Les Négriers: ou le trafic des esclaves.* Paris: Hachette, 1948.

Duchemin, Jacques. *Histoire du F.L.N.* Paris: La Table Ronde, 1962.

Eckstein, Harry. *Internal War.* New York: Macmillan Co., 1964.

Edwards, Lyford P. *The Natural History of Revolution.* Chicago, 1927.

Erikson, Erik H. *Gandhi's Truth on the Origins of Militant Non-Violence.* New York: Norton, 1969.

Favord, Charles-Henri. *La Révolution algérienne.* Paris: Plon, 1959.

Feieraband, Ivo K., Roasalind L., and Ted R. Gurr with Charles Ruttenberg.

*The Conditions of Civil Violence: First Tests of a Causal Model.* Princeton: Princeton University Press, 1967.

Feraoun, Moulad. *Journal 1955-1962.* Paris: Editions du Seuil, 1962.

Feuer, Lewis S. *Marx and Engels: Basic Writings on Politics and Philosophy.* Garden City, New York: Doubleday, 1959.

Fischer, Louis. *The Life of Mahatma Gandhi.* New York: Collier Books, 1973.

Fischer, Louis, ed. *The Essential Gandhi: His Life, Work and Ideas.* New York: Vintage Books, 1962.

Furnivall, J.S. *Netherlands India: A Study of Plural Economy.* Cambridge University Press, 1939.

——————. *Colonial Policy and Practice: A Comparative Study of Burma and Netherlands India.* London: Cambridge University Press, 1948.

Gallagher, Charles F. *The United States and North Africa.* Cambridge Mass: Harvard University Press, 1963.

Gandhi, Mohandas K. *An Autobiography: The Story of my Experiments with Truth.* Trans. Madadev Dessai, Boston: Beacon Press, 1957.

Geismar, Peter. *Fanon.* New York: Dial Press, 1971.

Gendarme, René. *L'Economie de l'Algérie.* Paris: Armand Colin, 1959.

Gendzier, Irene L. *Frantz Fanon: A Critical Study.* New York: Pantheon Books, 1973.

Gillespie, Joan. *Algeria: Rebellion and Revolution.* London: Ernest Benn, 1960.

Girault, Arthur. *Principles de colonisation et de législation coloniale.* 3rd ed. Paris, 1907.

Gisler, Antoine. *L'Esclavage aux antilles française (XVIIe - XIXe siècle): Contribution au problème de l'esclavage.* Fribourg: Editions Universitaires Fribourg, Suisse, 1964.

Gordon, David C. *North Africa's French Legacy.* Cambridge, Mass: Harvard University Press, 1962.

——————. *The Passing of French Algeria.* London: Oxford University Press, 1966.

——————. *Women in Algeria: An Essay on Change.* Cambridge, Mass: Harvard University Press, 1968.

Graham, Hugh D. and Ted R. Gurr, eds. *Violence in America: Historical and Comparative Perspectives.* Beverely Hills, Sage Publications, 1979.

Greene, T.N. *The Guerrilla and How to Fight Him.* New York: Praeger, 1962.

Guérin, Daniel. *L'Algérie caporalisée?: Suite de "L'Algérie qui se cherche."* Paris: C.E.S., 1965.

_____. *L'Algérie s'insurgeait, 1954-1962: Un anti-colonialiste témoigne.* Claix: Pensée Sauvage, 1979.

Gurr, Ted R. *Why Men Rebel.* Princeton University Press, 1970.

Hadj Ali, Bachir. *Qu-est-ce que c'est qu'un Révolutionnaire algérien en 1963?* Paris: Editions Sociales, 1963.

_____. *L'Arbitraire.* Paris: Editions de Minuit, 1966.

Hansen Emmanuel. *Frantz Fanon: Social and Political Thought.* Ohio State University, 1977.

Harmand, Jules. *Domination et Colonisation.* Paris, 1910.

Heggoy, Alf A. *Insurgency and Counterinsurgency in Algeria.* Bloomington: Indiana University Press, 1972.

Hegel, G.F.W. *Philosophy of Right.* Trans. by T.M. Knox. London: Oxford University Press, 1967.

_____. *Phenomenology of Spirit* (1807). Trans. A.V. Miller, text and forward by J.N. Findlay. Oxford University Press, 1977.

Hill, J.E. Christopher. *Lenin and the Russian Revolution.* Harmondsworth, England: Penguin Books, 1971.

_____. *Anti-Christ in Seventeenth Century England.* London and New York: Oxford University Press, 1971.

_____. *The World Turned Upside Down: Radical Ideas During the English Revolution.* London: Temple Smith, 1972.

Hobsbawn, Eric J. *Primitive Rebels: Studies in Archaic Forms of Social Movements in the Nineteenth and Twentieth Centuries.* New York: The Norton Press, 1956.

Howe, Irving. *Beyond the New Left.* New York: McCall, 1970.

Huberman, Leo, and Paul M. Sweezy, eds. *Régis Debray and the Latin American Revolution.* New York: Monthly Review Press, 1968.

Humbaraci, Arslan. *Algeria: A Revolution that Failed.* New York: Praeger, 1966.

Humphries, Donald H. *The East African Liberation Movement.* Adelphi Papers, no. 16. London: London Institute for Strategic Studies, 1965.

Huntington, Samuel. *Political Order in Changing Societies.* New Haven, Conn: Yale University Press, 1968.

Ibn Khaldun. *Histoires des Berbères.* Trans. Baron de Slane. 3 Vols. Paris, 1925.

Isaacman, Allen F. *Mozambique: The Africanization of a European Institution.* Madison: University of Wisconsin Press, 1972.

Isambert, F.A. *et al. Receuil général des anciens lois français,* 29 vols. Paris, 1821-1833.

Iyer, Raghavan. *The Moral and Political Thought of Mahatma Gandhi.* New York: Oxford University Press, 1973.

Jackson, Henry F. *The F.L.N. in Algeria: Party Development in a Revolutionary Society.* Westport, Conn: Greenwood Press, 1977.

Johnson, Chalmers. *Peasant Nationalism and Communist Power: The Emergence of Revolutionary Power.* California: Stanford University Press, 1962.

——————. *Revolution and the Social System.* Stanford: Hoover Institution Studies, no. 3, 1964.

——————. *Revolutionary Change.* Boston: Little Brown, 1967.

Julien, Ch-André. *L'Afrique du Nord en Marche.* 2nd ed. Paris: Juillard, 1953.

——————. *Histoire de l'Algérie contemporaine: La Conquète de les débuts de la colonisation (1827-1871).* Paris: Presses Universitaires de France, 1964.

——————. *L'Afrique du Nord en Marche; nationalismes musulmans et souveraineté française.* 3rd ed. Paris: Juillard, 1972.

Jung, C.G. *Four Archetypes.* Trans. R.F.C. Hull. Extracted from *The Archetypes and the Collective Unconscious.* IX, part 1, *Collected Works.* Princeton: Princeton University Press, 1969.

Kamenka, Eugene, ed. *A World of Revolution?* Canberra: The Australian National University, 1970.

Kaunda, Kenneth. *The Riddle of Violence.* San Francisco: Harper and Row, 1981.

Kedourie, Elie. *Nationalism in Asia and Africa.* New York: World Publishing, 1970.

Keramane, Hafid. *La Pacification.* Lausanne: La Cité, 1960.

Kessel, Patrick and Giovanni Pirelli. *Le Peuple algérien et la guerre: Lettres et témoignages d'algériens, 1954-1962.* Paris: François Maspero, 1962.

Kesteloot, Lilyan. *Intellectual Origins of the African Revolution.* Trans. from the French by Alexandre Mboukou. Rockville, Md.: New Perspectives, 1973.

Khaldi, Abdelaziz. *Le Problème algérien.* Algiers: Editions En-Hahda, 1946.

Khelifa, Laroussi. *Manuel du Militant algérien.* Lausanne: La Cité, 1962.

Kovel, Joel. *White Racism: A Psychohistory.* New York: Random House, Vintage Books, 1971.

Kraft, Michael. *The Struggle for Algeria.* New York: Doubleday, 1961.

Krasin, Iuriy A. *The Dialectics of Revolutionary Progress.* Moscow: Novosti Press Agency, 1972.

——————. *Sociology of Revolution: A Marxist View.* Moscow: Progress Publishers, 1972.

Kumar, Khrishnan, ed. *Revolution.* London: Weidenfeld and Nicolson, 1971.

Lacheraf, Mostefa. *L'Algérie: Nation et société.* Paris: Maspero, 1965.

Lacoste, Yves, André Nouschi and André Prenant. *L'Algérie passé et présent.* Paris: Editions Sociales, 1960.

Laroui, Abdallah. *The History of the Maghrib: An Interpretative Essay.* Trans. Ralph Manheim. Princeton University Press, 1977. Originally published as *L'Histoire du Maghrib: Un Essai de synthèse.* Paris: François Maspero, 1970.

Launay, Michel. *Paysans algériens: La Terre, la vigne et les hommes.* Paris: Editions de Seuil, 1963.

Lefort, René. *Ethiopie, la révolution hérétique.* Paris: François Maspero, 1981.

Lentin, Albert-Paul. *Le Dernier quart d'heure* Paris: Juillard, 1963.

Lerner, Daniel. *The Passing of Traditional Society.* New York: Free Press, 1958.

Lévy-Brühl, Lucien. *L'Ame Primitive.* Paris, 1927.

——————. *La Mythologie primitive: Le Monde mythique des australiens et papous.* Paris, 1935.

Le Tourneau, Roger. *Evolution politique de l'Afrique du Nord musulmane.* Paris: Armand Colin, 1962

Lucas, Philippe. *Sociologie de Frantz Fanon.* Algiers: Société nationale d'édition et de diffusion, 1971.

Maier, C.S. and D.S. White, eds. *The Thirteenth of May: The Advent of de Gaulle's Republic.* New York: Oxford University Press, 1968.

Mandouze, André. *La Révolution algérienne par les textes: Documents presentés.* Paris: François Maspero, 1961.

Mannoni, O. *Prospero and Caliban.* New York: Praeger, 1964.

Marçais, Georges. *La Berbérie musulmane et l'Orient au moyen âge.* Paris: Aubier, Editions Montaigne, 1946.

Marcuse, Herbert. *One Dimensional Man*. Boston: Beacon Press, 1966.

——————. *An Essay on Liberation*. Boston: Beacon Press, 1969.

Marx, Karl, and Frederick Engels. *Selected Works*. 2 vols. Moscow: Progress Publishers, 1969.

——————. *On Colonialism: Articles from The New York Tribune and Other Writings*. New York: International Publishers, 1972.

Mason, Philip. *Patterns of Dominance*. London: Oxford University Press, 1971.

May, Louis-Philippe. *Histoire économique de la Martinique*. Paris: Librarie des Sciences politiques et sociales, 1972.

Memmi, Albert. *The Colonizer and the Colonized*. Trans. H. Greenfield. New York: Orion Press, 1965.

——————. *Dominated Man*. New York: Orion Press, 1968.

Merleau-Ponty, Maurice. *Humanism and Terror*. Boston: Beacon Press, 1969.

Miller, Norman, and Roderick Aya, eds. *National Liberation: Revolution in the Third World*. New York: Free Press, 1971.

Mitrany, David. *Marx Against the Peasant*. North Carolina: Chapel Hill, 1951.

Mondlane, Eduardo. *The Struggle for Mozambique*. Baltimore: Penguin Books, 1969.

McKenzie Brown, D., ed. *The White Umbrella: Indian Political Thought from Manu to Gandhi*. Berkeley: University of California Press, 1958.

Merle, Robert. *Ahmed Ben Bella*. Paris: Gallimard, 1965.

Moore, Barrington. *Social Origins of Dictatorship and Democracy: Lord and Peasant in the Making of the Modern World*. Boston: Beacon Press, 1966.

Moss, Warner. *Violence*. Williamsburg, Va.: College of William and Mary in Virginia, 1968.

M'Rabet, Fadela. *La Femme algérienne*. Paris: François Maspero, 1965.

Murch, Arvin. *Black Frenchmen: The Political Integration of the French Antilles*. Cambridge, Mass.: Schenkman, 1971.

Nkrumah, Kwame. *Handbook of Revolutionary Warfare*. New York: International Publishers, 1969.

——————. *Consciencism*. New York: Monthly Review Press, 1970.

——————. *Class Struggle in Africa*. New York: International Publishers, 1970.

Nora, Pierre. *Les Français d'Algérie.* Paris: Juillard, 1961.

Odajnyk, Walter. *Marxism and Existentialism.* Garden City, New York: Doubleday, 1965.

Ollman, Bertell. *Alienation: Marx's Conception of Man in Captialist Society.* Cambridge: Cambridge University Press, 1971

Ottaway, David and Marina Ottaway. *Algeria: The Politics of a Socialist Revolution.* Berkeley and Los Angeles: University of California Press, 1970.

Paraf, Pierre. *Le Racism dans le monde.* 4th ed. Paris: Payot, 1972.

Pettee, George S. *The Process of Revolution.* (New York, 1938). New York: Harper and brothers, 1938.

Peytraud, L. *L'Esclavage aux antilles françaises avant 1789.* Paris: Hachette, 1897.

Quandt, William B. *Revolution and Political Leadership: Algeria 1954-1968.* Cambridge, Mass.: M.I.T. Press, 1969.

*Recueil des délibérations au congrès colonial national, Paris, 1889-90.* Paris, 1890.

Rosberg, Carl G., and John Nottingham. *The Myth of "Mau Mau": Nationalism in Kenya.* Nairobi: East Africa Publishing House, 1966.

Ruedy, John. *Land Policy in Colonial Algeria: The Origins of Rural Public Domain.* Berkeley: University of California Press, 1967.

Sartre, Jean-Paul. *Critique de la raison dialectique.* Paris: Gallimard, 1960.

——————. *Anti-Semite and Jew.* Trans. G.T. Becker. New York: Schocken Books, 1965.

Servan-Schreiber, Jean-Jacques. *Lieutenant in Algeria.* Trans. Ronald Matthews. New York: Greenwood Press, 1957.

Shaffer, Jerome A. *Violence.* New York: David McKay, 1971.

Shanin, Teodor. *Peasants and Peasant Societies.* Harmondsworth, Middlesex: Penguin Books, 1971.

Smith, M.G. *West Indian Family Structure.* Seattle: University of Washington Press, 1962.

——————. *Stratification in Grenada.* Berkeley: University of California Press, 1965.

——————. *The Plural Society in the British West Indies.* Berkeley: University of California Press, 1965.

Snow, Edgar. *Red Star Over China.* rev. ed. New York: Grove Press, 1968.

Sorel, Georges. *Reflections on Violence.* New York: Macmillan, Collier Books, 1961.

Sorokin, Pitirim. *The Sociology of Revolution.* Philadelphia, 1925.

Stein, Robert Louis. *The French Slave Trade in the Eighteenth Century: An Old Regime Business.* Madison: University of Wisconsin Press, 1979.

Taleb, Ahmed. *Lettres de Prison: 1957-1961.* Algiers: Editions Nationales Algeriénnes, 1966.

Tertre, Jean-Baptiste. ed. *Historie générale des antilles habitées par les Français.* 4 vols. Paris, 1667-1671.

Thrupp, Sylvia L., ed. *Millenial Dreams in Action: Studies in Revolutionary Religious Movements.* New York: Schocken Books, 1970.

Tillion, Germaine. *France and Algeria: Complementary Enemies.* New York: Alfred Knopf, 1961. Originally published as *Les Enemies Complémentaires.* Paris: Editions de Minuit, 1960.

Tocqueville, Alexis, ed. *The Old Regime and the French Revolution.* Trans. Stuart Gilbert. New York: Anchor Books, 1955.

Trotsky, Leon. *Literature and Revolution.* New York: International Publishers, 1925.

Vâlet, René, *L'Afrique du Nord: Devant le parlement au XIXe siècle (1828-1838—1880-1881).* Algiers, 1924.

Wertheim, W.F. *Evolution and Revolution.* Harmondsworth, Middlesex: Penguin Books, 1974.

Wiener, Philip P., and John Fisher, ed. *Violence and Aggression in the History of Ideas.* New Brunswick, N.J.: Rutgers University Press, 1974.

Woddis, Jack. *Africa: The Roots of Revolt.* New York: The Citadel Press, 1962.

_____. *New Theories of Revolution: A Commentary on the Views of Frantz Fanon, Régis Debray and Herbert Marcuse.* London and New York: International Publishers, 1972.

Wolf, Eric R. *Peasants.* Englewood Cliffs, N.J.: Prentice-Hall, 1966.

_____. *Peasant Wars of the Twentieth Century.* London: Faber & Faber, 1971.

Wolfenstein, Victor E. *The Revolutionary Personality: Lenin, Trotsky, Gandhi.* Princeton, N.J.: Princeton University Press, 1971.

Worsley, Peter. *The Trumpet Shall Sound: A Study of "Cargo Cults" in Melanesia.* London: MacGibbon and Kee, 1957.

Yacef, Saadi. *Souvenirs de la bataille d'Alger.* Paris: Juillard, 1962

Yetman, Norman and Hoy Steele. *Majority and Minority: The Dynamics of Racial and Ethnic Relations.* Boston: Allyn & Beacon, 1971

Zahar, Renate. *L'Oeuvre de Frantz Fanon: Colonialisme et Aliénation dans l'oeuvre du Frantz Fanon.* Trans. from the German by Roger Dangeville. Paris, François Maspero, 1970.

# Bibliography

## *Articles and Chapters**

Abel, Lionel. "Seven Heroes of the New Left." *New York Times Magazine* (5 May 1968), 30-31, 128-33, 135.

Abrash, Barbara. "Frantz Fanon." *African Library Journal*, 11, no. 3 (Autumn 1971), 9-12.

_____. "Fanon: Political Philosopher as Mythmaker." In Emmanuel Hansen and Adele Jinadu, eds. *Frantz Fanon: The Man His Work and His Thought* (Forthcoming).

Adams, Paul L. "The Social Psychiatry of Frantz Fanon." *American Journal of Psychiatry*, 127 (Dec. 1970), 109-14.

_____."Dehumanization and the Legitimization of Violence." In Jules H. Masserman and John J. Schwab, eds. *Man for Humanity: Concordance and Discord in Human Relations*. Springfield, Ill.: Charles C. Thomas, 1972. pp. 162-70.

Ahmed, Jamal M. "The Islamic Factor in the Awakening of Algeria." In Christopher Allen and Richard W. Johnson, eds. *African Perspectives: Papers in the History, Politics and Economics of Africa*. Cambridge: Cambridge University Press, 1970, pp. 113-42.

Alavi, Hamza. "Peasants and Revolution." *Socialist Register* (1965), 241-77.

Alsop, Joseph. "Passing of New Left's Hero: An Old Facet in U.S. History." *Washington Post* (21 Feb. 1969), 21.

_____. *Letter to New Statesman* (30 Jan. 1970), p. 150.

Amghar, Mohammed. "Fanon et la pensée occidentale." *El Moudjahid* (2 June 1971), 4-5.

Ansprenger, Frantz. Review of *Les Damnés de la terre. Journal of Modern African Studies*, 1 (1963), 403-5.

* Much of this material comes from Emmanuel Hansen, *Frantz Fanon: Soul and Political Thought* (Ohio State University Press, 1977), bibliography.

Arendt, Hannah. "Reflections on Violence." *New York Review of Books* (27 Feb. 1969), 19-31.

Armah, Ayi Kwei. "Fanon: The Awakener." *Negro Digest*, 18 (Oct. 1969), 4-43.

Arrighi, Giovanni, and John Saul. "Nationalism and Revolution in Sub-Saharan Africa." *Socialist Register* (1969), 137-88.

Barbé, Raymond. "Les classes sociales en Algérie." *Economie et Politique*, Part 1 (Sept. 1959), 7-23; Part II (Oct. 1959), 22-45.

Barnard, Roger. "Frantz Fanon." *New Society* (4 Jan. 1958), 11-13.

Beaudoux-Kouvats, Edith and Jean Benoist, "Les Blancs créoles de la Martinique." In Jean Benoist, ed. *L'Archival inachevé: Culture et société aux Antilles françaises.* Montréal: Les Presses de l'Université de Montréal, 1972. pp. 93-132.

Beauvoir, Simone de. "Fanon chez Sartre." From Simone de Beauvoir, *La Force de chose.* Excerpted in *Jeune Afrique*, 162 (16-22 Dec. 1963), 25-27.

Becket, Paul A. "Frantz Fanon and Sub-Saharan Africa: Notes on the Contemporary Significance of His Thought." *Africa Today,* 19 (Spring 1972), 59-73.

—————. "Algeria vs. Fanon: The Theory of Revolutionary Decolonization and the Algerian Experience." *Western Political Quarterly* (26 March 1973), 5-27.

Benedict, Burton. "Stratification in Plural Societies." *American Anthropologist.* 64, no. 6 (1962) 1235-45.

Benoist, Jean. "Une Civilisation antillaise." In Jean Benoist, ed., *Les Sociétés antillaises*. Montréal: Centre de Recherches Caraïbes, 1975, pp. 7-12.

Bernard J. Siegal. "Defensive Cultural Adaptation." In Hugh D. Graham and Ted R. Gurr, eds. *Violence in America: Historical and Comparative Perspectives.* Beverly Hills: Sage Publications, 1979, pp. 445-71.

Blackey, Robert. "Fanon and Cabral: A Contrast in Theories of Revolution for Africa." *Journal of Modern African Studies,* 12 (June 1974), 191-209.

Bondy, François. "Frantz Fanon." *Encounter*, 53 (August 1974), 25-29.

Braithwaite, Lloyd. "Social Stratification and Cultural Pluralism." Reprinted in Michael M. Horowitz, ed. *Peoples and Cultures of the Caribbean.* Garden City, New York: The Natural History Press, 1971, pp. 95-116.

Bundy, Colin. "Emergence and Decline of a South African Peasantry." *African Affairs*, no. 285 (Oct. 1972), 369-88.

Butterworth, Charles E. "Frantz Fanon and Human Dignity." *Political Science Reviewer,* 10 (1980), 257-327.

Capouya, Emile. "Time to Turn a Tide of Violence." *Saturday Review* (24 April 1965), 33-34.

Caute, David. "Philosopher of Violence." *Observer* (10 October 1965), p. 26.

Césaire, Aimé. "La Révolte de Frantz Fanon." *Jeune Afrique,* no. 63 (13-19 Dec. 1961), 24-35.

Cherif, Mohamed. "Frantz Fanon: La Science au service de la Révolution." *Jeune Afrique,* no. 295 (4 Sept. 1966), p. 24.

Chodak, Szymon, "Social Classes in Sub-Saharan Africa." *Africana Bulletin,* no. 4, (1966), 7-46.

_____. "The Birth of an African Peasantry." *Canadian Journal of African Studies,* V, no. 3 (1971), 327-47.

_____. "Social Stratification in Sub-Saharan Africa." *Canadian Journal of African Studies,* 7, no. 3 (1973), 401-17.

Cohen, Robin. "Class in Africa: Analytical Problems and Perspectives." *Socialist Register* (1972), 231-55.

_____, and David Michael. "The Revolutionary Potential of the African Lumpenproletariat: A Sceptical View." *Bulletin of Institute of Development Studies,* Sussex University, 5, nos. 2-3 (1973), 31-44.

Coser, Louis. "The Myth of the Peasant Revolt." *Dissent.* XIII, no. 3 (May - June, 1966), 298-303.

_____. "Fanon and Debray: Theorists of the Third World." In Irving Howe, ed. *Beyond the New Left.* New York: McCall Publishing Co. 1970, pp. 120-134.

Cranston, Maurice. "Sartre and Violence: A Philosopher's Commitment to a Pledge." *Encounter,* 29 (July 1967), 18-24.

Daniel, Jean. Review of *Les Damnés de la terre. L'Express* (30 Nov. 1961), 36.

Davidson, Basil. "African Peasants and Revolution." *Journal of Peasant Studies.* 1 (April 1974), 269-90.

Davies, James C. "Toward a Theory of Revolution." *American Sociological Review,* XXVII (Feb. 1962), 1-19.

_____. "The J-Curve of Rising and Declining Satisfactions as a Cause of Revolution and Rebellion." In Hugh D. Graham and Ted R. Gurr, eds. *Violence in America: Historical and Comparative Perspectives.* Beverly Hills: Sage Publications, 1979, pp. 690-730.

Debien, Gabriel. "Engagés pour les Antilles (1634-1715)," *Révue d'Histoire des Colonies*, 25 (1951), chapter 7, "Causes de départs: salaries elevés? promesses de terres? réclames?" 185-70.

Deming, Barbara. "On Revolution and Equilibrium." *Liberation* (12 Feb. 1968), 10-12.

Desparmet, J. "Les Réactions nationalitaires en Algérie," chapter 1, "Le Vieux génie maure." *Bulletin de la Société de Géographie d'Alger et de l'Afrique du Nord* XXXIV, no. 123 (1933), 173-84.

_____. "Les Réactions nationalitaires en Algéria," chapter 11, "La Vielle poésie nationale." *Bulletin de la Société de Géographie d'Alger et de l'Afrique du Nord*, XXXIV, no. 134 (1933), 437-44.

_____. "Les Réactions nationalitaires en Algéria," chapter IV, "Elégies et satires politiques de 1830 à 1914." *Bulletin de la Société de Géographie d'Alger et de l'Afrique du Nord*, XXXIV, no. 136 (1933), 35-54.

Dieng, Amady Aly. "Les damnés de la terre et les problèmes d'Afrique noire." *Présence Africaine*, no. 62 (1967), 15-30.

Domenach, Jean-Marie. Review of *Les Damnés de la terre. Esprit*, no. 304 (March 1962), 454-63.

Dubois, Françoise. Review of *Pour la révolution africaine. Tiers Monde*, 5 (July - Sept. 1964), 55-56.

Eckstein, Harry. "On the Etiology of Internal Wars." *History and Theory*, 4, no. 2 (1965), 133-63.

Elizabeth, Leo. "The French Antilles." In David Cohen and Jack P. Green, eds. *Neither Slave Nor Free*. Johns Hopkins University Press, 1972. pp. 134-71.

Epstein, David G. "A Revolutionary Lumpenproletariat." *Monthly Review*, (Dec. 1969), 54-56.

Fallers, L.A. "Are African Cultivators to Be Called 'Peasants'?" *Current Anthropology*, 2, no. 2 (1961), 108-10.

Fanon, Josie. "A propos de Frantz Fanon, Sartre, le racism, et les arabes." *El Moudjahid*, 10 (June 1967), 6.

Feierabend, D. and Rosalind L. "Aggressive Behaviors Within Politics, 1948-1962." James C. Davies, ed. *When Men Revolt and Why*. New York, 1971, pp. 229-49.

Feldman, Arnold. "Violence and Volatility: The Livelihood of Revolution." In Harry Eckstein, ed. *Internal War*, New York: Macmillan Co., 1964, pp. 111-129

Flacks, R. "Protest or Conform: Social Psychological Perspectives on

Legitimacy." *Journal of Applied Behavioral Science*, 5 (1969), 127-50.

Fontenot, Chester. "Frantz Fanon: The Revolutionary." *First World*, 2, no. 3 (1979), 24-28.

Forsythe, Dennis. "Frantz Fanon: Black Theoretician." *Black Scholar*, 1 March 1970), 3-10.

Franklin, Bruce. "The Lumpenproletariat and the Revolutionary Youth Movement." *Monthly Review*, 21 (Jan. 1970), 10-25.

Freeman, Michael. "Review Article: Theories of Revolution." *British Journal of Political Science*, 2 (1972), 339-59.

Furedi, Frank. "The Social Composition of the 'Mau Mau' Movement in the White Highlands." *Journal of Peasant Studies*, 1 (July 194), 486-505.

Furnivall, J.S. "The Political Economy of the Tropical Far East." *Journal of the Royal Central Asiatic Society*, 29 (1942), 95-210.

_____. "Some Problems of Tropical Economy." In Rita Hinden, ed. *Fabian Colonial Essays.* London: Allen and Unwin, 1945, pp. 161-84.

Geismar, Peter and Peter Worsley. "Frantz Fanon: Evolution of a Revolutionary. Biographical Sketch." *Monthly Review*, 21 (May 1969), 22-30.

Gendzier, Irene. "Frantz Fanon: In Search of Justice." *Middle East Journal*, 20 (Autumn 1966), 534-44.

Gert, Bernard. "On Violence." *Journal of Philosophy*, 66 (1969), 616-28.

Gordon, David C. "Frantz Fanon: Voice of the Algerian Revolution." *Middle East Forum* (Sept. 1963), 17-20.

Gottheil, Fred M. "Fanon and the Economics of Colonialism: A Review Article." *Quarterly Review of Economics and Business*. 7 (Autumn 1967), 73-82.

Gottschalk, Louis. "The Causes of Revolution." *American Journal of Sociology*, 1 (1944), 1-8.

Greki, Anna. "Les Damnés de la terre." *Jeune Afrique*, no. 63 (13-16 Dec. 1961), 25.

Grohs, G.K. "Frantz Fanon and the African Revolution." *The Journal of Modern African Studies*, 6 no. 4 (1968), 543-56.

Grundy, Kenneth. "The 'Class Struggle' in Africa: An Examination of Conflicting Theories." *Journal of Modern African Studies*, 2 (Nov. 1964), 379-93.

Hansen, Emmanuel. "Frantz Fanon: A Bibliographical Essay." *Pan-African Journal*, 5 (Winter 1972), 387-405.

Heggoy, Alf Andrew. "The Evolution of Algerian Women." *African Studies Review*, XVII, no. 2 (Sept. 1974), 449-56.

"Homages to Frantz Fanon." *Présence Africaine*, 21, no. 40 (1962), 130-52.

Hook, Sydney, "The Ideology of Violence." *Encounter*, 34 (April 1970), 26-38.

Irele, Abiola. "Literature and Ideology in Martinique: René Maran, Aimé Césaire, Frantz Fanon." *Research Review*, 5, no. 3, Trinity Term. Ghana University: Institute of African Studies, 1969, 1-32.

Isaacs, Harold R. "Portrait of a Revolutionary." *Commentary*, 40 (July 1965), 67-71.

Ishinger, Barbara. "Negritude: Some Dissident Voices." *Issue: A Quarterly Journal of Africanist Opinion*, IV, no. 4 (1974), 23-45.

Jackson, Henry. "Political and Social Ideas of Frantz Fanon: Relevance to Black Americans." *Pan-African Journal*, 5 (Winter, 1974), 473-91.

Jinadu, L. Adele. "The Moral Dimensions of the Political Thought of Frantz Fanon." *Second Order: An African Journal of Philosophy*, V, no. 1 (Jan. 1976), 30-43.

Johnson, Douglas. "Algeria: Some Problems of Modern History." *Journal of African History*, 5, no. 2 (1964), 221-42.

Jones, John Henry. "On the Influence of Fanon." *Freedomways*, 8 (Summer 1968), 209-14.

Kamenka, Eugene. "The Concept of a Political Revolution." In Carl Friedrich, ed. *Revolution*, New York: Atherton, 1966. pp. 122-35.

Kaplinsky, Raphael. "Myths About the 'Revolutionary Proletariat' in Developing Countries." *Bulletin of the Institute of Development Studies* (Sussex University), 3 (August 1971), 15-21.

Klein, Norman. "On Revolutionary Violence." *Studies on the Left*, 4 (May-June, 1966), 62-82.

Kramanic, Issac. "Reflections on Revolution: Definition and Explanation in Recent Scholarship." *History and Theory: Studies in Philosophy of History*, 11, no. 1 (1972), 26-63.

Kuper, Leo. "Theories of Revolution and Race Relations." *Comparative Studies in Society and History*, 13 (Jan. 1971), 87-107.

Lacan, Jacques. "Le Stade du miror comme formateur de la fonction du 'Je': Telle qu'elle nous est révélée dans l'experience psychoanalytique." *Ecrits*, 1 (1970), 89-97.

Lacheroff, Mostefa. "Nationalism algérien." *Les Temps Modernes* (Sept. - Oct. 1956), 214-55.

_____. "Constantes politiques et militaires dans les guerres coloniales d'Algérie (1830-1960)." *Les Temps Modernes* (Dec. 1960 - Jan. 1961), 727-800.

Lafon, Monique. "Le sucre des Antilles de la Réunion." *Economie et Politique*, (Oct. 1959), 46-64.

Lasky, Melvin J. "The Birth of a Metaphor." *Encounter*, 34 (Feb. 1970), 35-45; 34 (March 1970), 30-42.

Ledda, Romano. "Les Classes sociales et la lutte politique." *Révue internationale du socialisme*, Rome (August 1967), 594-615.

Lewis, Martin Deming. "One Hundred Million Frenchman: The 'Assimilation' Theory in French Colonial Policy." *Comparative Studies in Society and History*, 4 (Jan. 1962), 129-53.

Leys, Colin. "Politics in Kenya: The Development of Peasant Society." *British Journal of Political Sciences*, 1 (July 1971), 307-37.

Lowenthal, David. "Race and Color in the West Indies." *Daedalus*, (Spring 1967), 580-621.

Mair, Lucy, "Independent Religious Movements in Three Continents." *Comparative Studies in Society and History*, 1, no. 2 (Jan. 1959), 134-5.

Mannoni, O. "La Plainte du Noir." *Esprit*, 19 (Jan. - June, 1951), 739-49.

Maquet, Jacques J. "La Participation de la classe paysanne au Movement d'Indépendence de Rwanda." *Cahier d'Etudes Africaines*, 4, no. 16 (1964), 552-68.

Marcuse, Herbert. "Ethics and Revolution." In Richard T. De George ed. *Ethics and Society*, Garden City: New York: Doubleday, 1966. pp. 133-47.

Martin, Guy. "Fanon's Relevance to Contemporary African Political Thought." *Ufahamu*, 4 (Winter 1974), 11-34.

Memmi, Albert. "Frantz Fanon and the Notion of 'Deficiency.' " In Albert Memmi. *Dominated Man.* New York: Orion Press, 1968. pp. 84-89.

_____. "La Vie impossible de Frantz Fanon." *Esprit* (Sept. 1971), 248-73.

Mili, M. Mohammed El. "Frantz Fanon et la révolution algérienne." *El Moudjahid* (20 March 1971), 3.

Mittleman, James H. "Mozambique: The Political Economy of Underdevelopment." *Journal of Southern African Affairs*, III, no. 1 (Jan. 1978), 35-54.

Museveni, Yoweri T. "Fanon's Theory of Violence: Its Verification in Liberated Mozambique." In Nathan Shamuyarira, ed. *Essays on Liberation of Southern Africa*. Dar-es-Salaam: Tanzania Publishing 1971, pp. 1-24.

Mulambu-Mvuluya, F. "Introduction à l'étude du rôle des paysans dans les changements politiques." *Cahiers économiques et sociaux*, 8, no. 3 (Sept. 1970), 435-50.

Nighe Nguyen. "Frantz Fanon et les problèmes de l'indépendence." *La Pensée*. no. 107 (Feb. 1963), 23-36.

Nursey-Bray, Paul. "Marxism and Existentialism in the Thought of Frantz Fanon." *Political Studies*, 20 (June 1972), 152-68.

O'Brien, Conor Cruise. "The Neurosis of Colonialism." *Nation*. 200 (June 1965), 674-76.

Opello, Walter C. Jr. "Guerilla War in Portugurese Africa: An Assessment of the Balance of Force in Mozambique." *Issue: A Quarterly Journal of Africanist Opinion*. IV, no. 2 (1974), 29-37.

Pablo, Michel. "Les Damés de la terre." *Quatrième Internationale*, 20 (Feb. 1962), 57-63.

Perinbam, B. Marie. "Fanon and the Revolutionary Peasantry: The Algerian Case." *Journal of Modern African Studies*, 2 (Sept. 1973), 427-45.

_____. "Violence, Morality and History in the Colonial Syndrome: Frantz Fanon's Perspectives." *Journal of Southern African Affairs*, III, no. 1 (Jan. 1978), 7-34.

_____. "Frantz Fanon's View of the West Indian and Algerian Woman." *Journal of Ethnic Studies*, 1, no. 2 (1973), 45-55.

Posinsky, S.H. Review of *The Wretched of the Earth* and *Studies in a Dying Colonialism*. *Psychoanalytic Quarterly*, 35 (1966), 600-02.

Potekhin, I. "Land Relations in African Countries." *Journal of Modern African Studies*. 1, no. 1 (April, 1963), 35-59.

Pouillon, Jean. "Decolonisation et révolution." *Les Temps Modernes*, no. 191 (April 1962), 1554-63.

Ralston, Richard "Fanon and His Critics: The New Battle of Algiers." *Cultures et développement: revue internationale des sciences du développement.* Louvain, VIII, no. 3 (1979), 463-93.

Ranly, Ernest W. "Frantz Fanon and the Radical Left." *America*, 121 no. 14 (1 Nov. 1969), 348-88.

Ridell, William R. "Le Code Noir." *The Journal of Negro History*, 10, no. 3 (July 1925), 296-314.

Rohdie, S. "Liberation and Violence in Algeria." *Studies on the Left* (May-June 1966), 83-89.

Saul, John, and Roger Woods. "African Peasantries." In Teodor Shanin, ed., *Peasants and Peasant Societies*. Harmondsworth, Middlesex: Penguin, 1971, pp. 103-14.

Saul, John "African Peasants and Revolution." *Review of African Political Economy*, no. 1 (1974), 41-68.

Schaff, Adam. "Marxist Theory on Revolution and Violence." *Journal of the History of Ideas*. 34 (April - June 1973), 263-70.

Siegal, J. E. "On Frantz Fanon." *American Scholar*, 38 (Winter 1968), 84-96.

Silver, Burton D. "Social Mobility and Intergroup Antagonism: A Simulation." *Journal of Conflict Resolution*, 17, no. 4 (Dec. 1973), 605-23.

Smith, M.G. "A Framework for Caribbean Studies." *Caribbean Affairs Series*. Extra-Mural Department, University College of the West Indies, 1955. Reprinted in M.G. Smith, *The Plural Society in the British West Indies*. Berkeley: University of California Press, 1965, pp. 18-74.

_____. "Social and Cultural Pluralism." In Vera Rubin, ed. *Annals of the New York Academy of Sciences*, 83, art. 5 (1960). Reprinted in M.G. Smith, *The Plural Society in the British West Indies*. Berkeley: University of California Press, 1956, pp. 75-91.

Smith, Robert. "Beyond Marx: Fanon and the Concept of Colonial Violence." *Black World* (May 1973), 23-33.

Stambouli, F. "Frantz Fanon face aux problèmes de la décolonisation et de la construction nationale." *Revue de l'Institute de Sociologie*, nos. 2/3 (1967), 519-34.

Staniland, Martin. "Frantz Fanon and the African Political Class." *Memo*, no. 13, Institute of Development Studies. Brighton (July 1968). Reprinted in *African Affairs* (Jan. 1969), 4-25.

Stone, Lawrence. "Theories of Revolution." *World Politics*, 18 (Jan. 1966), 159-76.

Sutton, Horace. "Fanon." *Saturday Review* (17 July 1971), 16-19.

Talmon, Yonia. "Pursuit of the Millenium: The Relation Between Religious and Social Change." In Barry McLaughlin, ed. *Studies in Social Movements*. New York, 1969, pp. 400-27.

Thompson, Willie. "Frantz Fanon." *Marxism Today* (August 1968), 245-51.

Troare, Barbary. "On 'Les Damnés de la terre.'" *Présence Africaine*, 17, no. 45 (1963), 88-95.

Turner, H.W. "A Methodology of Modern African Religious Movements." *Comparative Studies in Society and History*, 8, no. 3 (April 1966), 281-94.

Turner, Ralph H. "Integrative Beliefs in Group Crises." *Journal of Conflict Resolution*, XVI, no. 1 (March 1972), 25-40.

Wallerstein, Immanuel. "Review of Studies in a Dying Colonialism." *New World Quarterly*. 3, no. 3 (1967), 76-77.

_____. "Frantz Fanon: Reason and Violence." *Berkeley Journal of Sociology*, 15 (1970), 222-31.

_____. "Class and Class Conflict in Contemporary Africa." *Canadian Journal of African Studies*, 7, no. 3 (1973), 375-80.

Weinstein, Brian. "The French West Indies: Dualism from 1848 to the Present." In Martin L. Kilson and Robert I. Rotberg, eds. *The African Diaspora*. Cambridge: Harvard University Press, 1976, pp. 237-90.

Wilson, Bryan A. "Millenarianism in Comparative Perspective." *Comparative Studies in Society and History*, 6, no. 1 (Oct. 1963), 93-114.

Wolff, Robert P. "On Violence." *Journal of Philosophy*, 66 (1969), 601-16.

Wolin, Sheldon S. "Political Theory as a Vocation." *American Political Science Review*, LXII, no. 4 (Dec., 1969), 1062-82.

Worchel, Philip, Philip G. Hester and Philip S. Kopala. "Collective Protests and Legitimacy of Authority." *The Journal of Conflict Resolution*, 18, no. 1 (March 1974), 37-54.

Worsley, Peter. "Revolutionary Theories." *Monthly Review*, 21 (May 1969), 30-49.

Zagorin, Parez. "Theories of Revolution in Contemporary Historiography." *Political Science Quarterly*, 88 (March 1973), 23-52.

Zolberg, Aristide R. "Frantz Fanon: A Gospel for the Damned." *Encounter*, 27 (Nov. 1966), 63-65.

_____ and Vera Zolberg. "The Americanization of Frantz Fanon." *Public Interest*, no. 9 (1969), 49-63.

_____. "Frantz Fanon." *The New Left*. Ed. Maurice Cranston (New York, 1971), 119-36.

# Index